THE GLASGOW DIARY
BY DONALD SAUNDERS, MAINLY

POLYGON BOOKS
EDINBURGH

First published in 1984 by
Polygon Books,
1 Buccleuch Place, Edinburgh EH8 9LW.

Copyright © Donald Saunders and individual contributors.

ISBN 0 904919 75 7

Typeset by E.U.S.P.B.,
1 Buccleuch Place, Edinburgh, EH8 9LW.

Printed by Redwood Burn, Trowbridge, Wiltshire.

PROLOGUE

The Glasgow Diary has its origins in the appearance in 1981 of *A Diary of Edinburgh*, a collection of 365 true incidents culled from the history of the Scottish capital, each presented in its appropriate calendar setting by the compiler, Trevor Royle. Its popular success persuaded the publishers that a Glasgow equivalent would be equally well received. But there are differences between Edinburgh and Glasgow which the new venture would inevitably reflect.

At some point in the nineteenth century, the weird and scandalous events that make history interesting stopped happening in Edinburgh or if they did not, it became bad manners to talk about them. As a result, the Edinburgh diary contains few twentieth-century events more interesting than the Queen's opening of the Commonwealth Swimming Pool. In Glasgow, however, it is obvious that the weird, the scandalous and the remarkable still happen. Some people, out of a misguided sort of local patriotism, wish us not to believe this and would happily censor all information that falls short of suggesting that the only things about Glasgow are the unselfish and far-seeing devotion of the local government officers, the beauty of the architecture and the friendly courtesy of the inhabitants. If a certain irreverence is found creeping into the text it may be at least partly in response to such an attitude.

"To create a little flower," says William Blake, "is the labour of ages." To collate this book in less time than it took God to evolve the forget-me-not the author has welcomed the following entries from contributors listed alphabetically below, most of whom have helped further by offering useful background material. Thanks must also go to Hamish White for his valuable criticism of the text, to David Manderson, Fiona Malcolm and Duncan McVicar for help in assembling the typescript, and to Ann McKeown for her tolerance and encouragement.

Finally, it should be made clear that the diary's use of the first person plural is not a matter of regal pretension, nor even of archaic journalistic convention, but an expression of the book's truly communal nature. *Floreat Glasghu.*

DONALD SAUNDERS

CONTRIBUTORS

CHRISTOPHER BOYCE
Native of Baillieston, librarian, author of three science fiction works and the speculative work *Extraterrestrial Encounters*. 8 July.

RICHARD FLETCHER
An immigrant to Glasgow, he lectures in engineering at Glasgow University and is the author of short stories, many of which have appeared in *Scottish Short Stories*. 11, 14 May; 6 August; 15 December.

ALASDAIR GRAY
Author, illustrator and muralist, he has received glittering prizes and critical acclaim for his novels *Lanark* and *Janine 1982* and his short story collection *Unlikely Stories Mostly*. 2 April; 24 May; 19 September; 14 October.

CLIFF HANLEY
Author of *Dancing in the Streets* and many other novels, he is also known as scriptwriter, broadcaster, wit and raconteur. 16 June.

ARCHIE HIND
Author of *The Dear Green Place*, writer of revues, his recent adaptation of *The Ragged Trousered Philanthropists* enjoyed great success at the Citizens Theatre. 1, 5, 6, 8, 10, 11, 18, 20, 24, 25, 27, 28, 29, 30, 31 January; 3, 4, 5, 6, 7, 15, 22, 25, 26 February; 8, 14, 16, 24 March; 10, 15, 17 April; 8 June; 14 September; 15 November; 1, 21 December.

JACK HOUSE
Glasgow's best known and best liked writer and broadcaster upon the city and its ways. 11 October.

ELSPETH KING
As Curator of Glasgow's People's Palace local history museum, she has done more than almost anyone to preserve the evidence of Glasgow's life and culture. 2, 22 January; 21 May; 6 October.

TOM LEONARD
Conceptual poet, sound poet, poet in both received standard English and in the Glasgow patois, he is currently writing a critical biography of James Thompson. 3 December.

CARL MacDOUGALL
Former journalist and editor, short story writer, playwright and children's author. He is not well known for his verses except among folksingers and "Hoi Polloi". 26 March; 5 April; 9 July; 6 September; 28 November; 26 December.

JACK
McLEAN

Best known (outside the classroom) as Glasgow's "Urban Voltaire". His column in the *Glasgow Herald* irritates the few and delights the many.

12 July.

ALEX
MITCHELL

A Glasgow journalist whose weekly column "Tales from the Glasgow Police Courts" is a source of great entertainment. He wrote the scripts for Stanley Baxter's popular "Parliamo Glasgow" series, which has been successfully adapted into book form.

ANGELA
MULLANE

Office worker, librarian, Special School teacher, freelance journalist, wife, mother and more.

25 July, 27 September.

Good for Glasgow

Bad for Glasgow

Act of God

Battle

Buffoonery

Church of Rome

Episcopalian Church

Execution

Fire

Football

Football Disaster

Literature

ILLUSTRATIONS

indicate the subject matter or moral tone of the entry.

Judiciary

Masons

Murder

Music

Riot

Police Action

Political Defiance

Reformed Church

Smoking

Shipping

Union of Parliament Riot

Weather

Ne'er Day. New Year's Day. The day after Hogmanay. This day is one of the great lay holidays of the year, having no connection with the church calendar, though it is probably connected with the pagan ceremony marking the passing of the winter solstice. Perhaps because of the strong Celtic influence in Glasgow the most fervent celebrations seem to be secular and pagan in character. Certainly the Hogmanay/Ne'er Day holiday, like those at the summer Fair or Hallowe'en, seems to be a time when the pulse of the Glasgow soul beats in harmony with all creation.

There are a few attendant customs. Nobody goes to bed. After that the most important is the first foot. Even the most rational and free-thinking Glaswegian prefers the first person over his doorstep to be both male and dark. Visitors to the house, be they friends or strangers, are expected to bring gifts symbolising those things which make survival possible through the dreich days of the winter, namely shortbread, "black bun", coal and whisky. The shortbread, "black bun" and coal are token gifts standing for fire and food. The whisky is meant to be taken seriously.

To those outsiders who visit Glasgow during this time the ferocity with which the holiday is celebrated is surprising, though they are often cheered by the geniality which the locals display to one another and to mankind in general. There is, for instance, the unbroken convention that even mortal enemies when they meet will shake hands, embrace, forgive and swear undying friendship. Some of these restored relations will remain unfractured until about a quarter to three.

To those wholly taking part — the Glaswegians —it is a descent into an abyss of commitment to joyfulness, drunkenness, sentimentalism, confession, nostalgia, amnesia, mawkery and misjudgement of reality, a festival of contradiction in which the tone-deaf sing, the clumsy dance, wallflowers are kissed, insomniacs sleep, the temperate swill, the meek are blessed, the joyful cry, the sad laugh, sinners behave, the good act in a contradictory fashion, the poor spend, the rich gi . . . but that would be going too far. Nevertheless we get drunk and musical and loving and speculative and hopeful and sentimentally miserable. In fact it's a *rerr terr*, which in the Sassenach tongue means jolly good fun. Everybody hates it.

---

2 January 1848

In the Australian bush, a Glasgow exile was labouring over a painful letter to his younger brother.

> "Dear James you will no dout be surprised to be accosted by your exiled (brother) the 3d time but on account of your unnaitrale conduct towards me I cannot but let you know that it surprises me verey much. I have got one Argus in 1846 and one in 1847. I have every rason to supose that you sent them but no letter . . . all I asked was you would let me know what of my Famaly was alive and when my Father Died but I supose that you disdaind to rite to me but I am sure that I never did anay thing to make you or anay of my Famaly to disspise me, onley What I was sent here for and if I had the same to do I would do it again altho the Radicals of Glasgow have used us all very ill. . . ."

Benjamin Moir (b. 1780) was one of the 22 people tried and convicted of high treason after the Radical Rising and Battle of Bonnymuir in 1820 (see 30th August). Baird, Hardie and Wilson suffered public execution, and by 1848 were regarded as national heroes. Their 19 compatriots who were sentenced to transportation to New South Wales were in some respects less fortunate. Benjamin Moir regarded his exile as a living hell.

> "Dear James I am now 68 years of age and I have not one spot or sore on my bodey. I am now 28 years in exile . . . for all I have got throw I would be happy if I could get home to die in my native land. . . . I am fairly tired of this country and has been this many years. . . . If I could Enjoy one year in my native country it would be better than a lifetime here. . . ."

Moir was the only labourer among the group of Scots who were transported in 1820. The others were weavers and skilled artisans, and some of them managed to find their way home after serving their sentence. Moir's wife and two daughters had joined him in Australia in 1823, but by the time he had served his 14-year sentence, he did not have the means to return home.

> "The crie here is for want of labor. . . . I ashure you it is a poor place for a working man as 7 shillings is the wadges for a good man at present and scarce to be got. . . . If you know of any person desirous of emigrating advise them not to come for this country is miserable and no prospect of getting any better. . . ."

The hypocrisy behind the lionisation of the dead radicals while the living were ignored rankled with Moir:

> "Dear James I say today in the Edenburgh weekly Jornal that the Friends of Reform has remuved the Bones of Harde and Baird from Stirling to Glasgow efter 27 years in the grave. But I think if they were as they pretend to be so good to the case they wuld trie to remuve this olde Bodey out of Exile. . . ."

While Moir's desperation to return home is evident in every letter, it is commuted to a desperate plea to his brother at least to send news of the family if nothing else. A year later, he got a neighbour to write on his behalf:

> "He is anxious that you should distinctly understand that his anxiety to hear from you is not to be construed into any hint as to getting pecuniary assistance. He as yet has never stood in need of assistance from anyone, and he is particular in wishing you should know this in case such a belief might keep you from writing him and relating those family and friendly news he is naturally anxious about. In your last newspaper he has seen with great delight that you have been elected a member of the Glasgow Town Council knowing as he does that this event has been in some measure occasioned by the popularity you seem to have acquired in the active advocacy of those various political changes which in his case 30 years ago brought upon him so much evil. . . . Sending the newspapers shows you have not forgotten him — But at the same time he is mortified and dissa-pointed you never write him. . . ."

Why his brother James Moir (1806-1880) acted in this inhuman fashion is a mystery. A successful tea merchant, ħe was active in the Chartist Movement and the Scottish National Reform League. Elected to Glasgow Town Council in 1848, he became a Bailie in 1871. He was noted for his radicalism and his championship of civic reform. A street in Glasgow still bears his name, his portrait is in the Art Gallery and his library was gifted to the city. In 1848 he was undoubtedly a man of considerable means and political power, and had he so chosen, he could have brought his exiled brother home in triumph and at no cost to himself. Nevertheless, he chose to keep his brother as the political skeleton in the family cupboard. The dead radicals of 1820 were convenient heroes, but his brother was a living embarrassment whose sole memorial is a few sad letters which survive in the Mitchell Library.

---

3 January 1746

Mr Cameron and Mr Coats, Bailies of the City of Glasgow, depart on a tour of the Highlands. Their impressions of the trip are not recorded, but it is unlikely that they enjoyed it. They were hostages of Prince Charles Edward Stuart, whose army was vacating the city after a week-long visit of extreme unpleasantness for highland host and lowland hosts alike.

The Prince's army marched in on 26th December 1745, made themselves at home, and demanded 6,000 coats, 12,000 shirts, 6,000 pairs hose (ditto shoes) and 6,000 blue bonnets (for holding up their cockades). Thus equipped, they held a review on Flesher's Haugh, on the east of Glasgow Green, before a sullen and resentful populace. But it seems they did not get all the quartermaster asked for, so Messrs Cameron and Coats aforesaid were taken as security for the balance.

Despite the perks of the visit — the comforts of Shawfield House, the charms of Clementina Walkinshaw, who entertained him there—Prince Charlie was so disgusted with Glasgow it is said he seriously considered sacking it. The city may have owed its deliverance to the intervention of the kindly Lochiel who was, as teuchter rebels go, a gentleman. So, despite regular but inchoate attempts (every Saturday night) to demolish the fabric, Glasgow was not put to the sack until the 20th century, when Attila the Urban Planner descended on it like a wolf on the fold.

---

4 January 1714

Reference is made in the Burgh Records to the still-vexed question of the dispute between Glasgow's barbers and surgeons.

In the previous century, the city magistrates had elevated them, jointly, to the status of a craft, with their own deacon. But they had their differences. While barbers continued to perform bloodletting and other simple operations, the surgeons came to regard themselves as somewhat more qualified, and to exclude their humbler colleagues from the craft. The Council ruled that excluded, but qualified, barbers were to be admitted. However, barbers were not to judge the qualifications of surgeons, while presumably surgeons refrained from interfering with a shampoo and blow-dry. Thus, for a time, peace was restored. It hardly needs to be said that the two professions have since become quite distinct. The blood-and-bandage of the traditional barber's pole is a rare sight nowadays, and many haircuts are conducted in Glasgow without anaesthetic.

---

5 January 1899

Horse-drawn tramways had been operating in Glasgow since 1872, first run by private companies, then, after 1894, by the Corporation, who had purchased over 3,000 horses. The first Corporation tram left the Dalmarnock depot on 1st July that year.

As a result of a successful experiment carried out on 5th January 1899, it was decided to adapt the whole system to electric power. The Pinkston Power Station was opened in 1901 for this purpose, and from then on the electric-powered tramway service was developed and extended until it became one of the cheapest and best public transport systems in the world. It was also profitable.

In its heyday the service had 150 miles of track,

and the longest runs were over 20 miles. It was also possible to connect with other tram services as far as Balloch on Loch Lomond. The fares were incredibly cheap: pre-war one could travel from, say, Airdrie to Elderslie for tuppence ha'penny, or one pence decimal.

Glasgow was very proud of its tram service and in 1926 there was a song published by R. F. Morrison (the man who wrote "Just a Wee Deoch-an-Dorus" for Harry Lauder) called "Glasgow's Tuppenny Tram". One verse went:

> Don't use your hoard for a Daimler or a
>   Ford,
> Like the workers of Uncle Sam,
> Since Mr Dalrymple's made motoring
>   simple
> Wi' Glasgow's tuppenny tram.

This advice was, of course, eventually to be ignored.

In the mid-Thirties a new type of tram was introduced, "The Coronation". The first few models were introduced in a silver livery and, against the grey of Glasgow tenements, they seemed to the inhabitants like something out of the 21st century. Much has been said about these trams, and none of it exaggerated. They were the most comfortable vehicles of public transport ever made for the city — warm in winter, ventilated in summer, spacious, comfortable, smooth, safe, cheap. It was easy to conduct and run, and for the first time the driver was protected from the weather. Whether in the earliest double-decked tram or the single-decked "room and kitchen", he had previously been exposed to the mercies of the Glasgow climate.

Many in Glasgow thought of the trams as they did the sky or the sea, having a God-given existence — they would always be. But no. The Second World War interrupted the plan to build a fleet of 600 "Coronations", and after the war the people took to the streets on four wheels. The tram got in the way of the motor car. In 1962, amid a lot of ceremony, the last trams ran. There was much righteous grief at their passing (see 1st September).

From an article in the *Glasgow Herald* reflecting on the year 1856:

6 January 1857

"It is difficult to find a week among the last 52 not infamously distinguished by some huge commercial defalcation; some daring embezzlement; some startling bankruptcy; some atrocious breach of trust; some huge shape or another of avarice or rapacity. Senators, bankers, doctors, clerks, servants fighting in the drama of crime, occasionally diversified with an appalling suicide on Hampstead Heath or some frightful deed of blood. . . ."

This can only add strength to our public nostalgia for good old Victorian values!

A Papal Bull of Nicholas V approved the foundation of a university (*generale studium*) at Glasgow, which, he ordained, should flourish "in all time". Modelled on that of Bologna, it was perhaps intended primarily for legal studies, but extended to include theology, canon and civil law, arts etc. And more was to come!

7 January 1450

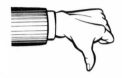

We are in the middle of the notorious Glasgow Cotton Spinners Trial which lasted from the 3rd to the 11th January 1838.

8 January 1838

In his *Conditions of the Working Classes in England*, Frederick Engels notes the proceedings:

"It appears that the Cotton-Spinners' Union, which existed here from the year 1816, possessed rare organisation and power. The members were bound by an oath to adhere to a decision of the majority, and had during every turnout a secret committee which was unknown to the mass of the members, and controlled the funds of the Union absolutely. This committee fixed a price upon the heads of knobsticks and obnoxious manufacturers and upon incendiarism in mills. A mill was thus set on fire in which female knobsticks were employed instead of men; a Mrs MacPherson, mother of one of these girls, was murdered, and both murderers sent to America."

Finally, in 1837, in May, disturbances occurred in consequence of a turnout in the Oatbank and Mile End factories, in which perhaps a dozen "knobsticks" or blacklegs were maltreated. In July of the same year, the disturbances still continued, and a certain Smith, a "knobstick", was so maltreated that he died (see 22nd July).

The committee was arrested, found guilty and transported for seven years (see 29th July). Engels, who had published this account in Germany, asks the rhetorical question: "What do our good Germans say to this story?" He then goes on to quote Carlyle:

> "What kind of wild justice must it be in the hearts of those men that prompts them, with cold deliberation, in conclave assembled, to doom their brother's workmate, as the deserter of his order and his order's cause, to die a traitor's and a deserter's death, have him executed, in default of any public judge and hangman, then by a secret one; like your old Chivalry Fehmgericht and Secret Tribunal, suddenly revived in this strange guise; suddenly rising once more on the astonished eye, dressed not now in mail shirts, but in fustian jackets, meeting not in Westphalian forests, but in the paved Gallowgate of Glasgow! Such a temper must be widespread among the many when, even in its worst acme, it can take such form in the few."

So we at least know what a Good Scotsman thought of it all.

---

9 January 1971

Three thousand attended a memorial service in Glasgow Cathedral today, one week after the appalling disaster at Ibrox stadium that shocked the city. A further 600 outside the Cathedral heard the service relayed by loudspeakers. Appropriately enough, all religious denominations were invited.

What had happened that Saturday was still something of a mystery. About 80,000 had attended the Old Firm game, and behaviour was remarkably good, only three arrests. Towards the finish, it seemed certain that Celtic had the game in the bag. Sections of the crowd began moving off, fatalistically, before the final whistle. Then, in the last few seconds, Rangers scored. There was an upsurge of excitement, those who were leaving turned about . . . on Stairway 13 someone must have fallen, tripping others up. From then on it was bloody chaos, people were smothered or broken in the crush, Sixty-six died, 145 were injured. The biggest emergency accident procedure seen in the city was mounted, though ambulances were delayed in reaching the victims by the crowds leaving.

Then the dismal aftermath, the cleaning and patching up, the difficult questions. As flags flew at half-mast over the city, the Lord Provost opened a disaster fund to help victims and their families, and a fatal accident inquiry was promised. For a time, matters of religious and sectarian difference were set aside, and Rangers and Celtic clubs and supporters alike joined in mourning.

Did it last? Did it hell. When a Catholic plays for Rangers we will take the change of heart seriously.

---

10 January 1844

The Free Trade banquet could muster only a paltry 2,000 Liberals to toast the (hopefully impending) repeal of the Corn Laws and to offer the Freedom of the City to William Cobden, a champion of Free Trade. This compares with a few years earlier in January 1837, when Glasgow's biggest-ever banquet was held. Sir Robert Peel having recently been elected Rector of the University, 3,483 Tories congregated to celebrate in style. The venue was a specially erected pavilion on the empty site which was to become Prince's Square. The toast: "Our determination to resist the inordinate desire for change that threatens to subvert our Constitution". Nowadays they would probably be called "wets".

---

11 January 1814

At a meeting of the Board of Green Cloth, the following was noted in the minutes:

> Mr H. Monteith bets a guinea and a Bottle of Rum with Mr Douglas that the Americans are not in possession of Montreal in six months.

(This refers to the invasion of Canada by American forces during the war of 1812-14. The Americans took a beating from a quite inferior British force, so that they failed to take Montreal and Mr Monteith gained his guinea and bottle of rum.)

The Board of Green Cloth was a whist and supper club founded in Glasgow around the middle of the 1780s. It lasted until almost 1820. Samuel Hunter, editor of the *Glasgow Herald*, and Kirkman Finlay (see 4th March) were both members. They met usually about five o'clock in the afternoon and drank, played whist, discussed important affairs, made silly bets and, at 10.15 exactly, had supper. In a memoir written in 1886, a Mr Colin Dunlop Donald said of the BOGC and its ilk:

> "These clubs had nothing in common with the palatial buildings of today, where men gather to scowl at each other, abuse the cook, and grumble at the committee."

If the amount of liquor consumed by the members is anything to go by, then this statement is true and the members were all good fellows. It hardly needs to be stressed that they were exclusively male.

---

12 January 325m B.C.

We were surprised to learn that a shark from Bearsden had, not so long ago, made big news. After all, isn't the area hoaching with them, with their flashy expensive cars and their big jobs in the city and all? This one, admittedly, had a better pedigree than most.

Imagine if you can the entire midland belt of Scotland submerged under the shallow seas of the Early Namurian age. Quite a seductive image, you'll agree. Imagine, in the area that will later be known as Bearsden, a primitive shark swimming contentedly around eating primitive shellfish. His name, though he doesn't know it, is *stethaconthus*, and he is destined for posthumous fame. And in case you are wondering how we are so confident of his gender, the characteristic paired penis is quite distinct . . . but we are going too fast.

One day in 1981 A.D. a Youth Opportunity Programme Supervisor was walking his dog, as even Youth Opportunity Programme Supervisors must do, beside a small stream in the middle of a Bearsden housing estate, when he came across *stethaconthus*, much older and turned to stone but otherwise amazingly well. Fortunately, the YOP Supervisor, being attached to Glasgow University's Hunterian Museum, knew he'd hit on something important. In fact it proved to be the oldest entire shark ever found, and the first complete specimen of his family. He has been voted Best-Preserved Shark from the Carboniferous era.

He is now proudly displayed in the Hunterian Museum, and a queer thing he is to be sure. Instead of the triangular dorsal fin associated with sharks, he has something like a parasol with teeth. The detail is extraordinarily fine — you can make out his last meal of crustaceans quite clearly in the gut.

The Bearsden Shark is the star, but there are other unique fossils that were discovered along with him: 11 examples of a new type of *palaeoniscoid* fish, several types of shrimps and what might be a giant fish louse. Also, lots of interesting *coprolites*, literally, fossilized shit. Trust Bearsden to pull it off!

According to Bishop Jocelyn, who is the only real source for the life of Glasgow's patron saint, St Mungo died on this day. According to the *Book of Saints* of the Benedictines, he died while taking a bath, but that is neither here nor there.

13 January 603

As a saint, and a pioneering, missionary-type saint at that, it is only to be expected that Mungo's life should be packed with miracles, and Mungo was miraculous a lot of the time. In fact, take away the miracles and the narrative tends to fall to pieces. He was born in miraculous enough circumstances, considering the rather ludicrous nature of his conception. His mother was a saint too, his father an innocent young girl. At least that's what he dressed up as to get into her bed. She was a bit simple. She was called St Thenew, later corrupted to St Enoch. Having been a Gate, a Chapel and a

This coat of arms, in the form authorised by the Lord Lyon King in 1866, is still familiar to most Glaswegians because it was stencilled in gold, silver and colours on the side of all public tramcars and transport vehicles from the end of the 19th century until 1974, when the reorganisation of Scottish local government turned Glasgow from a city into a Statutory District. Since the city had not flourished by preaching the word but by the vending of tobacco, slaves and machinery, God has been dropped from the motto and the Saint (though not the instruments of his miracles) moved upstairs.

The arms of the Statutory District of Glasgow, granted by the Lyon King in 1975. The baronial helmet has been replaced by a coronet or open crown of Scottish national thorns; the bird is a more convincing robin; a branch of the tree is now stripped of leaves to let the bell hang on it; the tree has been given visible roots; Saint Mungo grips his crozier more firmly, blesses the shield with his thumb tucked in, and has grown long hair. None of these changes are for the worse, but nowadays only advertisements and an ugly modern logo appear on the Statutory District transport vehicles.

Hotel, she is now only a Square and a Subway Station.

Mungo ("dear one") or Kentigern ("chief lord") — you may call him either — was brought up in the monastery of St Serf, where he soon made cordial enemies with all his fellow pupils. It seems they mistook the saint for a snob, a swot and a teacher's pet, as boys will. They made life so hard for him he decided he might as well go west and found a city or something.

On the way, he stopped off at Kernach to visit an old saint called Fergus, who made the visit memorable by dying that same night. Next day, Mungo put his body in a waggon, harnessed two wild bulls to it (this sort of thing was no trouble for a saint) and followed where they led. The bulls plodded on for about 30 miles before stopping at the tiny settlement called Cathures, "which is now called Glasgo" (Jocelyn), on the banks of a little stream. There happened to be a Christian burial ground nearby, so Mungo buried St Fergus, on the site of what would be the South Transept of Glasgow Cathedral. Then he built himself a cell near the stream, which was the Molendinar, and settled down to a life of exemplary asceticism.

Unfortunately the idyll did not last. Mungo fell foul of King Morken of Cumbria, a born-again pagan who had lately extended his dominion over the area. Mungo was forced to seek refuge in Wales, where he sojourned for twenty years near a river called, intriguingly, Clwyd ("Clyde"). Around the year 573, Rydderch Hael, or "Roderick the Liberal", came to power in the Kingdom of Strathclyde, with his seat of government at Pertnech, or Partick. Being a Christian, he was keen to have a Christian community re-established in the area. He invited Mungo to return. The saint did so, and followed his pastoral calling here until his death. His reputation grew, and Columcille, St Columba, visited him near the Molendinar. The saints swopped gossip and crosiers.

Four episodes from St Mungo's life are depicted on the Glasgow coat of arms (see also 23rd October and 26th November). The BELL is supposed to have been given him by the Pope when he was in Rome. Though it's highly unlikely he was in Rome, a small rectangular bell did exist in Glasgow and was attributed to him. The BIRD, a robin, was strangled by his classmates and brought to life by the saint. The TREE also dates from this period. The same obnoxious boys doused the school fire, which he'd been given the job of looking after. Mungo simply went outside, brought in a frozen branch, and commanded it to burst into flames. It knew better than to argue. As for the single FISH with the ring in its mouth, this is not, as some ignorant outsider suggested, a ring-pull haddock, but a salmon which featured in a marital dispute between King Rydderch and his wife, Languoreth. She had given the ring to her fancy man, in whose pocket her husband discovered it. He threw it in the Clyde, then threatened Languoreth with death if she didn't produce it. Understandably alarmed, she sought out Mungo. "Keep the heid, my child," he said, and told her to send a fisherman down to the river to cast his line in. She did, he did, and pulled out a fine big salmon with, yes, the ring in its mouth.

We have always felt this last trick more worthy of a Fairy Godmother than a Patron Saint.

---

14 January 1739

Glasgow did not escape damage during a great storm which engulfed Scotland. The top of the Tolbooth steeple was blown off. Many buildings were wrecked. Part of the spire of the cathedral fell through the roof into the church below. Trees were bowled over in the churchyard and on Glasgow Green. Wherever one turned, wreckage and desolation met the eye. And this just when they thought they were getting over the New Year hangover.

---

15 January 1918

This month, an estimate of £33½ million was given as the cost of constructing what would be one of the world's major waterways. It would be a canal joining the North Sea to the Atlantic via the "waist" of Scotland, capable of handling the biggest warships and merchant vessels.

Though the belligerent condition of Europe that year lent it urgency, the idea had been under discussion for years. The great commercial, strategic and maritime possibilities of such a route, avoiding on the one hand the crowded English Channel and on the other the foggy Pentland Firth, were obvious.

The proposed dimensions of the canal were 150 ft. broad and 45 ft. deep (the Panama Canal was 41 ft. deep, the Suez Canal only 28 ft.).

There were two possible routes. The first, the Loch Lomond route, would go from north of Grangemouth on the east, across to the south of Loch Lomond, up through the loch itself and out at Arrochar, from where it was a mere 1¾ miles to the natural deep water of Loch Long on the west coast. The canal would be protected by two locks only, one at each end, to control the tides. Only two major cuttings would be necessary, of 8 miles at Balfron and 1¾ miles at Tarbet. It would be crossed by three railway lines and 11 roads, while Glasgow's water supply would be led over by aquaduct.

The second, or direct, route involved simply following alongside the barge canal of the Forth and Clyde from Grangemouth to Bowling. This could be either a freshwater canal slightly above sea level, or a saltwater one on sea level. The dimensions would be the same as the Loch Lomond version, but it would have only one-sixteenth of its capacity for traffic.

Needless to say, neither of these plans were ever implemented. Our NATO allies found quite different and quite exclusive uses for our south-western seaboard. A canal would have no military function at this stage in our "defence", and as for trade . . . well, there's no point in living in the past.

Death of Sir John Moore at La Corunna in Spain.

16 January 1809

Not a drum was heard, not a funeral note,
As his corse to the rampart we hurried;
Not a soldier discharged his farewell shot,
O'er the grave where our Hero we buried.

Born in Glasgow in 1761, Moore rose to become a Lieutenant-General in the British Army. Aside from his death, about which every schoolboy and girl knows from Charles Wolfe's poem, Moore was distinguished by his humane and decent treatment of his troops and is reputed to be one of the greatest trainers of infantrymen in military history.

During the Peninsula campaign, Moore had his route of withdrawal cut off by Napoleon's troops, and he led his army to safety over snow-covered mountains to the coast at Corunna where they embarked. It was during this embarkation that the French attacked and Moore was mortally wounded. After his death he was severely criticised for retreating, but military historians now believe that his withdrawal was a brilliant strategic move which so tied up Napoleon's army that the Emperor's conquest of Spain was delayed by a year.

The Dean of Guild Court last week ordered the cleaning up and paving of one of the city's most notorious addresses, No. 32 New Street, Calton, better known as the "Whisky Close". They described it as:

17 January 1849

> "... a long narrow close, five feet in width, a four storey brick tenement on one side, and a lower house on the other. This five foot tunnel is the only access of light and air to a dense population of Irish and Scotch poor. There is an ashpit on the ground floor . . . it is the greatest plague (i.e. cholera) spot in the East End."

At the same meeting, they discussed one tenement near the High Street which was the most densely populated within the Parliamentary boundary. There, one apartment 7 feet by 15 feet, regularly accommodated nine adults. For 2d. per head, they each received bed and board (the same thing, probably) and just over 11 square feet of living space.

---

18 January 1908

The Glasgow District Committee met to consider letters from the Glasgow and District Unemployed Workers' Committee asking that men who were sent to the Palacerig public works daily be given something to eat other than bread and coffee.

During this consideration the following bit of light parsiflage took place:

> Councillor Cohen: I suggest porridge or peasmeal. (Laughter.)
> Councillor Carson: I suggest kitchen such as margarine.
> Baillie Steele: Ham and eggs. (Laughter.)
> Councillor Cohen: Porridge with milk or tea. (Laughter.)
> Councillor Pratt: I move that the men be given jelly with their bread.

On a vote the motion of Councillor Pratt was carried by 14 votes to 5.

---

19 January 1932

One of the most notable, and influential, of Glasgow gangs, the "Billy Boys", was founded by William Fullerton, in Bridgeton. His initial motive was one of revenge: he had been beaten up by rival supporters after scoring the winning goal for Bridgeton in a football match with the Calton team, Kent Star, and had decided to organise reprisals. Swelled by recruitment from Airdrie, Coatbridge and Cambuslang, as well as its native Bridgeton, the gang's membership reached a peak of around 800. It was exclusively Protestant, loyalist and anti-papist and its natural rivals were the Catholic "Norman Conks" (the "Conquerors" from Norman Street).

On 19th January 1932, around 300 Norman Conks marched in the Billy Boys' territory in Abercrombie Street using an unemployment march as a cover. They were armed with pickshafts.

Although taken by surprise, the Billy Boys managed to muster some 200 supporters and a pitched battle got under way. Several policemen were injured, several arrests were made and some fines imposed. These fines were met by levies on the local shopkeepers. Those who refused were beaten up and had their shops destroyed around them — it was estimated that this operation could be completed in around ten minutes. During the General Strike of 1926, a number of the Billy Boys organised themselves on the side of law and order, for which they received grateful recognition from the authorities. Their leader, William Fullerton, was a member of the Fascist Party for a time.

There were several things which caused the decline of the traditional gangs, particularly the coming of World War II. One individual who was most dramatically in opposition to them was Police Sergeant Morrison — 'Big Tommy from the Toll". He was an enthusiastic pioneer of reciprocal hardware capacity in on-going hard-edged interface situations. The testimony of court witnesses became quite monotonous: ". . . then Big Tommy from the Toll hit me, and that's the last I remember."

Two ladies (sic) who gave their names as Annie Swan (35), Bell Street, and Lily Scott, of 2 Carnarvon Street, both Glasgow, turned up at the Western Court according to a newspaper report of this day.

When a Woman (sic) appeared at the bar charged with importuning it was suggested that the ladies (sic) leave the court as was usual in such cases.

The Suffragettes, for such they were, refused to leave though Baillie Shaw Maxwell said that they had best consult their dignity by retiring. They stated as the reason for their protest that *women* were being tried by men with man-made laws.

Although professing to sympathise with the Suffragettes, Baillie Shaw Maxwell remarked that

20 January 1908

he believed that they should attempt first to convert those of their own sex.

---

21 January 1919

A concert was advertised in the Glasgow papers at the St Andrew's Hall, where Patuffa (sic) and Marjory Kennedy-Fraser were to sing Celtic songs to the Celtic harp in aid of the Stornoway disaster fund.

Tragedy struck during their performance of the "Song of the Seals", when the soloist was culled.

---

22 January 1898

On this day, the People's Palace was formally opened to the public "for ever and ever" at a special ceremony at which Lord Rosebery did the honours. A concept fed by the writings of Walter Besant and inspired by the ideas of William Morris and John Ruskin, it was to be the first of a series of cultural centres for the working people of Glasgow. Modelled on the People's Palace in the East End of London, it was not an ideal which many municipalities embraced, and indeed, the Corporation forgot their original intention of providing "palaces" in every area.

By the 1960s, the combination of museum, art gallery, winter gardens and music hall, where art and nature met for the benefit of the working classes, had been largely abandoned. Glass houses were felt to be anachronistic, and in 1966, the Winter Gardens were closed for demolition. Public outcry prevented so drastic a step, but the gardens remained closed, opening once or twice a year or the odd occasion. The museum soldiered on, half an institution struggling in an area which had become depopulated and desolate, half a People's Palace with no people to serve.

The museum staff hoped for better days, and in spite of the entire building being officially scheduled for closure, took the attitude that Lord Rosebery's word would rule. Preparations were made for an 80th birthday celebration, and Glasgow artists

Alasdair Gray was commissioned to paint a series of portraits of Glaswegians of 1977/8 — the famous, the infamous, and the anonymous. This was to open to the public on 22nd January with the optimistic title of "The Continuous Glasgow Show" and the invitation card to the opening intimated that the Winter Gardens would reopen at the same time. The Parks Department did not look on that prospect with the same enthusiasm, and the offending words had to be hastily obliterated from the invitation.

Nevertheless, the "Continuous Glasgow show" did prise open the doors of the Winter Gardens to the general public on a regular basis, and for the next 18 months the gardens were used and visited to such an extent that when they were again closed for demolition or repair, the outcry was enough to persuade the council that the building should be kept at all costs. The show still continues. . . .

---

23 January 1590

Magistrates and Councillors of Glasgow were shocked to learn that squatters had taken over the Tolbooth, the town prison. Some careless officer had forgotten to lock the doors.

Homelessness is still a serious problem in Glasgow, but we can't imagine anyone willingly taking up residence in the "Bar-L". Mind you, that "Special Unit" sounds not too bad, but it's murder to get into.

---

24 January 1919

As a result of alleged preferences given to British seamen who were signing on as crew to a ship in the Glasgow Harbour, a riot broke out between white and coloured seamen in the Broomielaw.

About 30 "coolies" (that was the word used in the newspaper reports) were set upon by a white mob. They took refuge in the Sailors' Home in James Watt Street, were ejected from there and found their way to a house nearby where they usually lodged. They were besieged there by the mob until help arrived from the police who had to draw reinforcements from all parts of the city. The riot lasted for an hour, several people were stabbed and shots were fired. One Duncan Cowan was shot in the neck and quite seriously injured. The black man who shot him had also quite serious wounds in his back.

In the end 30 people were arrested, mostly "coolies", and they were charged with forming part of a riotous mob, firing revolvers, brandishing knives to the danger of the lieges. The black man was also charged with shooting Cowan.

---

25 January 1906

At a meeting of the Toynbee Musical Association Choir a motion was put by a Mr H. S. Roberton, who was their conductor, that from then on they should be known as the Glasgow Orpheus Choir. A few years earlier Hugh Roberton had this to say about the choir's first warbles: "They threw it at me in slabs. . . . So it was the loudest noise I have ever heard or wish to hear in the name of music."

From this beginning the Glasgow Orpheus Choir went on under the continual leadership of Roberton to create for themselves an international reputation. The name was abandoned shortly after his death in 1951. During this time the choir gained its reputation both through the making of gramophone records and, especially in Germany and the United States, through touring.

Under Roberton there were certain songs, hymns and airs like "All in an April Evening", "Crimond", or "The Eriskay Love Lilt", which became almost definitive versions and to this day recordings are regularly played in radio request programmes. This pleasure was denied listeners to the BBC for some time in the early part of the Second World War when the Orpheus was banned from the air because of conductor Hugh Roberton's pacifist views. Roberton's case was taken up by the Council for Civil Liberties and Vaughan Williams, the composer, went on strike and refused to work for the BBC until the

"Orpheus" was reinstated. The ban lasted for about a year.

No account of the "Orpheus" can explain why it was such a loved and admired institution and why Glasgow people are so proud of it. There is the story of the schoolboy who when asked what were Scotland's Honours Three answered, "Rabbie Burns, Rangers, and the Orpheus Choir."

---

26 January 1839

Benny Lynch, Jim Watt, Ken Buchanan — a bunch of sissies. Boxing used to be a *man's* game, back early last century, none of your namby-pamby "rules", wet nurses for referees, gloves like sleeping bags and your nappy changed each round.

Deaf Burke. Now there was a boxer. His best fight was with Simon Byrne. Deaf Burke won by killing him in the 99th round. And Byrne wasn't rubbish — he'd killed Sandy McKay in the 47th.

In 1839 the *Glasgow Herald* says "this deaf blackguard" was disqualified for fighting foul. Shame!

---

27 January 1795

Report in *The Glasgow Mercury:*

> "For these eight days last we have had a very heavy fall of snow and last night a very intense frost. Now is the time for the wealthy and generous, during the present very rigorous and inclement season, to give immediate relief to the indigent who are perishing with hunger and cold in the cheerless tenement of poverty.
>
> "On Friday a guinea was sent by an unknown person to the keeper of the Tolbooth to purchase coal for the prisoners."

This was an untypical entry, as the burghers in Glasgow were not characterised by stealthy acts of public generosity. Usually, while declining to advertise their wealth, they liked to have their names listed, with the amount they contributed to charity. Every winter when the weather was bad long lists of the names of public benefactors were printed.

28 January
1868

Birthday of Frederick Lamond, one of Liszt's last pupils. He was a pianist of great distinction and a link with the Romantic piano of the mid-19th century. Lamond returned to his native country and was still giving concerts in Glasgow up until a few years before his death in 1949. The present writer heard two of these concerts and remembers that Lamond played pieces by Liszt as encores. One of his noted pupils was Agnes Walker, the Scottish concert pianist. Like his contemporary and fellow Glaswegian D'Albert (see 10th April) Lamond was considered a Beethoven specialist. He did make

some records which show him as a pianist of considerable imagination and style though he was said by some to have lacked the formidable technique that was often expected of Liszt's pupils. In contradiction to this is the claim that the breakthrough to the modern convention of playing such pieces of virtuoso material as the Hammerklavier not as a mere technical challenge but as a coherent and shapely musical composition can be attributed directly to Lamond.

Lamond was introduced to music by his father, who was a self-taught musician. He was brought up in the East End of Glasgow. In his mature years he became a friend of some of the most important 19th-century musicians and composers.

---

29 January
1918

At midnight on the morning of this day a demonstration was held in George Square in protest against the war. The previous evening the Clyde Workers' Committee had met with a Government representative who tried to persuade them to drop opposition to the Manpower Bill which provided for conscription of men over the age of eighteen.

The committee refused the Government's request and after a rousing speech by James Maxton spontaneously marched to George Square where they held their protest.

Bridge Street Railway Station was one of the first proper railway passenger stations in Glasgow. Cast iron urinals had been installed at the station in 1856 but shortly afterwards complaints were being made about "the insanitary sanitary conditions". On this day a self-regulating register was employed to count the numbers of men using the urinals and a charge of one penny was introduced.

The Clyde Workers' Committee organised a strike in January 1919 which was to become known as the "40 Hours Strike". Aside from their advocacy of a 40-hour working week, they had made other demands in respect of pay and working conditions.

Towards the end of the month, the committee persuaded the Lord Provost of Glasgow to ask the Government to intervene in the strike. Bonar-Law's reply was unequivocal: "In these circumstances the Government is unable to entertain requests for intervention."

On 31st January a large crowd gathered in George Square where they listened to speakers such as Willie Gallagher, David Kirkwood and Emmanuel Shinwell. These men were among a deputation allowed into the City Chambers.

Many of Glasgow's tram drivers had refused to join the strike and as a result the trams were still running. The authorities were well aware of this, as they were aware in advance of the meeting. While the deputation was inside, the police, under the pretext of clearing the way through the square for a tramcar, charged the crowd with drawn batons. Gallagher and Kirkwood were beaten up by police as they came back out of the City Chambers.

A Sheriff Mackenzie read the Riot Act, which he addressed not to the police but to the crowd. Peace was achieved because both injured leaders addressed their supporters from a window of the Town Clerk's office appealing for them to disperse to Glasgow Green.

That day has since been known in Glasgow as "Bloody Friday". Although the scenes were described as "riotous", the intention of the men who assembled was to support their cause in a completely lawful manner. It is one of the disgraces of Glasgow history not only that it happened, but that the behaviour of the police and those who gave them their orders was not subjected to proper legal scrutiny.

The following letter appeared in today's *Glasgow Herald*. If it seems strange how the smallest of things can merit the attention of the great and pre-occupied, we must remember how the rulers of the Roman republic used to divine the future from watching the flight of birds, even guiding their policy by such augury.

> "Sir,
> On Sunday, January 29, at 2.45 p.m., I spotted a cloud of midges in my Pollockshields garden. Is this a record? What are the implications for the summer?
>> Dr Michael Kelly,
>> Lord Provost,
>> City Chambers, Glasgow."

Ominous, Dr Kelly, ominous.

Glasgow's old Grammar School, founded way back in 1450, was no doubt a very venerable and useful thing, but it perpetuated some deplorable traditions.

Every year, on this day, a ceremony took place in the Common Hall known as the "Candlemas Offering". All the pupils and staff would be present, with the Rector presiding. One at a time, the pupils would arise and make an offering of cash to the Rector and to his class teacher. The Rector would call out the amount presented.

If the offering was 5s., the Rector cried *"vivat!"* (let him live) and the pupils would stamp their feet once. If it was 10s. the Rector cried *"floreat!"* (let him flourish) and he got two stamps. For 15s. he got *"floreat bis!"* (let him flourish twice) and three stamps, while 20s. earned the cry of *"floreat ter!"* (let him flourish thrice) and, yes, four stamps. But for the little sook with the Tobacco Lord for a daddy who gave a guinea or over, it was *"gloriat!"* and six hearty, if thoroughly jealous, stamps.

It is not difficult to imagine which pupils got the best treatment. By 1786, the Town Council was getting embarrassed by the whole disgraceful performance, and banned the public pronouncements. The offerings themselves continued, though

— they had no desire to mitigate inequalities in education, merely to be more tactful about them.

3 February 1946

Buses replaced night tram services running from George Square at 1.00, 2.15 and 3.30 a.m. Waiting for these buses after a night at the "jigging" is one of the Glaswegians' fondest memories. It takes more than blizzards, hypothermia and cold wet feet to kill *Romance*.

4 February 1925

Operators of bus companies were forbidden from this date to use stances in any part of the city as termini, other than those at Calton Place, Cathedral Street and Renfrew Street. This was to prevent out-of-town buses from crossing the city centre. There had been an increase in motor traffic and along with the start of motor bus services on 9th December 1924, this restriction was deemed necessary by the Chief Constable.

The order was ignored by the operators and did not come into effect until several of them were fined under the relevant Police Act. Even then some cases were taken as far as the Appeal Court.

5 February 1908

At a Local Government Enquiry into the administration of Ruchill Hospital, a Nurse Leslie gave evidence of a ward of 75 patients being looked after by two nurses and a probationer. Other evidence of a similar kind was given. This was in the middle of a long enquiry which became a *cause celebre* for a while in Glasgow.

The matron was reported as addressing her overworked staff with these words: "I am matron of Ruchill Hospital. *My power is absolute* (our italics). I will staff the wards with what I like and with whom I like."

She also kept a bathroom in one of the wards from being used because she kept her dogs in it.

After evidence being given for days about the dispute between the said matron and the rest of the hospital staff, a report was sent to a Local Government Board who were to decide whether or not another enquiry should be held.

John MacLean arrested and charged with sedition (see 30th November). He had been speaking at a meeting in Bath Street when he was seized by the police. He was taken by the police next day to Edinburgh Castle as "a prisoner of war" where he was told he was to be held under the Defence of the Realm Act. He had the choice of being tried by the High Court or by Court Martial.

He wrote in a letter, "Naturally I'll select the High Court. . . ."

6 February 1916

Two Glasgow detectives set sail for Belfast where, meeting some officers of the Royal Irish Constabulary, they travelled further to the shores of Belfast Lough. There in a cave near the shore they arrested four Glaswegians. The hideout had been given to the police by an informant in Glasgow.

The four were James Rollins, Albert Fraser, Helen White and Elisabeth Stewart. The women were prostitutes and the two men were their ponces. A few days previously Rollins and Fraser had induced White to pick up someone for the purposes of robbery. Their victim was a man from Govanhill whom White picked up in Hope Street.

The two ponces waylaid the victim, one Henry Senior, holding him up with a revolver. Senior fought with them and eventually he was killed by blows from the revolver butt.

The charges against White were dropped when she became principal witness for the Crown. The two men were found guilty after a two-day trial and were hanged at Duke Street prison in May. It was the last double hanging to take place in Duke Street.

7 February 1920

8 February 1830

Moved along for the last time today was Alexander MacDonald, better known as "Blind Alick" or, more extravagantly, as the "Glasgow Homer". This popular and successful busker made his living by composing occasional verse on matters of current interest, such as the French wars. After much whisky and rehearsal he would sing these up and down the Trongate, accompanied by a fairly rough fiddle. His verse had quite a number of faults, but chiefly a tendency towards overstatement:

> *I've wandered the world over,*
> **And many a place beside;**
> *But never saw a more beautiful city*
> *Than this on the navigable river Clyde.*

It might be supposed that MacDonald had been blind from birth, but no, his handicap was the result of an attack of smallpox as a young boy.

---

9 February 1779

On the occasion of the King's fast day a mob, later to become known as "Bagnall's Rabble", congregated round his house in the Gallowgate where Catholics had been worshipping. The mob set fire to the house and broke into Bagnall's shop, wrecking it and its contents. Order was not restored until the following day.

The immediate cause of "Bagnall's Rabble" was the Reform Bill which was then being discussed in Parliament. Magistrates issued a proclamation that the Bill had been dropped. They also offered 100 guineas reward for the arrest of the ringleaders and even arrested some of the rioters. However, they were not diligent in the pursuit of the matter and no one was prosecuted.

To counteract the menace of Catholicism no fewer than 85 societies were formed, consisting of about 12,000 members! This to oppose any form of change to the existing anti-papist legislation. At that time the entire Catholic population of Glasgow was estimated to be about *twenty*, consisting mostly of Highlanders and their families.

"Rules and Regulations to be Observed by the Debtors confined in the Upper Storey of the Tolbooth of Glasgow" (approved by the Provost's Court).

A glance at this extraordinary document shows dramatically the difference between the attitude of the Glasgow establishment to civil debtors and to other prisoners. While the latter, in the cells below, enjoyed conditions typical of any 18th-century town gaol, i.e. appalling, the former were able to form an exclusive, and not uncomfortable, club. Rule 3 makes it plain that membership of this upper storey was not just open to anyone who owned a bob or two. No less a person than the provost called a court, and it was put to secret ballot whether the applicant might join. If accepted (Rule 4) he had to pay a "garnish" of 2s. 6d. (3s. 6d. if between 15th September and 15th March), or equivalent security. This procured such items as coal, candles, pen and ink, soap, salt, mustard — in short, all those little extras that make confinement less irksome for the gentleman debtor. Rule 6 offered a bargain package for the recidivist. If he was reincarcerated within 12 months of his release, his "garnish" was a mere 1s. 6d. Rule 7 allowed that prisoners other than civil debtors could be admitted "if of good character", and could vote with the court. But they had to pay a garnish of 6s. In accordance with the convivial nature of this fellowship, Rule 9 required each person, on the occasion of his liberation, to treat his fellow prisoners with 1s. worth of the liquor of their choice — unless "on his word of honour" he could not afford it. Rule 22 confirms the delicacy of the virtuous debtor: "It is firmly and irrevocably agreed upon, that the member of these rooms shall not permit the jailor or turnkeys to force any person or persons into their apartments who are thought unworthy of being admitted". That the top of the Tolbooth was at least as much a sanctuary as a prison, is made explicit in Rule 24: "Seeing that debtors suffer sufficient punishment by being imprisoned, it is unanimously agreed, that if any creditor or creditors shall presume to come into these apartments and insult any of the members, it shall be made a common cause, and everyone shall aid and assist to turn such creditor downstairs with sufficient marks of indignity."

11 February 1829

Mrs Hare, wife of half of the celebrated duo of surgical suppliers, was under the protection of the Glasgow police. She had travelled by foot from Edinburgh, carrying her young female child and sleeping by the roadside on the way. On reaching Glasgow, she was lodged in a Calton police cell to keep her from the sight and vengeance of the public. She succeeded in remaining incognito for four nights, waiting for a vessel to take her to Ireland, but was recognised in Clyde Street by a woman who shouted "Hare's wife — *burke* her!" and threw a stone at her. A crowd gathered and set upon her. Only the arrival of the police saved her from a fate named after another Irish killer, Judge Lynch. She was detained in protective custody until 12th February, when she sailed to Belfast on the steamer *Fingal*.

12 February 1574

The city's accounts for this date show that 12 shillings were paid out of the civic purse for "futt balls" for the use of revellers in the Glasgow Green on Fastern's E'en, or Shrove Tuesday.

These festivities, in marked contrast to the rigours of Lent, were actually supported by the Corporation, which also paid for pipers and jesters. Six footballs per annum were provided out of the common good fund until the financial year 1589-90, when the supply was privatised.

13 February 1810

Mr M. Monteith bets with Mr Colquhoun a bottle of rum that Glasgow Jail is not thirty feet wide over the wall. Mr Colquhoun lost and settled the bet.
(Minutes of the Board of Green Cloth.)

14 February

St Valentine's Day, and all very soppy it is too. But how many of the lovesick are aware that St Valentine is a resident of the Gorbals? His official relics are contained in an oaken chest in St Francis' Franciscan Church, having been moved there when the church was built in 1881.

Why is there not an annual pilgrimage to the Gorbals? It could work wonders for tourism.

---

15 February 1793

Fire left the Session House and Tron Church completely gutted when "Disciples of Tom Paine who were roystering and excited by liquor entered in a frolic".

Apparently some drunken louts from the Hellfire Club entered the church and started making bets as to who could stand nearest the fire for the longest time. They started to stoke up the fire, probably to make the ordeal harder, and eventually it got out of control and burned down everything but the steeple which, of course, is standing to this day. Whether they were "disciples of Tom Paine" is doubtful. They could as easily have been members of Bearsden Rugby Club, and it didn't even exist then. But even then the media were in the habit of blaming everything they could on members of radical political organisations.

---

16 February 1865

A terrible riot occurred on this day at the Old College in High Street. A number of students gathered to throw snowballs at the public, which missiles they discharged shockingly "at all classes of persons", as the press report put it. The police became involved and were set upon by *both* sides. A number of anatomy students heard the commotion and, leaving the classroom, belaboured the police with the bones they had been studying.

---

17 February 1849

At the Theatre Royal in Dunlop Street, *The Surrender of Calais* was playing to a packed house. Around 500 occupied the cheap threepenny seats in

the upper gallery. At the close of the first act, a trifling fire, caused by a gas-pipe leak, was discovered and easily extinguished. But not before the cry of "Fire!" had caused a full-scale panic in the gallery. As the audience rushed to the exit, 65 were smothered on the stairs, one a child of three.

18 February 1746

At an away match at Falkirk yesterday, Jacobite Rovers chalked up a convincing win against Hanover United in what was to be their last success of the season. Commentators complained that the game was marred by some over-physical tackling of the Glasgow wingers (two volunteer regiments) by the Highland lads. Manager Charlie Stuart was "unavailable for comment", but Dougal Graham (see 20th July), our man on the terraces with the hunchback and the big bell, summed up the situation in the second half:

> *Glasgow and Paisley volunteers,*
> *Eager to fight, it so appears,*
> *With the Dragoons advanced in form,*
> *Who 'mong the first did feel the storm.*
> *The Highlanders, seeing their zeal,*
> *Their Highland vengeance poured like hail.*
> *On red coats they some pity had,*
> *But 'gainst militia were fighting mad.*

Could it be they harboured a grudge against their former hosts? (see 3rd January).

19 February 1932

Writing in the *Sunday Mail* last week, John Clarke, MP, described his narrow escape from the crash of the R101 airship in France, a disaster which claimed 47 lives out of its 54 passengers. Not that he was on it himself; he had to cancel his flight at the last minute, happily securing the survival of one of Glasgow's most unusual zoopolitical specimens. John S. Clarke, an Englishman by birth, was to trade a lion tamer. He was also a political radical and versifier, involved with Maxton etc. in the left-wing politics of his adopted city. These two strands of his life came together when he earned Lenin's gratitude by curing his dog. He was reckoned to have a way with animals, and in the General Election of 1929 he was elected ILP Member for Maryhill. In his two and a half years in the House, he was not particularly active. In fact, he never got round to making his maiden speech, though he did participate when the issues of capital punishment and captive animals arose. When Wilson's Zoo in Glasgow was burned down in 1944, he tended the lions, soothing their nerves and bathing their eyes. After this, he performed regularly at the Kelvin Hall circus, retiring only at 67, by far Britain's oldest left-wing lion-tamer.

Mr Carnegie bets a bottle of rum and a Guinea dry with Mr Middleton that the French are in possession of Cadiz on or before the 1st of April next. Mr Carnegie lost and paid his debt.

(Minutes of the Board of Green Cloth.)

20 February 1810

At a special meeting of the Glasgow Chamber of Commerce held on this date, Mr W. A. Smith moved the following resolution, which was seconded by Mr J. L. Mitchell, viz:

21 February 1888

> "That, as the directors of the Chamber have passed a unanimous resolution on the 30th May 1887 in favour of the principle of the Decimal System, not only in the currency, but also as regards Weights and Measures, it is the opinion of this Chamber that the unit for the decimalisation of the Coinage should be £1 sterling, subdivided into 10 florins and 1,000 mils;* and that this resolution be communicated to the London Chamber forthwith."

The motion, after debate, was carried by 26 votes to 13.

This was not the first occasion on which Glasgow's businessmen had recommended decimalisation. As early as April 1855, the Merchants' House petitioned Parliament to introduce a system of coinage, weights and measures on similar lines to the US and the continent. They proposed two new coins, a silver cent and a copper mil (with value as above). The pound, half sovereign, shilling and sixpence would remain. It goes without saying that Glasgow's businessmen were ahead of their time.

* At 1,000 to the pound, the mil would have been worth fractionally less than a farthing — which would have bought you something then.

---

22 February 1615

John Ogilvie, the Roman Catholic martyr who was canonised on 17th October 1976, had been arrested in Glasgow as a Papal spy. He had come from France, and would not provide an explanation of his presence in that city that satisfied his interrogators. Furthermore, a number of Catholic books and a holy relic (a lock of the hair of St Ignatius) had been found among his belongings. To cap this damning, if circumstantial, evidence, he affirmed that the Pope's authority was above that of the king. This was enough to have him found guilty of treason and sentenced to death.

On 22nd February, he wrote a letter to a friend on the Continent describing his treatment: "While in prison I lay under a load of 2 cwt. of irons, looking for death, unless I accepted the proffered favour of the king . . . viz., a rich preferment and another religion." He stated that he had been kept for eight days and nine nights without sleep and fully expected more torture before his death.

He was hanged in the street outside the Tolbooth on 10th March.

---

23 February 1968

Patricia Docker, a 25-year-old nursing auxiliary, set off for a night's dancing at the Majestic Ballroom in High Street. At least, that is where she said she was going, but it appears she went instead to the Barrowland Ballroom. This turned out to be an unfortunate choice. Her naked body was discovered this morning in a garage doorway in Carmichael Lane. She had been strangled — the first victim of the enigmatic, mysterious and finally elusive killer who came to be known as "Bible John".

The centrepiece of the triptych of murder was that of Jemima McDonald, a 32-year-old mother of three. She lived near the Barrowland Ballroom and went there regularly. Her last visit was on Saturday, 10th August 1969. Her strangled body, partly clothed, was found in a derelict flat not far from her home on Monday evening.

Helen Puttock came from Scotstoun. She was 29 years old, and a mother of two. She often went dancing at the Barrowland on Thursdays. On 30th October 1969, she took her sister Jeannie along with her. At the dancing (this is Jeannie's recollection) they met a rather unusual person called John (he gave a second name, but it wasn't clear). He was sharply dressed, sober and well spoken — in fact, he stood out, Jeannie remembered, because of his *niceness*. He got dancing with Helen and offered to run her home. Jeannie was dropped off en route, after hearing the strange young man's puritanical, bible-paraphrasing talk in the taxi. She never saw her sister again. At 7 a.m. the next morning, her body was found near a railway embankment in Scotstoun. She too had been strangled.

The hunt for "Bible John" has been the most intensive in Scottish history. Despite a massive publicity campaign, maximum media involvement and the interviewing of thousands of members of the public, it has been singularly fruitless. For any reader who wishes to join in the search, cold now though the scent may be, we offer an alternative artist's photofit impression from our forensic department, painstakingly reconstructed from contemporary rumour:

For over a fortnight, Bayne and Duckett have been advertising in Glasgow a type of boot called the *"Eukmenida"*, "warranted absolutely water-proof, without differing in appearance from the usual polished and pointed-toed article". A fine

24 February 1884

article no doubt, but it'll never catch on in Glasgow with a name like "Eukmenida". How about "Wellies"?

___

25 February 1949

The first trolley-bus arrived in Glasgow. This was the first of a delayed delivery of 64 buses and the actual service did not begin until later. This group of trolley-buses were of two different kinds — one lot were numbered TB1 to 34 powered by English Electric motors and the other numbered TD1 to 30 which were powered by Metro-Vick.

The TD series had in fact a rather sluggish pedal action and could be difficult and unresponsive to drive. This made it particularly hard on the "Wine Special". It was usual for this run to be stowed out on to the platform, up the stairs and along the top. There was a stop just at the bottom of the slope going up Royston Road and many a time the TD series bus would not take its over-regulation load. The technique used by at least one driver was to persuade the roysterers on the platform to get off and shove. Once the bus picked up speed they could jump back on — that is, if they were fast, agile and sober enough. If they weren't, the crew would see them on the return journey and give them a wave. Nobody ever took it too hard.

In 1951 the single-deck trolley was introduced. Though this vehicle was meant to have a pay-as-you-enter system, it was not entirely satisfactory. Brian T. Deans in his *Glasgow Trolleybuses* mentions that the internal congestion forced some conductors to move around instead of sitting to collect fares. Our own memory is that most conductors did this all the time and that the pay-as-you-enter system on these buses was a complete failure. Another thing about the single-decker was that because of the overhang at the front of the bus and the type of suspension used, it was possible to get seasick while driving it.

The biggest practical difficulty for the driver of the trolley-bus was keeping the trolleys, or "booms" as they were called, on the wires. If they jumped off while the bus was at speed they could be quite dangerous as they sometimes pulled down the electric wires. They had to be replaced by using a long pole with a hook at the end. This was a tricky and embarrassing task, especially when the booms came off in the middle of High Street or Glasgow Cross on a Saturday afternoon. There were also dead sections of wire wherever there were intersections and these had to be coasted without the use of power. The turn from St Vincent Street into West Nile Street was particularly difficult, being a right-handed uphill turn, and buses often held up traffic there by getting stuck.

These technical problems were not insurmountable and it was for other reasons that the trolley-bus was withdrawn in 1967. During its period in Glasgow it had served no more than eight routes.

For a while the old Dunlop Street theatre was in the charge of an actor-manager called Alexander who was considered by the public to be a less than satisfactory performer. On this date the *Dramatic Review* carried an article noticing one of his performances:

26 February 1845

> "In the character of 'Scamp' Mr Alexander interlarded the author with a superabundance of his own good things and the laughter which his grotesque and absurd personation drew from the galleries encouraged him to introduce an extra quantum of his own peculiar dancing. He also busied himself in giving loud voice directions in stage minutiae."

After being greeted from the stalls by a "universal hiss", he finally stepped out of the part he was playing completely and made a speech to the audience, accused the orchestra leader of being drunk, abused the other actors, threatened to call the police, and created general mayhem.

A few nights previously he had played Cassius in *Julius Caesar* in his own inimitable style. So much so that a member of the audience who occupied a box was unable to stop laughing at his performance. Inevitably, Mr Alexander was piqued and had an altercation with the gentleman. This was too much for the actor who was playing Brutus. "I," cried Brutus, "can't stand this sort of thing," and discarding his part, his toga and his dignity, he got over the footlights, climbed into the box, engaged in anti-classical fisticuffs and then ejected the offending customer from the theatre.

The *Dramatic Review* doesn't inform us as to whether on any of these occasions the cast ever actually managed to finish the play.

---

27 February 1868

The *Glasgow Herald* reported that in future policemen in Glasgow would be allowed to wear contact lenses like their Metropolitan counterparts. No doubt some saw this as a lamentable sign of decadence; others must have felt it held out some slender hope of the right people being arrested. We also learn that the first recruits of the new minimum height requirement of 5 ft. 8 ins. had been accepted. Hitherto, the typical Glasgow polis was a 7-foot mesomorph from Benbecula. The men were worse.

---

28 February 1800

This month saw the "Bread Riots" flare up at last in Glasgow. The latest harvest having failed, the city was suffering its worst food shortage. Many were in real danger of starving, and each family had been restricted to a dole of one peck of meal. The dwindling store was guarded by a force of militia.

Such a situation, the Provost pointed out, could mean trouble, particularly when the writings of that seditious Tom Paine were being circulated. So the Council took measures. It started a guarantee fund, and set up a committee to import and distribute food. In all, £117,500 worth of supplies was brought in to relieve the city. David Dale (see 17th March) played a major part by shipping in grain at his own risk and expense. But whereas the authorities brought in the familiar oats, wheat, barley, beans, peas, flour and potatoes (in that order of quantity), Dale introduced maize, or Indian corn.

Glaswegians, highly suspicious of this novelty,

dubbed it "sma' pease", and probably made it into a sort of porridge. Having neither the recipes nor resources for chicken Maryland, crab and sweet-corn soup, or even buttered corn-on-the-cob, we must imagine them, like Ruth, in tears amid the alien corn.

The "meal mob" did considerable damage to persons and property before the problem was resolved, quite simply, by a harvest as bountiful as its predecessor had been disastrous.

1 March 1793

Following the establishment of a regular London-Glasgow mail coach, the gentlemen of the city began looking forward to the delivery of news and other public papers as one of the day's highspots. The chronicler "Senex" tells of the excitement that built up in the fashionable Tontine coffee house; how the waiter Charles Gordon would take delivery of the bag of around 60 papers from the post office. Locking himself in the bar, he would sort them into a heap. Then, unlocking the door, he would run out into the middle of the room and toss them into the air. A mad scramble ensued, as they were snatched, torn, fought over. The ritual became something of a civic scandal, and one facetious observer was moved to suggest that the town circus, which at least had a licence, was getting unfair competition. During February 1793, the following was posted up at the Exchange:

"TO BE SEEN AT THE
GLASGOW TONTINE COFFEE ROOM
Every day except Wednesday, about 11 o'clock
forenoon

or

Immediately after the arrival of the London Mail,
An entire New Entertainment.

A SCRAMBLE

This Exhibition consists of Flips, Flaps, Cuffs, Slaps, Kicks, Trips and other feats of *Gentlemanlike* agility, which need only be seen to be admired. It is not performed in any other town in the Kingdom, and is perfectly adapted to the polished manners of this flourishing city.

The performance can only be done by very *young people*; and as the Exhibition subjects the youths to many accidents, and has been hitherto performed without the permission of the Magistrates, they are afraid it may not continue long in this place; they therefore flatter themselves the curious Public will take the earliest opportunity of encouraging this very ingenious Entertainment.

Admittance with a basin of soup, 3d."

The custom was soon discontinued in favour of more sedate methods of distribution.

With the imminent completion of the *Notable Places of the Scriptures Expounded*, Zachary Boyd's lifetime of sacred literary labours was nearing its close. The following day he wrote in a trembling hand, "Heere the author was neere his end, and was able to doe no more." He died shortly after, probably later that year.

Boyd's output of religious writings was prodigious, and included such things as versions of the Psalms in his own excruciating metres and cheering dialectics like the *Last Battel of the Soule in Death*. He left behind a vague folk belief, mercifully exaggerated, that he had put the whole Bible into English verse. He did, however, grow the *Flowers of Zion*, doggerel rhyming versions of episodes from the Old and New Testaments. These are not very suitable for quoting, but we believe they are among the funniest things he wrote.

The year before his death, Zachary gave over £20,000 Scots to build a new High Street home for Glasgow University — previously, its accommodation had been makeshift to say the least — and to support three Bursars in Theology (what else). The grateful University installed a rather clumsy bust of him above its entrance. When the old college buildings were demolished (see 30th July) this was rescued, and can be seen today in the Hunterian Museum. If you really want to, that is.

Mr Connel bets against Mr Finlay a bottle of rum that Mr James Dennistoun will rout as a cow louder and better than Mr Henry Monteith.

(Minutes of the Board of Green Cloth)

The death occurred today at the age of 70, of Kirkman Finlay, the merchant prince who dominated Glasgow's business life in the first half of the 19th century.

In 1790, he had inherited from his father the cotton mills of James Finlay & Co. By 1801 this was the largest cotton firm in Scotland, and the largest supplier of cotton yarn to Europe. The latter was quite a feat, as the Napoleonic wars were in progress. Kirkman Finlay simply smuggled the goods through Bonaparte's blockade and into the occupied countries. He did such brisk business that in 1809 he opened up a London office solely to handle this contraband trade. The flouting of his blockade probably worried Napoleon considerably more than the Glasgow volunteer force known as the "Sharpshooters" that Finlay commanded, raised to meet the threat of French invasion.

Finlay again showed his flair and initiative in 1813 when, as a Member of Parliament for Glasgow, he attacked the East India Company's monopoly of the India and China trade. His campaign was vigorous and successful — Parliament abolished the monopoly. The way East was wide open for the Clyde merchants, who were not slow to take advantage of the new markets. Finlay himself, characteristically enough, was among the first in there.

Whatever the undoubted benefits Finlay brought to Glasgow's merchant class, he was a vicious reactionary when it came to politics, and in particular the movement for reform. It was he who, while Provost of Glasgow, was given the responsibility by the Government of investigating the West of Scotland radicals and collecting information against them. It was he who organised the iniquitous system of spies and *agents provocateurs* — in particular, the fifth columnist Richmond — that led to the persecution of many courageous and forward-thinking men and precipitated the disasters of 1820.

Clearly, your opinion of Finlay would depend on whether you were a wealthy burgher or one of the crowd that hung him in effigy from the Tontine pillars, and laid siege to his house in protest against his support of the Corn Laws. Whatever else he was, he was a busy man. As well as being Provost and MP, he was President of the Chamber of Commerce, Governor of the Forth and Clyde Canal, Dean of Faculty and Rector of the University. He died in

Castle Toward, which he had built for himself. The firm of James Finlay & Co. survived him, and has flourished into the 20th century, particularly in the tea business, where they are noted for the enormous wages they pay the workers on their Sri Lankan plantations.

Glasgow's Chamber of Commerce likes to remember Kirkman Finlay as the "Beau Ideal of a Glasgow Merchant". We might say, a capitalist's capitalist.

---

5 March 1967

John Fagan, of 35 Penston Road, Easterhouse, lies dying of cancer. His wife, Mary Fagan, along with members of the Legion of Mary, pray for the intercession of the Blessed John Ogilvie, martyred in 1615 (see 22nd February).

Father John Fitzgibbon has previously sought his intercession at Masses said for the cancer victim. Fagan is not expected to survive the night. In the early hours he complains he is hungry and eats a boiled egg. From then on, his recovery is rapid, eventually complete, and medically inexplicable. It is directly instrumental in the canonisation of St John Ogilvie on 17th October 1976.

---

6 March 1810

Mr Blackburn bets a bottle of rum with Collector Corbet that General Graham who has recently sailed that the object of his Voyage is Cadiz.

Mr Corbet lost and settled.

(Minutes of the Board of Green Cloth)

---

7 March 1696

A meeting of the Town Council and Magistrates to deal with the nagging question of The Poor and "What To Do With Them" concluded that the only way was for the merchants to look after their own poor (who were possibly not *quite* so poor), the trades to look after theirs, and, for those who didn't fit into either category, well, the Kirk Session would have to maintain them. A committee consisting of the Provost, four members of the Town Council and four of the Kirk Session, would meet "from tyme to tyme" to organise their welfare. Money would come from "that part of the stent formerly imposed upon such as are residents and neither merchants nor traders". Constables were to be appointed to keep strange beggars away from the city, to prevent abuse of the system. Apart from such would-be intruders, though, all poor and disabled persons were to be catered for, and all foundlings taken into care. The committee would build or purchase almshouses, and establish rules for their management. Vagabonds, and those who could not give an account of themselves regarding their employment, would find that civic hospitality had its price. They were to be lodged and fed, and set to work also. If they refused, they would be physically punished — but "not extending to life and limb, or mutilations of any member" said the Council in a fit of benignity.

The bulk of the community of Glasgow being found to be happy with the scheme, the order was to be put into action the following year.

---

8 March 1817

The newspapers today carried the final account of the trial of Alexander McLaren, a weaver, and Thomas Baird, a shopkeeper, which had taken place over the previous three days. McLaren was accused of making a seditious speech in Kilmarnock which invoked the spirit of Bannockburn and Baird had published the same. McLaren said, among other things:

> "Let us lay our petitions at the foot of the throne where sits our august prince, whose gracious nature will incline his ear to listen to the cries of the people, which he is bound to do by the laws of the country. But should he be so infatuated as to turn a deaf ear to such a petition, he has forfeited their allegiance. Yes, my fellow townsmen, in such a case, to hell with our allegiance."

In spite of the fact that the speech in defence of McLaren by his advocate Jeffrey was said to be one of the finest defence speeches of the time, and Lord Gillies the presiding judge being an old friend of the radical lawyer Muir of Huntershill, both men were sentenced to six months' imprisonment and ordered to find caution for a period of three years. McLaren at the time was earning five shillings a week for a 15-hour day.

After being burned down in January 1978, in one of the tragic conflagrations that have so dogged its owners, the Reo Stakis Organisation, over the years, the Grosvenor Hotel reopened for business in style.

The destruction of the grade-A listed building, so long a landmark of elegance in Glasgow's West End, shocked local residents, conservationists and insurers. Fortunately, the Norwich Union were able to spend the £6 million required to recreate the Victorian facade in glass-reinforced concrete, using moulds from the original stonework. It still looks more like glass-reinforced concrete than stone, but the proportions have been accurately preserved.

At the opening ceremony, Lord Provost Dr Kelly spoke of the new Grosvenor's importance to Glasgow. "We should concentrate (he said) on new and growing industries rather than those which are outdated," meaning, presumably, high-class tourism and catering rather than shipbuilding and engineering. Mr Stakis evidently agreed with him. The hotel, he prophesied, would be showing a profit within the year.

9 March 1982

The Town Council renewed an act ordaining every able man of substance to have a hagbut, with "graitht", powder and bullet effeiring thereto, and all others to have long spears, jacks, steel bonnets, sword and buckler. Deacons of each craft were appointed to report on how many were so provided. Baillies were required to report on the non-craftsmen. On the same date, the old ports of the burgh were ordered to be repaired.

10 March 1577

11 March 1831

Since July of 1825, Glasgow's Chief of Police had been Mr John Graham, a city merchant, who also held a commission in the army. He was the first incumbent of the post to hold the rank of superintendent. Being, moreover, a City Marshal, he was commonly know as Marshal Graham, and cut an impressive military figure in trades processions and the like: "in full uniform . . . mounted on a grey horse and (carrying) a large handsome truncheon". Present-day Chief Constables, though far from despising public acclaim, have tended to be less showy.

Graham's term of office appears to have been an eventful one. Twelve persons were executed for various felonies, the "resurrectionists" were active, and public morals were a continual cause for concern. An article in *Blackwood's Magazine* of June 1831 claimed Glasgow had 2,850 public houses (about one to every 14 persons) and half as many brothels — 1,425. It further claimed that from ten to twenty thousand Glaswegians got helplessly drunk every Saturday night and remained in that condition until the following Tuesday when they would dribble into work looking extremely pale and interesting. (See also *The Moral Statistics of Glasgow*—7th June.)

Three months prior to this shocking exposé (perhaps not entirely accurate as the author's main purpose was to attack the Reform Bill) the bold Marshal Graham had at least attempted a clean-up. On this date he ordered that all "loose women" found walking the streets be rounded up. Seventy were arrested between 11 p.m. and 6 a.m. the following morning.

12 March 1833

Glasgow Necropolis, destined to be one of the city's livelier developments, was formally opened on this date. It covered that area of wooded declivity formerly known as the Fir Park, the property of the Merchants' House. In a wordy advocacy of the site, the City Chamberlain, Mr James Strang, described it as:

". . . . suitable for every sort of sepulchral ornament. The individual, for example, who might wish for the burial of patriarchal times could there obtain a last resting-place in the hollow of the rock, or could sleep in the security of a sandstone sepulchre; while he who is anxious to mix immediately with his kindred clay, could have his grave either in a grassy glade, or his tomb beneath the shadow of some flowering shrub."

It was laid out in the design of the celebrated Père la Chaise on Mount Louis in Paris, and divided into sections from "Alpha" to "Omega" in a pleasant and symbolical circularity. What immortal hand or eye could frame that fearful cemetery? Why, Lord Provost James Ewing, in 1829. (See also 12th September, 17th October, 10th December.)

---

13 March 1683

Glasgow's Burgh Records mention the payment of £5 sterling "to the mountebank for cutting off umquhile Archibald Bishop's legg". A mountebank was originally someone who got up on a bench to extol the merits of some medicinal formula that would cure everything from herpes to cholera, a sort of Barrowland Roche & Co. Inevitably the word came to suggest a rogue, a trickster, a charlatan. On this occasion these derogatory implications may have been all too appropriate: "umquhile" means "late" or "deceased".

---

14 March 1941

On the morning of this day there was a beautiful moon — "a bombers' moon" as it was called by airmen and pilots of these days. From about half-past nine the previous evening a German force had been attacking Clydebank. Two hundred and thirty-six bombers attacked along the length of the Clyde and dropped 272 tons of high explosive and 1,650 incendiary containers. The German pathfinder unit which led the Junker and Heinkel bombers to the west coast of Scotland was the same unit which had led the previous terrible raid on Coventry the year before.

The British had radio countermeasures which

interfered with the German navigation devices by jamming their signals but as they operated only over English cities the Germans had a clear run up to Glasgow and Clydebank. Unfortunately, among the first targets hit by the Germans were stores of highly inflammable material: Singer's timberyard and the distillery at Yoker. These fires were able to attract some of the later bombers who were not instructed to look for specific targets. As a result of this the blaze which later developed in Clydebank could be seen as far as Dyce in Aberdeen by RAF planes flying there.

As usual in wartime, the overt purpose of the bombing, the destruction of industrial targets, was not nearly so successful as the Germans would have expected or liked, and the toll in human misery and suffering was everything. Schools, churches, hospitals and people's homes turned out to be more vulnerable than the supposed targets and the fatalities among the civilian population of Clydebank and Glasgow were horrendous. The bombers returned to Clydebank and Glasgow the following evening and bombed again until the morning.

In Glasgow, according to a report which was at the time kept secret, there were 647 deaths and 390 serious injuries; Clydebank 358 deaths and 973 serious injuries and in Dumbarton and other counties 78 deaths and 239 serious injuries.

---

15 March 1693

A breakthrough occurred in Glasgow's public transport facility when the Town Council authorised the Provost to agree with a coachman to serve his city with "Haickna choches". London had already acquired Hackneys in 1634. The one-man operated GGPTE was called John Taylor, and had an annual budget of 200 merks.

---

16 March 1926

Steamship *Dalriada* launched on this day. She was the fastest single-screw steamship ever built, doing the Gourock-Campbeltown run in less than three hours. She was sunk in the Thames during the Second World War while on service as a salvage vessel.

David Dale, one of the most popular, successful and versatile businessmen and philanthropists Glasgow has produced, died on this day.

Dale, the son of a small shopkeeper, started out as a cowherd before being apprenticed to a weaver in Paisley. From there he came to Glasgow, where he worked as clerk to a silk mercer. He set up a small business of his own in linen thread. To begin with, he would tramp around the country buying up small quantities of the thread from farmers' wives, but was soon importing it in bulk from Holland and France.

He became interested in cotton. In 1775, when Arkwright, the inventor of the "Spinning Jenny" came to Glasgow, he showed him the land by the Falls of Clyde at Lanark, amply supplied with water power to drive cotton mills. Arkwright agreed that the site was ideal. The two men went into partnership. By 1793 the four "New Lanark"

mills were the largest in Britain, employing 1,334 men, women and children. These included children from orphanages and poorhouses Dale had taken under his protection, cared for and trained, as well as 200 destitute would-be emigrants from the Highlands whose ship had been driven back by the weather. Other mills were started at Blantyre, Katrine, Oban and Stirling, and cotton became solidly established as the staple industry of the West of Scotland. Thirty years after Dale's death, there were no fewer than 134 cotton factories in the country, almost all within a 25-mile radius of Glasgow.

In 1799, Robert Owen visited Glasgow to negotiate the purchase of the New Lanark mills, which he bought for £66,000. He also married Dale's eldest daughter. Owen's pioneering of industrial welfare at New Lanark has tended to overshadow Dale's own contribution, though the work of the two men is best seen as complementary.

Not all Dale's ventures were successful. He tried to bring cotton manufacture to the Highlands, building an entire village (called Spinningdale) and factory on the Dornoch Firth in the expectation of cashing in on the cheap Highland labour in the area. Its failure to attract a sufficient workforce was put down to the incompatibility of the Gaelic temperament with organised labour: to put a Highlander in a factory, they said, was like putting a stag to the plough. Whatever the reason, the experiment failed. The plant was sold for a song, insured, and conveniently burned down. Dale tried his hand at coal mining, sinking £20,000 into a Barrowfield pit, but the seam was never reached. Much more successful was his involvement with George Macintosh in "Turkey Red" dyeing (see 18th March).

During all this, Dale found time to be a city magistrate, to be the Royal Bank's first Glasgow agent, to help found the Glasgow Chamber of Commerce and the Humane Society, and to be a lay preacher. Regarding the last, he seceded from the established church in 1769 and, not finding one to his liking, founded his own — the "Old Scotch Independents". This attracted some derision, but he took it seriously, teaching himself Greek and Hebrew and building a church in Greyfriars Wynd, the so-called "Caunel Kirk".

Dale put as acceptable a face on capitalism as it could wear in his day, and possibly since. His philanthropy may have been largely enlightened self-interest, but it was enlightened.

He is generally supposed to have been the model for Bailie Nicol Jarvie in Walter Scott's *Rob Roy*.

---

18 March 1797

The City Magistrates, fearing it might interfere with their own efforts (and reduce the consequent glory) yesterday refused George Macintosh's offer to raise a volunteer corps of 500 Highlanders for the war with France. Three years later, however, he helped substantially to fill the ranks of the Gordon Highlanders, the 133rd and 78th Regiments, and the North Lowland Fencibles, raised the Glasgow Highland Volunteers and, in 1804, when the Canadian Fencibles mutinied in the city, persuaded them (in Gaelic) to return to their duty. The Scottish Highlands at that period were suffering such dire poverty and overpopulation that there was no shortage of kilted cannon-fodder for Macintosh's homicidal hobbies.

But Macintosh was an amateur of more peaceable arts, and is better known for his partnership with the great David Dale and the development of "Turkey Red" dyeing.

Born in 1739 to a Ross-shire farmer's family, Macintosh came to Glasgow to seek his fortune. Having begun as a junior clerk in a tannery, by the age of 34 he was at the head of a rival shoe factory, employing 500 workmen. He became interested in the process of making dyes from lichen. Crotal, a rock lichen which had been used for dyeing sheep's wool in the Highlands for generations, had been recently developed by the chemist Cuthbert Graham, who discovered a process for extracting the dye in concentrated form. This came to be known as "Cudbear" after its originator. Macintosh had the foresight and the capital to cash in on the process. In 1777, he bought 17 acres of land in the Easter Craigs, near the Molendinar Burn, and began working in conditions of the utmost secrecy. It is said that for security reasons he employed only Highland workmen who had no word of English. Soon demand for "Cudbear" dye was so great the works were consuming around 250 tons of lichen a year, and Macintosh had to look abroad, to Norway and Sweden, for supplies.

"Cudbear" dyeing had its drawbacks. The cost of foreign lichen tended to grow with the demand. And it stank, so abominably in fact that it became the custom in the drafting of title deeds to property to forbid the manufacture of cudbear by the buyer or the feuer. And, above all, it could not be used to dye that most important and up-and-coming fabric, cotton. Looking around for an alternative, Macintosh discovered a madder dye called adrianople, or "Turkey Red", a pleasing, robust but ungaudy red originating perhaps in India. In 1775 he brought from France a M. Papillon who had practised Turkey Red dyeing at Rouen and, in partnership with his friend David Dale (see 17th March), set up Britain's first Turkey Red dye-works at Barrowfield. Though the secret of the immensely popular Turkey Red eventually seeped out via the mercenary Papillon, dyeing grew, alongside textiles, to be one of the city's greatest industries.

It was George Macintosh's son, the chemist Charles Macintosh, who struck a major blow in the war against the weather (or, in Glasgow, Weather) with his invention of the waterproof cloth that bears his name.

---

19 March 1746

For as long as people remembered, the journeyman wrights and masons of the city had worked a 14-hour day, from 6 a.m. to 8 p.m. Now they were demanding that an hour be knocked off in the evening, with no reduction in wages, and several had downed tools until this was agreed to. The Deacons and Masters of Trade were outraged. They responded by forbidding any foreman of the city to hire them except on previous terms, under a penalty of 10 merks a time. They called the wrights' demand "an imposition, not only on the freemen of the craft, but upon the lieges, and a species of oppression". The matter was brought before the Magistrates and Town Council, who interposed their authority on the bosses' behalf. Glasgow's first strike was quelled.

It was fairly obvious that the trade incorporations were associations of employers rather than workers, but by 1748 Glasgow had what might reasonably be regarded as its first trade union as we understand the term. The "porters and workmen" of the city applied, successfully, to the Magistrates and Council for authority to enforce the rules of a proposed society. Its main purpose was to provide support for "decayed" members and widows, to which end they sought fund-raising powers. They also had an early version of the closed shop: no one was to be employed unless he was a member of the society, and had given caution for his honesty and good behaviour.

In 1685, as a spin-off from their famous Whale-fishing Company which operated from Greenock, Sir George Maxwell and his partners established a soap factory or "soaperie" in the Candleriggs. Those distillers of blubber-based beauty products must have run into financial difficulties for on 20th March 1727, 66 firkins of soap were poinded against arrears of feu duty. However, on appeal, an agreement was arrived at. Whether the Town Council was loth to jeopardise a valuable Glasgow industry, or whether they just didn't want their citizens turning into dirty wee middens, Maxwell and his partners managed to soft-soap them into waiving not only the arrears, but all future feu duty for a lump sum of £60. And they got their firkined soap back.

The "soaperie" continued in business for another 50 years, before it was burned down in the usual way.

20 March 1727

A travelling menagerie put up at the Bear Tavern, above Glasgow Cross, and advertised:

> "a grand and surprising collection of real wild beasts, including the noble rhinocerine or real unicorn, a work of nature not to be paralleled, weighing upward of 70 cwts. taken from the great Mogul by the noted Kouli Kan (sic), all in its coat of mail or armour; and many more too tedious to mention".

Well, they could hardly follow that for a pedigree.

21 March 1748

Most Glasgow newspapers carried a brief account of the conviction of one Peter Manuel. He was sentenced to 12 months' imprisonment on 18

22 March 1946

charges of theft. This was Manuel's first conviction in Scotland. Later that year, while still in prison, he was charged with assault and rape and sentenced to eight years' penal servitude.

This was, of course, merely the beginning of the Glasgow lad's anti-social behaviour. He ended up on the gallows in Barlinnie on 11th July 1958, convicted of the murders of nine people, all within the space of two years. There were some who thought fewer. Unsolved murder cases are always an embarrassment, not to mention the terrible clutter they make in the files. It would be perfectly natural if the most strenuous attempts were made to clear one up, particularly if it could be ascribed to someone who was going to hang anyway.

---

23 March 1650

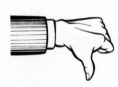

An advance of £5 sterling was awarded to an "Inglis clothiar" called Simon Pitchersgill (or Pickersgill). This was part of an agreed salary of £45 to be paid by the Town Council "for the erecting of the manufactorie and placeing him thairin", that is, for setting up a municipal factory and waulk-mill in the Drygate. Initially, the city fathers were full of enthusiasm for the scheme and made considerable financial outlay. Orders were given for work looms and for the construction of a mill lade. £500 went to purchasing mill furnishings from Holland, around £1,000 for wool, and so on. But by the following year, the venture had run into difficulties, not least as a result of bureaucratic obstruction. An Edward Robinson was employed to sell the cloth and to collect accounts, but each piece of cloth had to be inspected and measured by a *committee* before it was sold. By April 1652, the Town Council had decided the venture was failing and sent the town drummer around with the news that the "manufactorie" would be leased to the highest bidder. By the following year they were thoroughly fed up with all the expense and worry. The shrewd Pitchersgill took over on bargain terms. Thus an early experiment in manufacturing industry passed out of civic hands.

On this day Chief Superintendent Pearce wrote to the Lord Provost of Glasgow as follows:

24 March 1848

> "I observe with deep regret and painful interest the feeling of dissatisfaction lately evinced in regard to my direction of the police under my charge during the late riots, and although I am convinced that the grounds of this dissatisfaction would disappear after the first feelings of indignation on the part of the inhabitants, caused by the disgraceful scenes which have been witnessed, have been allowed to subside and the whole circumstances were dispassionately investigated and considered, I feel no longer I have the confidence of the public, without which I cannot perform the duties of my office and therefore tender my resignation."

The "disgraceful scenes" happened earlier in the month after an assembly of people in Glasgow Green. Although the assembly itself was peaceful enough, it seems that afterwards there were riots and looting taking place so that the magistrates were compelled to call in a troop of cavalry and to go about the city reading the Riot Act. In one incident in the city, a body of army pensioners, commanded by constables, opened fire on the crowd, killing three and wounding several of them seriously. One of the dead men turned out to be an "innocent bystander". He was in fact a special constable. Although 46 people were actually committed for trial there were 150 people arrested during the two days of rioting. As a result of these matters Pearce's successor decided that the police force needed reorganisation and managed to get for his officers and men a new style of uniform.

Today the voters of Glasgow Hillhead indulged in an orgy of "mould-breaking", a suggestive but ultimately meaningless term beloved by the media and the recently formed "Social Democratic" Party. And it was the Rt. Hon. Roy Jenkins of the SDP, in a profitable "Alliance" of convenience with the Liberals, who did the damage, ousting a Conservative majority of 2,038 to take the seat with a comfortable 10,106 votes. (The Tory got 8,068, Labour 7,846 and the SNP 3,416.) The result was

25 March 1983

received with some amazement, not least in Hillhead constituency itself, a strange and socially divisive place of seemingly random outlines. Perhaps the glamour and flattery involved in being in a position to change the course of British politics had gone to their heads. Perhaps they even believed it.

At any rate, it was a lively campaign, thanks largely to the minor contenders. At the forefront of these was the indefatigable Pastor Jack Glass (see 25th May), who took 388 votes for the "Protestant Campaign Against the Papal Visit". He was obviously toning down his message — normally we'd expect something along the lines of "Holy Crusade against the Scarlet Whore of Rome and the Coming of Antichrist". (It didn't succeed — see 1st June.) He was followed by a cad who unsportingly set out to resemble the front-runner as much as possible, but Roy Harald Jenkins (SDP) didn't fool more than 282 voters. Dr Nicolette Carlaw (Glasgow Ecology) managed a mere 178 votes — someone should have told her there *is* no Glasgow ecology. Finally, an Englishman with a good Glasgow surname, William Boaks, of the "Public Safety Democratic Monarchies White Residents", hit a British record low of five votes.

It was a silly by-election — we may not look upon its like again.

---

26 March 1656

According to John K. McDowall, author of *The People's History of Glasgow* ("compiled in classified form and issued at a popular price"), in 1899, on this date the City Treasurer was repaid £10 sterling, which he had given a friend in Edinburgh "for daing the toun ane guid turne". McDowall is typically coy regarding his sources, and what the "guid turne" was remains a mystery. And, while this gracious act on behalf of a citizen of Edinburgh gives us a nice warm feeling inside, we must confess our most exhaustive enquiries have failed to come up with another like instance.

When Provost Andrew Cochrane presented the Glasgow office of the Bank of Scotland with £900 worth of notes and requested they be changed into coin of the realm, he got quite a nasty surprise.

"Sorry," they said, "we've nane."

It transpired that two-thirds of their capital, and all of their notes, had been lent out on bonds and they were quite unable to provide immediate cash. Moreover, its rival, the Royal Bank (which was stoutly Hanoverian in its leanings, and run largely by Campbells, whereas the Bank of Scotland was Tory and had Jacobite leanings) was suspected of engineering a run on their cash, and effectively emptying their tills.

The bank in Glasgow insisted that, while it was prepared to pay interest in the interim, it was quite within its rights to defer payment. The Court of Session agreed with them, but the bold Provost appealed to the House of Lords, who took his side. Banks, they said, were bound by their promises in the same way as the private individual.

This was a useful precedent, valuable to all bank users, which means most of us.

From the Burgh Records:

> "William Glen, sone to Johne Glen, is fund in the wrang for casting of ane stane at Robert Rank and hitting him therewith above the ey to the expulsion of his blude; and also Johne Glen, younger, and Johne Glen, brethir to the said William, are fund in the wrang for striking at the said Robert and casting him doun violentlie to the erd; and also Laurens Hoge for troublans done to Johne Glen, younger, in thrawing of his neis, and hitting him on his dhe with an irne pyle; and the said Johne Glen for invadying of the said Laurens with ane drawin quhinger, efter the furst tumult cesyng, and als George Layng for invadying of Johne Glen with ane drawin sword; and dwme given thairon respective."

Aye, hanging's too good for them!

On the death of Sir William Burrell at the age of 87, the community of Glasgow became the grateful if barely competent recipient of his vast private collection.

Burrell's career can be stated briefly. Of Northumbrian descent, he was born in Glasgow in 1861. Next to nothing is known of his early years, but in 1875 he entered the family's already thriving shipbuilding business. After his father's death, Burrell & Sons meant William and his brother George; George handled the technical side of the business and William the commercial and financial. From the outset, he showed singular business acumen, or to put it otherwise, an eye to the main chance. The business grew and grew, seemingly without effort, although Burrell was not scared of taking risks. He himself described it as "making money like slate stones". When the First World War broke out Burrell & Sons sold the government all but two ships of their fleet. Afterwards, although the firm stayed in business until 1939, William had effectively retired. While he still kept an eye on it, he concentrated on indulging his famous and fertile passion for collecting *objets d'art*, which, by then, he could well afford to do.

As a collector, Burrell was shrewd, idiosyncratic, lucky, narrowminded, broadminded and tireless. The end result was quite unique. After years of hesitation and uncertainty, its full glory is at last displayed in its fine new home in Pollok Park. We shall make no attempt to describe it — it has received plentiful attention elsewhere — but conclude this rather breathless account by simply recommending the reader to visit it. Satisfaction is guaranteed.

---

30 March 1813

Mr Connell betts wt. Mr Craigie five Guineas and a bottle of Rum that preliminaries of Peace between Britain and America are signed before the thirtieth of December next.

(Minutes of the Board of the Green Cloth)
Mr Connell lost. Although a Treaty of Peace was signed at Ghent on 24th December, it was not ratified by the United States until 17th February the

following year. In the interim, the British contrived to lose 2,000 men at the Battle of New Orleans.

The University of Glasgow made one of their happier decisions on this date when they accepted the petition of Robert Foulis to become official printer to the University.

Although Robert Foulis, along with his brother Andrew, had only been in the printing business two years, the pair had already established standards of clarity, accuracy and elegance that far outstripped anything in Scotland and vied with anything produced on the Continent.

The brothers were sons of a maltman and largely self-educated. Robert, the more energetic of the two, began his career as a barber, while Andrew trained for the ministry. Robert began attending moral philosophy lectures at the College. The lecturer was Hutcheson, who spotted Foulis's potential and encouraged him to set up in business as a printer and bookseller. But before doing this, the brothers travelled abroad, visiting and establishing connections in Oxford and France, where they studied the classics as well as printing techniques. They also collected books, which they sold on their return. In 1741 they set up as printers in Shuttle Street.

The output of the Foulis Press was phenomenal, both in terms of quantity and quality. In the course of their 30 years, they published 554 works, mostly Greek and Latin classics and religious works, but also poetry, plays and contemporary letters. Their fame as the "Elvezirs of Glasgow" went far beyond the confines of the city. Robert was admitted to the College's Literary Society, to the company of Hutcheson and Adam Smith.

Not all their productions were impeccable. In the year they became the University printers, they brought out an edition of Horace which they determined should be of perfect accuracy — the "Immaculate Horace". As it was completed, it was displayed in the University quadrangle and a reward of £50 offered to anyone who could find a mistake. It was left there for two weeks before publication. Although no one claimed the prize, it turned out that there were no fewer than six errors (as many as there had been proof readers), one on the first line of the first page.

Robert Foulis was keenly interested in promoting the Fine Arts in Glasgow. He conceived the idea of an Academy of Fine Arts. This would be the first of its kind in Britain, ante-dating the Royal Academy by about 15 years. Foulis travelled through the Continent, buying up hundreds of paintings attributed to the greatest of the masters. In 1754, the Academy opened in premises lent by the University. Artists were brought over from Europe to instruct in paintings, drawing and sculpture.

The Academy lasted for over 20 years, supported by private patronage such as that of Provost Ingram and by Robert Foulis's own money and labours. Posterity has been a harsh judge of its successes — perhaps Glasgow was "not ready for it" — but it did produce the portraitist David Allan and medallion maker James Tassie.

After the death of Provost Ingram in 1770 and Andrew Foulis in 1775, the Academy's days were numbered. Robert was forced to close it and sell the collection. The auction, held in London, was a disaster. After all his expenses had been paid, he was left with a profit of 15 shillings. It turned out that almost all the paintings by the "old masters" were fakes.

Robert Foulis died destitute on 2nd June the following year.

As the citizens of Glasgow were making their way to church this Sunday morning, they may well have thought themselves victims of an April Fool joke. nd perhaps they were. A notice inviting them to open rebellion had appeared all over the city, subscribed "By Order of the Committee of Organisation for Forming a Provisional Government". Certainly, the contents of the poster were substantially in keeping with radical aims, but it now appears that fifth columnists had deliberately published it early, to spring a trap for the conspirators.

If this was the case, it worked. The authorities in the West of Scotland were already in a state of military readiness, and following the proclamation, several Regiments of Foot, Hussars and Yeomanry were mobilised, not to mention the bold Glasgow Sharpshooters under Samuel Hunter, ebullient editor of the *Glasgow Herald.*

On the 6th April about 70 men gathered at the Fir Park, armed themselves, and marched towards Falkirk with the intention of occupying the Carron Iron Works, expecting to meet reinforcements on the way. When none were forthcoming, many of their number dispersed. While the remainder were resting in an enclosure near Bonnymuir, they were discovered by a troop of the 7th Hussars. They refused to surrender when called upon and formed an attempt at an infantry square. In the ensuing skirmish, all were wounded and all were taken prisoner. They were tried on 6th July that year for high treason. A second force which had mustered on Cathkin Braes disbanded when their expected reinforcements failed to arrive. A number of these were later taken prisoner, including James Wilson (see 30th August).

On this day died Dr Gregory, the famous Edinburgh surgeon. Born in Aberdeen, his only connection with Glasgow must have been encounters with patients therefrom. Shortly after his death this anecdote about one such encounter found its way into print.

Scene: Doctor's study. Enter a grave-looking Glasgow merchant.

Patient: Good morning, doctor; I'm just come to Edinburgh about some law business, and I thought, when I was here at any rate, I might just as well take your advice, sir, anent my trouble.

Doctor: And pray what may your trouble be, my good sir?

P: 'Deed, doctor, I'm no' very sure; but I'm thinking it's a kind of weakness that makes me dizzy at times, and a kind of pinkling about my stomach — I'm just no right.

Dr: You're from the west country, I should suppose, sir?

P: Yes, sir, from Glasgow.

Dr: Ay. Pray sir, are you a gourmand — a glutton?

P: God forbid, sir! I'm one of the plainest men living in all the west country.

Dr: Then, perhaps, you're a drunkard?

P: No, doctor; thank God, no one can accuse me of that: I'm of the Dissenting persuasion, doctor, and an elder; so ye may suppose I'm nae drunkard.

Dr: (Aside—I'll suppose no such thing, till you tell me your mode of life.) I'm so much puzzled with your symptoms, sir, that I should wish to hear in detail what you eat and drink. When do you breakfast, and what do you take to it?

P: I breakfast at nine o'clock. I tak a cup of coffee, and one or two cups of tea; a couple of eggs, and a bit of ham or kipper'd salmon, or maybe both, if they're good, and two or three rolls and butter.

Dr: Do you eat no honey, or jelly, or jam, to breakfast?

P: O yes, sir; but I don't count that as anything.

Dr: Come, this is a very moderate breakfast. What kind of dinner do you make?

P: Oh, sir, I eat a very plain dinner indeed. Some soup, and some fish, and a little plain roast or boiled; for I dinna care for made dishes; I think, some way, they never satisfy the appetite.

Dr: You take a little pudding, then, and afterwards some cheese?

P: Oh yes; though I don't care much about them.

Dr: You take a glass of ale or porter with your cheese?

P: Yes, one or the other, but seldom both.

Dr: You west country people generally take a glass of Highland whisky after dinner?

P: Yes, we do; it's good for digestion.

Dr: Do you take any wine during dinner?

P: Yes, a glass or two of sherry; but I'm indifferent as to wine during dinner. I drink a good deal of beer.

Dr: What quantity of port do you drink?

P: Oh, very little; not above half a dozen glasses or so.

Dr: In the west country, it is impossible, I hear, to dine without punch?

P: Yes, sir; indeed 'tis punch we drink chiefly; but, for myself, unless I happen to have a friend with me, I never tak more than a couple of tumblers or so, and that's moderate.

Dr: Oh, exceedingly moderate, indeed! You then, after this slight repast, take some tea, and bread and butter?

P: Yes, before I go to the counting-house to read the evening letters.

Dr: And on your return, you take supper, I suppose?

P: No, sir, I canna be said to tak supper; just something before going to bed; a rizzer'd haddock, or a bit of toasted cheese, or half a hundred oysters, or the like o' that; and, may be, two-thirds of a bottle of ale; but I tak no regular supper.

Dr: But you take a little more punch after that?

P: No, sir; punch does not agree with me at bedtime. I tak a tumbler of warm whisky toddy at night; it's lighter to sleep on.

Dr: So it must be, no doubt. This, you say, is your everyday life; but, upon great occasions, you perhaps exceed a little?

P: No, sir, except when a friend or two dine with me, or I dine out, which, as I am a sober family man, does not often happen.

Dr: Not above twice a week?

P: No; not oftener.

Dr: Of course you sleep well, and have a good appetite?

P: Yes, sir, thank God, I have; indeed, any wee harl o' health that I hae is about mealtime.

Dr: (assuming a severe look, knitting his brows, and lowering his eyebrows) Now, sir, you are a very pretty fellow, indeed; you come here and tell me that you are a moderate man, and I might have believed you, did I not know the nature of the people in your part of the country; but, upon examination, I find, by your own shewing, that you are a most voracious glutton; you breakfast in the morning in a style that would serve a moderate man for dinner; and, from five o'clock in the afternoon, you undergo one almost uninterrupted loading of your stomach till you go to bed. This is your moderation! You told me, too, another falsehood — you said you were a sober man; yet, by your own shewing, you are a beer swiller, a dram-drinker, a wine-bibber, and a guzzler of Glasgow punch — a liquor, the name of which is associated, in my mind, only with the ideas of low company and beastly intoxication. You *tell me* you eat indigestible suppers, and swill toddy to force sleep — I *see* that you chew tobacco. Now, sir, what human stomach can stand this? Go home, sir, and leave off your present course of riotous living — take some dry toast and tea to your breakfast — some plain meat and soup for dinner, without adding to it anything to spur on your flagging appetite; you may take a cup of tea in the evening, but never let me hear of haddocks and toasted cheese, and oysters, with their accompaniments of ale and toddy at night; give up chewing that vile narcotic, nauseous abomination, and there are some hopes that your stomach may recover its tone, and you be in good health like your neighbours.

P: I'm sure, doctor, I'm very much obliged to you — (taking out a bunch of banknotes) — I shall endeavour to—

D: Sir, you are not obliged to me — put up your money, sir. Do you think I'll take a fee from you for telling you what you knew as well as myself? Though you are no physician, sir, you are not altogether a fool. You have read your Bible, and must know that drunkenness and gluttony are both sinful and dangerous; and, whatever you may think, you have this day confessed to me that you are a notorious glutton and drunkard. Go home, sir, and reform, or, take my word for it, your life is not worth half a year's purchase.

(Exit patient, dumbfounded, and looking blue.)

Dr: (Solus) Sober and temperate! Dr Watt tried to live in Glasgow, and make his patients live moderately, and purged and bled them when they were sick; but it would not do. Let the Glasgow doctors prescribe beefsteaks and rum punch, and their fortune is made.

---

3 April 1887

The match between Abercorn and Arthurlie (Barrhead) football clubs for the final of the Renfrewshire Cup was halted yesterday in disgraceful circumstances. Arthurlie had disputed a goal against them (which would have made the score 2-1 for Abercorn) and left the pitch. A fight broke out between Tam Johnstone of Abercorn and one of the Arthurlie full backs. While some spectators rushed on to the pitch to join in the affray, others seized the money collectors and manhandled them. One threw his takings at the crowd to prevent further ill-treatment and later an estimated £20 were thus lost. Most of the money, however, had been placed in a vehicle and taken to the bank by the treasurer. The constables, helpless in the face of large numbers of opposing spectators fighting on the pitch, were not helped when the referee tried to abandon the match, for many more spectators, till then not involved in the skirmishes, invaded the pitch loudly clamouring the game continue. With hundreds now rioting for one reason and another, and Johnstone and his opponent lost from sight in a seething mass, reinforcements arrived and the game was at length resumed. Abercorn won by five goals to one.

Later, at a meeting of the Renfrewshire F.A. in Paisley, it was decided:

1. To reject Arthurlie's protest regarding bias of referee.
2. To expel two Arthurlie players from the Association "during its pleasure" for using abusive language to the referee.
3. The two players were censured for quarrelling during the game.
4. The Arthurlie secretary was censured for persuading his team to leave the field and for using bad language to the referee.
5. Both clubs were to make good the damage to the ground.

(From *Scottish Umpire*, 13th April 1887)

The first stone of the new University at Gilemorehill was laid, although the ceremonial laying of the foundation did not take place until October of the following year when the Prince and Princess of Wales attended and a contemporary bard was moved to enthuse:

Ye walls that massive rise on Gilmorehill,
With stately tower and many a turret
*   crowned,*
Soon shall the thronging youth these
*   precincts fill,*
Soon render these environs classic
*   ground.*

Well, perhaps, but the word "classic" is unfortunate since the end result, for better or worse, was that spiky pile of bogus Gothicism that dominates the skyline of the West End to this day.

4 April 1867

Amazingly, there was no competition for the design. It appears that the University authorities wanted a prestigious job rather than just a good one. It is hard to credit otherwise when, with architects of the quality of "Greek" Thomson, flourishing in the home city, they looked to London, to the expensive and fashionable George Gilbert Scott, for the designs. However, they did, and, despite Thomson's scathing comments, the building went ahead.

Scott's claims were somewhat weird. The building, he claimed, was "authentically mediaeval and Scottish" (presumably with the exception of little modern conveniences like the huge cast-iron beams built into the walls to support the upper floors). "We took that noble architecture which characterised the secular buildings in Scotland in the 16th century and worked it out with details of the 14th century in France, and in doing so I believe we very nearly succeeded in recovering what was the early architecture of Scotland." What on earth could he have had in mind?

Many faults have been pointed out: the inadequate opportunities for lighting (and other practical considerations as any student who has shivered in its dismal lecture halls will confirm), the boring South face, with its misproportioned tower, the poor spire (happily altered by Scott's son to the present open-work affair) and so on. Kindly apologists usually end up by saying it is not really as bad as it might have been. And the spires do dream in the manner proper to higher learning.

Some relics of the High Street College were salvaged and incorporated in the new building. The "Lion and Unicorn staircase", complete with beasts, was reconstructed in the Outer Quadrangle, while Pearce Lodge, at the foot of University Avenue, is composed of fragments of the old facade. An interesting trophy retained from the good old days is the "Blackstone Chair". This is a sort of electric chair without the electricity, or a combined throne and egg-timer. At examinations, the student-victim would be placed on it and searching questions fired at him in Latin until the sands ran out, by which time he would no doubt be done to a turn, scrambled or hard-boiled. We hear this ancient form of the third degree is still resorted to on ritual occasions. Yes, the heritage of barbarism is gruesome enough, but that of civilisation can be downright cruel.

Carl MacDougall is born just in time to get himself an income tax rebate. Hard to believe this smiling babe will one day so far forget himself as to be irrevocably connected with that disreputable street-ballad, greatly relished by the vulgar element, known as "Cod Liver Oil and Orange Juice". Indeed, many believe it to be a folksong of hazy and ancient origin;* however, we confirm it is wholly the handcrafted work of the aforesaid and present it here, as it were, from the horse's mouth:

COD LIVER OIL AND THE ORANGE JUICE

It was oot o the east[1] there came a hard man,[2]
Aw haw, aa the way fae Brigton.[3]

Chorus
Ah-ha, Glory Hallelujah,
The cod liver oil and the orange juice.[4]

He went intae a pub and he came oot paraletic,[5]
Aw haw, the VP[6] and the cider.

Does this bus go tae the Denny Palais?[7]
Aw haw, Ah'm lookin fur a lumber.

In the Palais he met Hairy[8] Mairy.
Aw haw, the flooer o the Calton.

He says tae her, Tell me hen[9] are ye dancin?
Aw naw, it's just the wey Ah'm staunin.

He says tae her, You're wan in a million,[10]
Aw haw, so's your chances.

Can Ah run ye hame? Ah've got a pair of sannies,[11]
Aw haw, you're helluva funny.

Up the back close and doon the dunny,[12]
Aw haw, it[13] wisnae for the first time.

Oot came her maw tae go tae the didgy,[14]
Aw haw, he buggered off sharpish.

She's tried tae find the hard man, he's jined the
  Foreign Legion,
Aw haw, Sahara and the camels.

So Hairy Mairy had a little baby,
Aw haw, its faither's in the army.

* The theme does owe something to the American
Spiritual "The Virgin Mary had a Little Baby".

Glossary of Terms

1   "East" — The percipient reader will note that our hero, in
    order to travel west from Brigton to the "Denny Palais"
    must first go west by north-west, veering north-easterly
    round about the Gallowgate. Such an indirect approach is
    frequently adopted by the "hard man" on a "Saturday
    night".
2   "hard man" — One insensitive to the claims of heart and
    conscience, as distinct from the demands of the genitals
    and belly.
3   "Brigton" — Site of the Battles of the Boyne.
4   "cod liver oil and the orange juice" see 6.
5   "paraletic" (a) 1. affected with, suffering from, or subject
    to paralysis; palsied: 2, of the nature pertaining to
    paralysis: 3, deprived or destitute of energy or power of
    action; powerless; ineffective; characterised by impotence
    or powerlessness. (b) Drunk.
6   "VP" — Whether of the ruby, white or tawny variety this
    reasonably priced colonial wine is at all times robust,
    congenial and well rounded, making up in hearty good
    spirits what it lacks in pedigree. Slight aftertaste but
    considerable after effect. Should be served straight from
    the pocket, slightly chambré, or *al fresco* with chips. Here
    it is imbibed contrapuntally with a "chaser" of wood-
    alcohol "cider" in what has become a classic combination.
    Some connoisseurs would argue, however, that the only
    accompaniment necessary is a good boke and "Same
    again, Jimmy".
7   "Palais" — From "Palais de Danse Macabre". Dennis
    MacAbre was its first manager.
8   "Hairy" — Not hirsute as such but female. (Pron: Herry.)
9   "hen" — Form of address used towards the fair sex. N.B.
    A "hairy" may be a "hen" but a "hen" cannot be "hairy"
    only "feathery" or in some instances, "plucked".
10 "one in a million" — The complex mathematical equation
    contained in this stanza can be expressed as follows: where
    Y="Hairy Mairy" and X="your chances":
$$Y = 1/1,000,000$$
$$X > Y$$
    Therefore $X => \times 1/1,000,000$.
11 "sannies" — gutties.
12 "dunny" — The communal stairs serving the Glasgow

tenement rises from a communal passage called the "close" linking the street entrance with a rear entrance to the communal drying green or back. Where this yard or back is on a lower level than the street, the close will have steps descending to a sunken area anterior to the rear entrance. This is the dunny.

13 "it" — Signifies a characteristic delicacy of nuance, whereby any event of particular physicality and/or emotional intensity is not so much explicated within the texture of meaning of the verse, as alluded to with the obliquity of suggestion, like a fart in a thunderstorm.

14 "didgy" — midden.

Glasgow began counting the cost after the appalling disaster — the worst to date — at Ibrox Park yesterday. During the Scotland-England game, with the packed crowd swaying from side to side, part of the western terracing, a high wooden structure, gave way. Hundreds fell to the ground below, The incident, though disastrous, was localised. Many of the rest of the crowd did not understand what had happened, and the game was played through to the end.

Twenty-five spectators were killed and 380 seriously injured. The score, if it matters, was a 1-1 draw.

6 April 1902

The Glasgow parking problems are nothing new. In the 18th century it was the practice of virtually all the carriers and carters to leave their unloaded carts and waggons in the streets through the night. As there were no street lights the lieges tended to run into them on moonless nights. So on this date the magistrates, under threat of dire penalties, ordered them to be removed. No one seems to have paid any attention, neither parking tickets nor traffic wardens having been established for the kindly enforcement of the regulations. The following year the Council and Magistrates were again fulminating against the obstructions which were preventing citizens laying paving stones outside their properties, but it was not until the passing of the Police Act that this nuisance was abolished.

7 April 1769

8 April 1611

Considerable consternation was aroused in Glasgow following the granting by James VI of a Charter to the town of Dumbarton in December 1609. The said Charter, if interpreted in the way its beneficiaries were likely to interpret it, would have given Dumbarton a practical monopoly of river traffic on the Clyde. Not surprisingly, Glasgow Town Council opposed this, and took legal advice the following year. A couple of meetings were arranged between representatives of the two burghs, but nothing came of them. Then, in a test case, Dumbarton charged certain shippers in Glasgow not to unload anywhere but at Dumbarton, as being the nearest Royal Burgh. The charge was suspended pending litigation which resulted in a decree of the Lords of Council and Session in Glasgow's favour. Glasgow Town Council applied to King James, and on 18th April 1611 were granted a historic Charter which clearly set out their city's rights and status. Glasgow was explicitly erected into a Royal burgh, "to be held of the King and his successors", and its possessions and privileges were confirmed. Whereas previous charters were granted in favour of the Bishop of Glasgow, this one was in favour of the Provost, Baillies, Council and community. Specifically, it granted them the privilege of the River Clyde "from Clochstane to the brig of Glasgow". Negotiations with Dumbarton were to be thereafter on a more even footing.

9 April 1851

Building gets under way of the Victoria Bridge over the Clyde. This, the third to link Stockwell Street to Gorbals (or Fishergate to Bridgend, in the old terminology) was opened for traffic on 1st January 1854, costing around £50,000.

The first bridge on this site was a much humbler affair, made entirely of wood some time in the 13th century. This was replaced by Bishop Rae in 1345. Rae's stone bridge was to be Glasgow's only one until 1768, when one was constructed at the Broomielaw (see 30th September). A mere 12 feet wide, its breadth was increased to 22 feet in 1777, and Thomas Telford added an iron framed footpath in 1821. Subsequent undermining of its foundations by the deepening of the river rendered a new structure imperative. But the old bridge — almost five centuries old — was used for pedestrians until its removal in 1850.

---

10 April 1864

Eugene D'Albert was born near Charing Cross of a French father and a German mother. He grew up to become a composer and was considered by many people to be the greatest piano virtuoso of his age. He became a pupil of Liszt who nicknamed him "Albertus Magnus" and referred to him as "our young lion". Considered to be the greatest executant of Beethoven's music in his time, Liszt wrote of him as an extraordinary pianist and that among his young pupils, "I know of no more gifted as well as dazzling talent than D'Albert". He later studied under Sir Arthur Sullivan who seems to have helped him very little. Before the First World War D'Albert wrote a letter to *The Times* withdrawing any allegiance to England, a country which he declared was unworthy to harbour any artistic talent. D'Albert's opera *Tiefland* was a tremendous success on the Continent. Bruno Walter considered D'Albert a titan in his playing and wrote of him: "In his intimate contact with his instrument he appeared to me like a new centaur, half piano, half man." He was a progressive composer and both encouraged and played the modern school of his day. A wild and tempestuous man, he was married six times. What his life was like in his home town or his attitude towards it is little recorded.

---

11 April 1735

Thomas Moore, master of the church music, having been brought to Glasgow from Manchester and given a salary to teach music here, and the venture having proved such a success, the said T. Moore petitioned the Council for further expenses, including the cost of "coall and candle" for his school. It was agreed also to provide the poorer scholars with music books out of the civic purse. Henceforth there would be no excuse for not knowing all the words of *The Old Rugged Cross.*

---

12 April 1757

> "The whilk day, and considering that the town officers have been in use to get the buns and ale upon the day on which the Lords of Council have come to town, by which sundry abuses have happened, and for remedying whereof in time coming, the Magistrates and Council ordain, that for hereafter, the officers be allowed one shilling sterling at each term the Lords come to town at the Circuit."

We can only speculate what the "sundry abuses" were that caused the city fathers to curtail so severely the ale-buying capacities of their functionaries. John Strang, in *Glasgow and its Clubs*, says the attitude of the Council of this period was particularly mean and penny-pinching. A few days later, the city's gravediggers were required to provide their own spades and shovels for making "the narrow-houses that last till doomsday", as they put it.

---

13 April 1951

The "Lia Fail", the Stone of Destiny, ended its brief sojourn in Glasgow. At any rate, a police car whisked a block of sandstone from here to London, to Westminster Abbey, which had been without one form some 109 days. But although positively identified in Glasgow on 12th April by the Abbey's Clerk of Works, accurate copies had been made. There is still some doubt as to whether the present stone, whose wretched doom it is to bear the bottoms of future British monarchs, is even the original substitute.

---

14 April 1884

The first of the Cluthas, or "penny steamers", had been plying for two days between Victoria Bridge and Whiteinch. The fare was one penny, and the steamer could carry about 300 passengers.

By 1903 the service was failing to make a profit

against the competition of the subway and tramcars and was discontinued. The last Clutha made its trip on 30th November 1903.

---

15 April 1746

Of all the tales of all the sons of Glasgow who were to take part in tomorrow's battle on the rain-soaked moors of Culloden, there is none more redolent of pride, let alone endurance (not to mention outrage) than that of Quentin MacLauchlan Compson.

The Compsons were Glasgow printers, but Quentin was orphaned young and brought up by his mother's family in Perthshire. He took part in the '45 Rising, and after Culloden fled to America, to Carolina, with, according to his American chronicler, "little more than a claymore and the tartan he wore by day and slept under by night".

During the War of Independence Quentin, reluctant to fight against an English king, sought sanctuary in the wilds of Kentucky with his grandson, grandiloquently yclept Jason Lycurgus.

In 1820 this grandson rode north up the Natchez Trace to the Chickasaw agency at Okatoba, Mississippi, on a "light-waisted but strong-hocked mare" which, being the fastest quarter-horse seen by the Indians, who still possessed the land, not to mention owning the title, he eventually swapped with their chief Ikkemotubbe for a square mile of that very land — "a solid square mile of North Mississippi dirt as truly angled as the four corners of a card table top".

On that square mile of dirt was founded the town of Jefferson, the Compson dynasty, and the County of Yawknapatawpha, Mississippi.

---

16 April 1746

When Nemesis overtook the Young Pretender on Culloden Moor, the city of Glasgow was unequivocably delighted. On the 21st of the same month the city held a cake-and-wine banquet to "solemnise" the occasion. A deputation was despatched to Inverness to congratulate Butcher

Cumberland on his heroic action and to present him with the Freedom of the City.

It was a different story when it came to persuading Parliament to cough up compensation for Jacobite levies (see 3rd January). Provost Cochrane and his aides had to struggle for four years before the full sum of £16,000 was finally awarded. The problem was a strong anti-Glasgow lobby among several of the English MPs who resented its success over their own constituencies in the matter of the tobacco and sugar trade.

---

17 April 1909

Scottish Cup Final replay between Celtic and Rangers. After a single-goal draw a riot started, apparently because the referee would not allow extra time to be played. When the rioters attacked the pavilion, after uprooting the goalposts and tearing up the nets, they were charged by mounted police. From there the riot grew until parts of the terracing were on fire along with some of the pay boxes. When the firemen arrived their hoses were slashed. Some witnesses claim that the firemen and police charged the rioters and stoned them in an attempt to protect the hoses. The riot continued until the early evening. Official police figures say that 45 men were injured, 14 of them seriously. Apart from police, firemen and ambulancemen who were hurt there were about 30 people detained in hospital, over 100 were treated for injuries. Scrapes, bruises and sore heids were uncounted. The SFA retained the Scottish Cup for that year and the players' medals were withheld from them.

---

18 April 1946

Some stories *ought* to be true. One such concerns one of Glasgow's early brushes with modernism in the shape of a Picasso-Matisse exhibition in Kelvingrove Art Galleries. A Glasgow man was seen fleeing down the gallery steps screaming, "Let me out, let me out! I'm beginning to like it!"

Scottish Tourist Board

GLASGOW CATHEDRAL

OPEN TO VISITORS

OCTOBER TO MARCH

Weekdays	Sundays
9.30 a.m. - 12 noon	
1.00 p.m. - 4.00 p.m.	2.00 p.m. - 4.00 p.m.

APRIL TO SEPTEMBER

9.30 a.m. - 1.00 p.m.	
2.00 p.m. - 7.00 p.m.	2.00 p.m. - 5.00 p.m.

SUNDAY SERVICES

11.00 a.m. and 6.30 p.m.
Visitors very welcome.

WEEKDAY SERVICES

Wednesday at 11.00 a.m.

The first stone built Glasgow Cathedral was dedicated in the presence of King David I in 1136. That building was destroyed by fire and a new building was consecrated in 1197. The Cathedral as we see it to-day was begun by Bishop William de Bondington (1233-1258) and was completed by Archbishop Blacader (1483-1508). Since that period the Cathedral has never been unroofed and the worship of God has been carried out within its walls for more than 750 years.

The splendid achievements of the architects and builders of those far off days can be studied and admired. Not everything, however, is old and the Cathedral has one of the finest post-war collections of stained glass windows to be found in Britain. In the Lower Church is a large tapestry designed by a Scot, Robert Stewart, and made in Edinburgh by the Dovecot Studios.

The Regimental Colours were carried by Scottish Regiments in peace and war. They include the original Assaye Colour of the H.L.I.

Glasgow Cathedral, which is Crown property, is not a monument, but a church with a regular and active congregation and no visitor to the city should leave without making a visit.

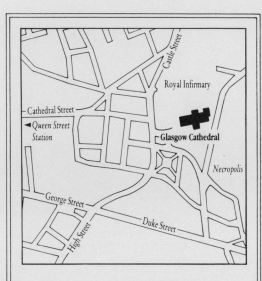

The Cathedral is about 1½ miles north-east of George Square. Car parking may be found in the vicinity and there are buses to it from Central Station, Argyle Street, Hope Street and Bath Street.

The Society of Friends of Glasgow Cathedral gratefully acknowledges the financial assistance of Tennent Caledonian Breweries Ltd.

Designed by Westpoint, Glasgow.

To commemorate the 850th anniversary of the dedication of the first stone built Glasgow Cathedral, and also the Jubilee of The Society of Friends of Glasgow Cathedral, 1986 will be a special Festival Year.

During the Year the undernoted events have been planned. Confirmation of the times and dates and details of programmes, prices of tickets and where they will be available will be given in separate leaflets and posters. All the events will be within the Cathedral.

1986

Wednesday	1st January	2.30 p.m.	**"Messiah"** by Handel.
Wednesday	5th February	7.30 p.m.	**"Columba"** — Opera with
Thursday	6th February	7.30 p.m.	music by Kenneth Leighton &
Friday	7th February	7.30 p.m.	libretto by Edwin Morgan.
Saturday	8th February	3.00 p.m.	Produced by Peter Ebert.
✻	March	✻	**Bands & Choirs of the Salvation Army.**
Friday	11th April	7.30 p.m.	World Premiere of a commissioned work **"The Kentigern Suite"** by Thomas Wilson with Scottish Baroque Ensemble & Moira Anderson.
Friday	2nd May	7.30 p.m.	**Concert by the Glasgow Cathedral Choral Society.**
Thursday	8th May	7.30 p.m.	**Recital by Benjamin Luxon with Geoffrey Parsons.**
Thursday	5th June	9.30 a.m.	
Friday	6th June	to	**Flower Festival.**
Saturday	7th June	7.00 p.m.	
✻	August	✻	Still to be arranged but probably a Celebrity Organ Recital & Exhibition of Munich Stained Glass.
Wednesday	10th September	7.30 p.m.	**Concert by the Scottish National Orchestra** conducted by Sir Alexander Gibson.
Thursday	23rd October	7.30 p.m.	**BBC Invitation Concert.**
Tuesday	11th November	7.30 p.m.	**Concert by Antonine Brass Ensemble**
Friday	19th December	7.30 p.m.	**Concert by Glasgow Cathedral Choral Society.**

✻To be arranged

This, the date of the skirmish at Lexington that began the American War of Independence, has a particular relevance to Glasgow, signalling as it did the downward trend in the fortunes of its giant tobacco trade. While the importance of the "Tobacco Lords" has perhaps been exaggerated and their rise and fall dramatically oversimplified, it remains true that for 40 or so hectic years Glasgow dominated the American trade and at least some of its citizens amassed personal fortunes on a previously undreamt of scale.

How was it, then, that a rather small town, remote from the traditional centres of trade, had within two generations captured half of the European tobacco trade against the combined rivalry of Bristol, London and Liverpool, who had controlled it for over a century?

Since the Navigation Act of 1660, Scotland had been denied trade with the English colonies. Its main outlet was Europe, in particular the Low Countries, and Glasgow was unfortunate enough to be on the wrong side of the country to benefit greatly. With the coming of the Union of 1707, bitterly opposed though it was in Glasgow, the Navigation Act was abolished and the way to the West thrown open.

There was no immediate breakthrough. Glasgow, financially and psychologically injured by its involvement in the Darien Scheme, had little capital to invest, though it had some connection with the Virginia plantations (including a tradition of smuggling goods past the English administration). But it had the great advantage of a shorter passage for its ships — 14 to 20 days shorter — with commensurate savings in food and wages for crews, wear and tear on ships, and rate of turnover of trade. Moreover, Glasgow was in a good position to send its vessels back laden with the goods the colonists needed, such as linen, woollens, blankets, stockings, shoes, metalware and a myriad of commodities from all over Southern Scotland and even the North of England. By 1725, the trade was beginning to expand significantly.

After 1735, as a result of the (mainly maritime) wars with France, the English Channel and the waters of the south-west were hoaching with privateers and virtually closed to traffic. Glasgow had no such problem. The north-west route to America was unassailed. War or no war, the French still needed their tobacco, and Virginia was the only source. Business being business, the protagonists agreed on safe conduct for ships bringing tobacco to France. The United General Farms of France, which held the monopoly for selling tobacco there, chose the Glasgow merchants as its suppliers, thanks to their ability to provide vast quantities at lowest prices.

Trade boomed. To illustrate its extraordinary growth, imports rose from about 300 tons per annum at the beginning of the century to a peak of perhaps 20,000 tons in the year before the colonists revolted.

The "Tobacco Lords" who benefited from all this were of course lords only in that they possessed the lordly attributes of wealth and power. The traditional landed gentry of the area continued to despise them as parvenus. No doubt the merchants were not unduly worried. They themselves formed a clannish sub-community, related by ties of marriage, kinship and business interest. They lived in some style, and their arrogance became legendary. A typical specimen would sport a three-cornered hat, flaxen wig (preferably made from the tresses of Swedish blondes), black satin coat and breeches, scarlet cloak and shoes with jewelled buckles. A gold-topped cane would complete the ensemble. The "Plainstanes" outside the Tolbooth, the only paved area of the city, they made their exclusive property, and would congregate there like a flock of parrots to conduct their daily business. If it was raining, they would use the piazza close by as their Exchange.

The "Tobacco Lords" were neither the first nor the last nobs to be seen in Glasgow, though they had the finest plumage. They left behind little of substance; a few street names, some folk legends.

What wealth they made they kept, or spent, or lost. But the export trade that grew up alongside the tobacco imports did inadvertently encourage the manufacture of goods in Glasgow as in much of Scotland. This was to prove a less ephemeral benefit to the society.

When the American colonists rebelled in 1775, the Glasgow merchants were not totally unprepared, although few expected the war would last more than a few months. Already many had diversified into other trades or had amassed stocks before selling their ships for transports. For the export side of things, it was a different story. The colonists repudiated all their debts, the export in manufactured goods vanished, and unemployment swept the city. Those who actually owned property in Virginia suffered a total loss — the colonists simply confiscated it. In 1777 the plantation-owning firms of Buchanan, Hastie & Co. and Andrew Buchanan & Co. crashed. It was the greatest collapse so far in Glasgow's commercial history, bringing down many other smaller firms.

The war lasted for seven years. The tobacco trade, though not obliterated, never recovered anything like its former prominence. It would be a mistake to imagine a huge vacuum left behind — the West Indies traffic in sugar and rum was already well established (plus the slave trade by way of a sideline) and King Cotton was about to come into his own.

"Good Friday", the supposed date of the death by crucifixion of Jesus Christ, founder of the Christian religion so popular in Glasgow and elsewhere. The image of that event most associated with Glasgow is that limned by the paranoic fringe surrealist Salvador Dali, and known as "Christ of St John of the Cross".

The 80″ by 45″ painting was purchased for the city's galleries in February 1952 and went on show

20 April 30

the following June. It caused quite a stir, from the financial, aesthetic and religious points of view.

First, there was the cost. This was £8,200, actually £3,800 less than the original asking price. Many canny Glaswegians thought that was just too much to invest in a single painting, one not even by an "old master" but by a living artist. Anyway, what business had a weirdo like Dali painting such a subject? The very idea was utterly distasteful — but wait, it turned out to be a big money-spinner. By 1971 it had brought in £33,000 via donations, royalties, sales of reproductions, postcards etc. How wrong first impressions can be!

Regarding its merits as a serious work of art, or a work of religious art, opinions continue to differ. It is an eclectic piece. The dominating figure of Christ crucified, dramatically foreshortened so that the divine visage is in mystic eclipse, is taken from a sketch by the 16th century Spanish visionary poet, S. Juan de la Cruz. This is one of the few original images of the Messiah which enables the viewer to look down on Him from a great height, a circumstance doubtless appreciated by the most idolatry-conscious Protestant. The whole assemblage hovers like a UFO over a seascape from Dali's home in Port Lligat, Catalonia. The figure on the shore is lifted from a painting by Velasquez. And so on. The texture of the work, like fine old linoleum, and the rather gluey twilit lighting seem to come not so much from the Da Vinci paintings like the "Virgin of the Rocks" which impressed Dali so much, as from the layers of dirty varnish that have accrued to them. Even fans of the Dalinesque are likely to be disappointed by the lack of paranoic-critical elements, or Nasty Things in the Corners. In fact, it's a rather peacefully symmetrical work which, if it wasn't for the unusual angle, would be over-bearingly academic.

It still draws the crowds.

---

21 April 1874

Stephen Mitchell, who has given his name to Glasgow's famous library, died on this date. He was born in Linlithgow in 1789, into a family well established in the tobacco trade, and moved to Glasgow with the business in 1825. He bequeathed the sum of £66,998 10s. 6d., which was to lie until it had reached a round £70,000. Accordingly, on 1st November 1877 the Mitchell Library opened at the corner of Ingram Street and North Albion Street. It had a stock of 14,432 volumes, of which it issued 186 on its first day. By 1889, when it moved to new premises in Miller Street, the collection had swelled through bequests and purchases to 89,000 volumes, and about 1,500 a day were being issued. In 1911, it moved to North Street, and on 3rd November incorporated the old St Andrew's Halls building as an extension.

The kirk session of Govan showed both foresight and compassion in passing an enactment that "whaever shall sell drink to drunken folks shall come under the same censure as drunkards, as shall also wha keep drunkards on their premises or fills drink to ony *save in cases of necessitee* (our italics) up till ten hour at evin".

22 April 1655

The pillory was first introduced to Glasgow, the master of works being ordained to make one "with all diligence". Other popular punishments were nailing the ear to a post, the stocks, jougs, branks (a kind of iron mask) and ducking in the river, the last less deadly to health than it would be today. As well as these, there were of course the usual imprisonments, banishments, floggings and hangings. A few of those executed were hung in chains, but there was only one recorded case of dismemberment; a limb of Hackston of Rathillet, one of the murderers of Archbishop Sharp, was fixed to the Cross steeple in 1680.

23 April 1647

In 1843, William Wotherspoon opened a small starch factory at Glenfield, Paisley. Prior to this,

24 April 1843

almost all the starch used in Scotland had been made in London or Nottingham. Soon Wotherspoon & Co. were by far Britain's largest manufacturers and exporters of starch. Around 480,000 packets per week of the pure sago product found their way to every corner of the civilised world, or British Empire. For the Victorians well knew how much the stiffness of their upper lips depended on the stiffness and unimpeachable laundering of their collars. Can we imagine any servant of Empire negotiating with some wily Pathan, or facing the Fuzzy-wuzzy's frenzied assault under the wretched handicap of a limp, creased or disordered shirt front? We cannot. By putting backbone into laundry, Glenfield starch performed an inestimable service to morale wherever the Union flag, undrooping, flew. At this point it is fitting that someone else should take over being carried away. In his awful *Commercial Enterprise*, an uncritical account of capitalism in major British cities, John Dawson Burns becomes positively ecstatic about Wotherspoon & Co.:

> "We can well imagine some of the fair daughters of Renfrewshire who are exiled from home, while manipulating their little articles of finery in their homely laundries chaunting 'Gloomy winter's noo awa' ' and thrilling their notes in reflective tones with their minds far o'er the deep. Some too may call up the reminiscences of home when beholding the labels of Glenfield. . . ."

Mr Burns goes on for a bit in this vein, before shrewdly anticipating a possible objection:

> "some of our readers may ask what connection there can possibly be between starch and poetry?"
> *(Pause)*
> "Our answer is, that whatever is calculated to afford music and pleasure to the ladies, whether by their domestic hearths, in the green fields, or in 'the joyous throng', must be pregnant with poetical sentiment. Our opinion is, that lovely women are nowhere to be seen to better advantage than when employed in those little domestic occupations where the genius of order and cleanliness presides. Depend upon it, gentlemen, if a woman attends to her washing tub, and understands the use of starch, she is sure to make a good wife, and therefore the noblest of man's poetical aspirations."

Oh, well put, sir! And while in the saccharine mode, it may be mentioned that Wotherspoon's firm subsequently opened up a large confectionery factory in Dunlop Street, Glasgow, inspired no doubt by "the increase in demand for luxury and refinement" (J.D.B.). On offer were 52 sorts of lozenges, 29 sorts of comfits and 18 of candied sugar. Medicated lozenges were a popular sideline, with 30 types of drug thereby rendered palatable, including calomel, Ipecacuanha, opium, morphia, quinine and rhubarb (sic). Glaswegians are still infamous for their sweet-tooth, and the state of the civic dentation is a constant disgrace.

---

25 April 1817

Two Irishmen, William McKay (or McCoy) and James O'Neil, were tried today in Glasgow for forgery and uttering a forged banknote. They had proferred a single guinea note, ostensibly of the Greenock Bank, for a bottle of porter in Govan Ferry house. The girl who served them was suspicious. She alerted the ferryman, who trailed the two men to Partick. With the help of some passers-by, he made a sort of citizen's arrest, and they were marched off to the police station.

The penalty for forgery was death, and the Greenock Bank were determined an example should be made. In his final, impassioned address to the jury, the accused's lawyer waved the offending guinea note and demanded of them, was this scrap of paper worth a man's life? He got his answer. O'Neil was acquitted, but McKay was found guilty and sentenced to the maximum penalty. He was hanged on 28th May that year. It was the last execution in Glasgow for the crime of forgery.

---

26 April 1539

Glasgow had two martyrs to offer the Reformation. One was a young man of 18 years from Ayr called John Kennedy, either a student at the College or, according to John Knox, a friar and a poet. The other was Jeremy Russel of the Grey Friars.

The Grey Friars, or Franciscans, had come to Glasgow in 1472. They settled in the High Street with the avowed purpose of "hearing the confessions of the students" from the nearby College. Their convent was opposite to and an exact contemporary of "Provand's Lordship", Glasgow's oldest surviving dwellinghouse, and probably erected by the same builders. The lodgings were far from palatial — in fact they were later deemed unworthy of looting — and their mode of life appears to have been exemplary, at least in comparison to that enjoyed by some other monastic foundations. Certainly, when he was arraigned for heresy, Brother Russel displayed admirable unworldliness. It is said that Archbishop Dunbar, who presided over the trial, showed unwilling to have the two men done to death. But four hardliners, "four sergeants of Satan" Knox calls them, were sent "to assist . . . in that cruel judgement, or at least to cause him to dip his hand in the blood of the saints of God". It was made clear to the Archbishop that if he attempted to spare the accused he himself would be liable to denunciation.

When Kennedy showed signs of recanting, Russel exhorted the younger man to stand firm, so successfully that Kennedy burst into spontaneous thanks to God who, through his servant Russel, had ensured his martyrdom. They were both burned alive at the east end of the Cathedral.

When in 1559 the Reformation swept the Grey Friars from the city, one Brother Baxter suffered a gentler martyrdom. This time it was for adherence to the Catholic Church. He was obliged to surrender in court all his properties and inheritance. These were quite substantial — perhaps the order had become more worldly in the brief interim?

"Bairn smooring" (wean smothering) must have been quite a common pastime in the 16th century, judging by the number of cases that the kirk (taking on the role of the "cruelty") had to deal with. That most were not infanticides but the results of drunkenness or neglect is suggested by the extreme lightness of the penalty the presbytery advised: "that smoorers of bairns mak their repentence two Sundays in sakclaith standing at the kirk door".

Certain persons of Rutherglen were admitted as burgesses of Glasgow with the usual fees or "fines" being waived. In fact, the Council was quite simply buying voters in connection with the forthcoming Parliamentary elections for the Glasgow district.

28 April 1741

The *Glasgow Herald* today published the results of a survey to determine the attitude of Glasgow's Catholics (three-quarters of those in Scotland) to sectarian education. It showed that, in startling contrast to the hierarchy's position, no less than 63 per cent favoured integration of schools.

29 April 1967

The issue of separate Catholic schools within the state system has been and continues to be a ticklish one, particularly for the Labour Party in Glasgow. During the programme of comprehensivisation in the '60s, the abolition of fee-paying selective Catholic schools in Glasgow was strongly resisted. Eventually, while loth to alienate a traditional source of votes on a matter of mere principle, Labour in 1976 endorsed integration as an eventual aim. The required agreement of the Catholic Church, however, has shown no sign of materialising.

The following scrap from a contemporary newspaper's property pages was dug up on the site of a toilet near the Molendinar. It casts a fascinating light on the earliest Glasgow settlements:

30 April 543

> "TO LET: a number of furnished circular HUTS, 7-8 ft. diameter. Natural pine exterior, with modish 'wattle'-style interior finish. 3-piece fallen logs, straw, etc. Reasonable terms. Suit large family with high infant mortality.

"TO LET: Limited number of unfurnished "WEEMS", semi-circularised for maximum ecology interface. Good area. No Picts.

"FOR SALE: (Busby) The last word in Sheltered Housing, this intimate individualised apartment, fully 12 ft. square with 5 ft. high earthen ceiling, is reached by an exclusive passageway handcrafted into the hillside. Fireplace centralised for optimum smoke/roof-orifice displacement capability. Suit retired person or monk."

Today, workers, trade unionists, supporters and sympathisers of the Left of all sorts take to the streets of Glasgow in a show of strength and solidarity.

"May Day" comes from the French *m'aidez*, a desperate cry for help uttered when in imminent danger of going under.

1 May

Beltane, or Bel's Fire, the festival of the pagan god Bel or Belenos, marking the spring of the Celtic year (Celtic, not Celtic). It comes as no surprise that this was still celebrated up until the 19th century by the godless people of Rutherglen at their Beltane Fair. In Glasgow itself, the Burgh Records show that even in the mid-18th century it was still used as one of the term days at which entry would be given to the tenants of various properties. But the fun had gone out of it (except, of course, in Rutherglen).

2 May

"Count Borulawski presents his respectful compliments to the ladies and gentlemen of Glasgow and the neighbourhood, and will deem himself honoured with their company to (*sic*) a public breakfast at the Assembly Room, on Friday the 8th inst., in the course of which the Count will perform some select pieces on the guitar. Tickets to be had at the Count's lodgings, Argyle Street, opposite Stockwell, or at the Rooms, at 3s. 6d. each."

3 May 1789

The elegant and accomplished Count, who normally lived in Edinburgh, was 38 inches high and had to make a living somehow. He had an average-sized wife and three average-sized children to support. Unfortunately, his marriage was none too happy. It was said that in the course of one of many disputes his wife stuck him up on the mantelpiece, and left him there until he (metaphorically) climbed down. The abuse of wee husbands by average-sized Scottish wives — and vice-versa — has ever been a blot on our national character.

4 May
1926

The General Strike, which began on this date, aroused as much solidarity in Glasgow and industrial Scotland as in equivalent areas of Britain. Yet with Clydeside's radical traditions and the recent experience of the wartime disputes, one might have expected more. In *Scottish Capitalism* (ed. Tony Dickson, 1980, London) some of the reasons for this relative lack of fervour are outlined:

> "Firstly, Scotland (and especially Clydeside) was no longer such a significant element in British capitalism. The collapse of demands for the products of heavy industry . . . meant that the Scottish working class no longer had the powerful base that existed during the war. Secondly, the centralisation of trade union organisation on a British basis meant that the General Strike was largely English-led and directed. Third, trade union leadership in Scotland, given the legacy of the CWC (i.e. Clyde Workers' Committee) and the 1919 General Strike in Glasgow, was unlikely to support a militancy based once again on rank and file activity, underpinned by the support of the Communist Party. Fourth, the occupations that might have given a more radical edge to the strike in Scotland were precisely those who were least involved. . . . The workers most affected by the strike, such as the miners, lay outside the Glasgow area which had provided the previous focus of radical activity. Finally, the most crucial period for radical action in Scotland had been the 1915-19 period. The failure of the CWC to effectively co-ordinate working-class activity had removed the chance of operating from a strong economic base. The challenge to bureaucratic centralism in the unions had also failed — leaving the strike to be directed by the official leadership."

Centralisation of trade union organisation on a British basis . . . bureaucracy and reaction in the union leadership . . . the failure of the radicals to maintain and mobilise their mass support . . . some of this is awfully familiar.

---

5 May
1752

A certain convivial club, which had been meeting since 1750, was formally constituted under the title of the "Hodge-Podge" and arrangements were made for it to meet fortnightly in Cruikshank's Tavern. The interests of its members, which included the soldier John Moore, the journalist

Sam Hunter and the capitalist Kirkman Finlay, were vaguely literary, but when poetasting got tedious, reverted to whist and blethers. Food and drink were not ignored. The name "Hodge-Podge" itself refers to a kind of obsolete dish, a sort of entropic broth of various ingredients (Zachary Boyd, writing of the rout of the Royalists at Newburn, says "All was made *hodge-podge . . .*").

This was just one of many in that brief golden age of the Glasgow clubs, when anyone with the money and leisure would seek out the society of the inns and taverns. It was a fairly self-indulgent business, and brought no particular credit to the city. The names of some of them give an idea of the life and preoccupations of the period: the Pig, the Rumble-gumpy; the Oyster; the Miss Thompson's Tea; the Driddle; the Jumble; the Council of Ten; the Badger (later the Western); the Crow; the Grog Club; the Accidental Club; the What You Please; the Coul; the Gegg; the Banditti; the French; the Duck; the Morning and Evening; My Lord Ross's; the Beefsteak, or Tinkler's; the Packers and Every-night; the Face; the Waterloo; the Post Office; the Sma' Weft; the Shuna; the Camperdown.

For the fullest treatment of the subject, we recommend Strang's fascinating *Glasgow and its Clubs*.

---

6 May 1873

At Mr Kibble's invitation, around 1,500 Glasgow gentlefolk attended a private viewing within the Crystal Art Palace and Conservatory, Botanic Gardens, prior to its public opening.

This was the glass structure known today simply as the "Kibble Palace" after its creator. Press reports of the opening describe something barely recognisable as the same place. For a start, the twin Victorian obsessions of cultural improvement and gadgetry were to be handsomely indulged. Instead of cacti and chrysanthemums, the transepts of the "Palace" were to house a collection of models of ancient ruins and buildings "such as the Parthenon, the Temple of Jupiter, the Colosseum etc.". The centre of the main dome was a 185-foot pond with a 14-foot diameter sunken chamber below it "where it is proposed to place an orchestra, whose music will form a melodious mystery to strangers". When this live *muzak* was not flooding the place with sound, a fountain with 40 water jets would be turned on, while electric lights playing over the spray would create marvellous rainbow effects.

A far cry from the oasis of greenery and humid peace that is the present Kibble Palace, a well of silence and vegetable contemplation. Goldfish hang suspended in their gelid pond. A sprinkler hushes over the gravel. High among the Trees of the World sparrows chatter in dialect. Green palms sweat, statues are cool. Thrill-seekers can sit and watch algae form on the marble.

---

7 May 1941

Death, at Cambridge, of the great social anthropologist, Sir James Fraser, author of *The Golden Bough*. He was a Glaswegian by birth and an MA graduate of Glasgow University. His major work achieved numerous editions, getting huger all the time. Although many of its arguments have been seriously challenged since, Glaswegians think the *Bough* is just magic.

---

8 May 1822

Sentence was this day carried out on one Richard Campbell, convicted of taking part in a huge popular riot on 17th February this year against George Provand, a merchant of the city who was suspected of being a "resurrectionist" or body-snatcher. There was no truth whatever in these suspicions. Provand traded in paints and oils, and lived in the mansion once inhabited by "Bob Dragon" (see 19th November) and since, it appears, by his ghost.

Certain nosy citizens, looking through the windows of the mansion, saw what they thought were tubs and pails of blood and bits of bodies. In fact, they were pots of red paint and other perfectly legitimate wares. This was quite enough for the gullible Glasgow mob to go on. They did a very thorough demolition job on Provand's premises and effects, and overpowered the police who tried to stop them. The cavalry had to be brought in and the Riot Act read before the rioters dispersed.

Two hundred guineas reward was offered; five were arrested. Only the luckless Campbell, though, was sentenced to be whipped through the city. Tied to the tail of a cart, he was given 80 lashes at four stops by the public hangman. This was the last time Glasgow was treated to such a spectacle, and starred the last hangman to be maintained by the city, the veteran Thomas Young.

---

9 May 1651

To:

The Magistrates, Council and
Community of Glasgow,
Glasgow, N.B.

Dear Loyal Subjects,
    Could you see your way to lending us £500? We'll see you all right come the Restoration. Thanks.

Carolus Rex (II).

(See 23rd May.)

---

10 May 1784

Some judicial murders strike one as being more disgusting than others because of certain details, perhaps poignant or macabre.

James Jack, aged 24 years, a stocking weaver, was tried in Glasgow for the robbery this month of William Barclay, a schoolmaster. He had readily confessed his guilt, but despite the jury's unanimous recommendation for mercy, was sentenced to hang on 7th July. His behaviour while awaiting execution gave rise to serious doubts about his mental stability: he made numerous pen drawings of himself being greeted in hell by the devil. These he gave to his visitors, and were later valued as curiosities. On the morning of his execution, he tried to kill himself with a knife. He was prevented from doing so, but not before he had wounded himself severely in several places. Bandaged and fettered, he was drawn in a cart to the Castle Yard, where he was *hoisted on a pulley* and left to hang for the stipulated time. This seems to have been the only occasion where the executioners of Glasgow saw fit to apply their knowledge of mechanics in this novel way.

11 May 1888

Glasgow does it again! The largest umbrella in the world is ready for despatch to its owner. Messrs Wilson, Matheson and Co., umbrella manu-facturers in Glassford Street, today put the finishing touches to a magnificent umbrella for a West African king. The canopy is a full 20 feet in diameter on a polished mahogany staff of a similar length. The cover is of Italian straw. The lining is of cardinal red and white, with a border of crimson satin. The crown of the canopy sports a pine-shaped straw ornament topped by a gilded cone. In use the umbrella will be fixed in the ground and can shield 30 guests at dinner from tropical sun or rainstorm. the firm have also made six palanquins of variegated silk for the same monarch.

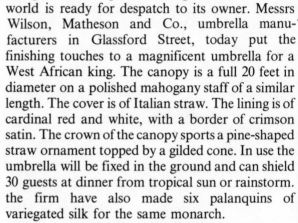

The *first* umbrella to appear in Glasgow was brought over from Paris in 1782 by a surgeon called John Jameson. It was apparently made of yellow or green glazed linen. Although neither as splendid nor as huge as the above model, it was large enough to shelter "a small family".

But the biggest ever was surely the "Highland-man's Umbrella", the railway bridge over Argyle Street. Under shelter of its grim iron girders, the Gaels of Glasgow would congregate, hip-pockets distended by half-bottles, to gossip and reminisce about the lone sheiling of the misty island, from which mountains divide them and a great waste of breath.

12 May 1568

Gorbals in the 15th and 16th century was famous for its manufacture of both swords (said to be almost as good as Andrea Ferrara's) and harquebuses, or handguns (on a par with any from Ghent, Paris or Milan). It is reported that the following ditty (whose triads irresistibly suggest some Celtic connection) was sung at Mrs Menzies', the chief tavern in Gorbals then, on the eve of the Battle of Langside:

THE GORBALS GUNMAKERS' SONG

Three things that do mak a man lean,
Sma beer, breid and cheese, and a bold quean,
    It's an auld sang, and a true sang,
    Never let a man trust a woman ower lang.

Three things that do mak a man fat,
Roast beef, boiled beef, and the ale tap.
    It's an auld sang, and a true sang,
    Never let a man trust a woman ower lang.

Three things that do mak a man poor,
Hunting, hawking, and keeping ane whure.
    It's an auld sang and a true sang,
    Never let a man trust a woman ower lang.

We should point out that "quean" here refers to any young woman, and not by any stretch of the imagination to Queen Mary Stuart, who was to meet such misfortune on the following day. We are quite certain on this point. But read on. . . .

"Merde," sighed the young Queen, as her richly caparisoned palfry shifted nervously beneath her. "Je suis bien undone! C'est vraiment un 'ba' on the slates' situation."

    In the distance, she could espy the hyaena-like keelies of the treacherous Regent driving her gallant but in-numbered band before them in disarray. Was it all over, then? Where were the high hopes she had nurtured as she approached the rugged shores of her new domain, hopes that had perished like the fleur de lys in autumn before the rude blast of the northern wind? Memories came flooding back — her happy childhood in the chateaux; that little restaurant in the Rue des Grenouilles; the Dauphin's cuirasses in the moonlight . . . memories, too, of dearest Darnley with his funny, boyish ways,

13 May 1568

of Rizzio strumming *Che Sera Sera* on his lute
. . . and darker memories; those coarse Scottish
barons; that horrible Knox man wagging his beard
at her. . . .

She shuddered involuntarily, the knuckles of her
slender fingers whitening as she clutched at the
cairngorm fastening of her plaid chemise. Had all
her sacrifices truly been in vain? Was it for this she
had had her loof crossed at Crossmyloof, for this
that her Poll (poor, loyal Poll!) had deed at
Polmadie, for this she had sighed lang, lang at
Langside? She had set her heart on Dumbarton,
would she ever see it now? A tear started from her
doe-like eye, but she dashed it away angrily. She
was still a Queen! She . . .

Just then, a figure came into view, struggling up
the hillock whereon she stood, a figure clad in
outlandish attire, a figure who clutched under one
arm a huge sheaf of papers, a figure whose face was
muffled, but around whose hat was written
P-O-S-T-E-R-I-T-Y in large, bright letters.

He addressed her breathlessly.

"Mary, Queen of Scots, isn't it? Well, have I got a
contract for you!"

It was all over.

NOTE: Within the space of 45 minutes, the three-
to four-thousand strong army of the Regent Moray,
fighting from the vantage point of Langside Hill,
had routed the Queen's force of five- to six
thousand under the command of the Earl of Argyll.
Moray lost four men in the action, Mary around
300. Most of the Glaswegians involved fought on
Moray's side, largely out of hostility to the Queen's
champion, Arran. A stone on Court Knowe, about
100 yards east of Cathcart Castle, marks the spot
from where Mary observed her downfall.

---

14 May
1887

Spring, making Glasgow's fair places green again,
finds a candy-traveller calling his wares in Pirratt's
Row off the Maryhill Road. At once the closes grow
loud with neighbours clamouring for mothers to
bring out children afflicted with whooping-cough.

A crowd forms round the candyman and his donkey and one by one the mothers pass their pathetic mites under the donkey's belly, face to the ground. A neighbour takes the child, somersaults him so that he faces the sky, passes him over the animal's back and so into his mother's arms. Three times the cure is repeated, the women counting carefully, for no part of the process must be neglected. Children dying as well as those less severely afflicted are treated, and quite a few in good health, for the treatment is said to ward off as well as relieve the pestilence. After each patient the donkey must be fed a titbit, heel of bread or similar, and the child a piece of candy. For half the morning the pedlar does a good trade, and the mothers declare themselves well satisfied with the enchantment.

---

15 May 1626

The groundstone of the "new" Tolbooth building was laid, and it was completed the following year. This replaced a previous Tolbooth, mentioned as early as 1454. This had been Glasgow's first municipal building, comprising a town hall, or court, and prison.

The Burgh Records name one James Naysmith as the new building's first jailor, at a salary of £2 4s. 5⅓d. per year.

All that remains of the Tolbooth today is the steeple, a central landmark of old Glasgow, but to traffic planners an abiding nuisance. Well, they have had their own way far too often in Glasgow. The steeple is a fine handsome old structure, with its steep lines and elegant "imperial crown". One ornament is missing though: until 1790 it sported spikes to accommodate the heads of malefactors, probably mainly parking offenders.

---

16 May 1810

Robert Tannahill set out from Paisley to visit his friend and fellow weaver Alex Borland in Glasgow. Tannahill was a sort of small-town bard, a laureate of the Glasgow and Paisley periodicals, as well as attracting the admiration of contemporaries such as James Hogg. His verse was generally sentimental and pastoral. A lot of his poems and songs described places he had never been to, although in such conventional terms it scarcely made any difference. He was not a very good poet, though one or two of his songs have entered the folk repertoire, but he was a sincere one, and an honest man.

James Hogg visited him towards the end of March 1810. They got on splendidly, and their parting was an emotional one. Tannahill, who suffered from periodic fits of melancholia, seemed to have a premonition of his death.

When Alex Borland saw him last, he found his speech slurred and almost incoherent. Concerned for his friend, he saw him home to Paisley. Tannahill wandered from his home around 3 a.m. on the morning of the 17th. His body was discovered in a local burn by his two brothers.

---

17 May 1780

The *Triton* from Dublin today discharged 60 tierces of French brandy at the Broomielaw, now an independent port. The duties are paid at the Custom House and Excise Office — this is the first vessel to make entry.

---

18 May 1968

Dismay and confusion reign among Rangers supporters as a shrewdly anonymous *Glasgow Herald* columnist reveals that the sacred name of Ibrox is, in fact, of Celtic provenance, being originally "ath bruic", the Ford of the Badger.

---

19 May 1715

Before the great Celtic immigrations of the 19th century complicated everything, the political and religious tendencies of Glasgow were fairly clear cut. As a prosperous south-west lowland town she was stoutly Protestant, Parliamentarian and Whiggish. By 1715, it was not to be expected that she would have any truck with Jacobite adventurers. Yet there seems to have been the occasional Glaswegian who, whether from partisan or mercenary reasons, contrived to help the Rising. In May of that year, some three months before King James raised his standard, Provost Aird received intelligence that arms destined for the Highlands were being put aboard a ship at the Broomielaw. On visiting the harbour in person, the bold Provost found three chests containing muskets, bayonets and pistols on a vessel owned by a man called MacDonald. These he had confiscated and locked in the Tolbooth.

Before long, the same weapons helped to arm the Glasgow volunteers who went to join Argyll's forces at Stirling. Rather to their disappointment, they didn't see any fighting. They were sent to guard Stirling Bridge (over which the outnumbered Argyll half expected to have to flee) and missed the fiasco at Sheriffmuir. In fact Glasgow suffered no casualties in the '15, though its attitude was to be remembered by a later wave of Jacobites.

---

20 May 1809

Mr Middleton says that Mr Blackburn went to Edinr. He has had communication with a lady or ladies. Mr Maxwell denies for a bottle of Rum.
    Mr Middleton lost. Settled.
                (Minutes of the Board of Green Cloth)

And wash your mouth out with soap and water, Mr Middleton.

---

21 May 1937

An era ended with the death of Alexander Wylie Petrie, the Glasgow Clincher, editor of the newspaper of that name, and the last in a long line of street vendors of broadsides and cheap literature who came to the fore with the advent of the printing press.

The Clincher died in the Victoria Infirmary, and the *Glasgow Herald* noted laconically that "his passing will be regretted by Glasgow people in many parts of the world". It was not as Petrie had envisaged it. His paper, in February 1899, had predicted a different scenario:

> "They were tolling the bell the other day and a gentleman seriously enquired, is the Clincher really dead? No, the man replied, the Clincher will never die, but when he passes away the raw grain whisky syndicate bailies will ring their old metal bells all over Glasgow."

The Clincher was a thorn in the flesh of the bailies and councillors of Glasgow Corporation. From the time his spasmodical broadsheet/newspaper burst upon the streets in July 1897, his witty, wicked and scurrilous comments were a torment to the city officials and representatives.

Petrie had a high opinion of his skills:

> "Since the battle of Bannockburn they have been wanting a real newspaper editor in this country. They have got one now, and he is the Clincher that clincheth."

Petrie maintained that by virtue of a silver cell in his brain he was able to clinch any argument. Since many of these arguments were against the city fathers, they immediately detained him in Woodielee lunatic asylum. Petrie struck back by consulting independent doctors, and obtaining a certificate as proof of his sanity. The authorities had no option but to release him, and he lost no time in flaunting himself in front of the City chambers as the only certified sane man in Glasgow.

The people of Glasgow delighted in Petrie's triumph, and sales of his paper went up. The City Magistrates were reduced to having the police detain him and fine him on minor charges from time to time, and the Clincher's contempt for both the police and the councillors was evident in every issue of the paper. Regular feature columns were "Woodielee Wanderings" and "Out on Bail", and the Clincher had a wonderful variety of correspondents to call upon.

> "Our Shellfish Correspondent says, 'The only difference between a camel and a policeman is that a camel can work nine days without drinking, and a policeman can drink nine days without working. . . .'"

In February 1902, Petrie applied for the post of

Chief Constable of Glasgow and printed his application in the newspaper in full:

> "I shall endeavour . . . to suppress crime, so that the police economy of Glasgow shall in future be a terror to evildoers from the Lord Provost down to the most humble Corporation official. I shall not persecute or oppress decent people . . . neither shall I insist in putting a philosopher in jails and lunatic asylums to please the scientific pickpockets of the city . . . I shall take no tips or perquisites of money, jewellery, clothes, boots, bread, beef and beer. . . ."

Needless to say, while he did not get the job, sales of his paper increased:

> "All the principal bowly-legged ladies in this country read the Clincher, from the Queen to the mill girls in Bridgeton . . . the Clincher is like Ballochmyle whisky — the older it gets, the better it gets."

Petrie's irreverence for the famous was legendary. Sir Thomas Lipton was "a pork ham slasher"; Sir William Bilsland was a "successful scone grocer"; Harry Lauder was dismissed as a comic singer with a crooked brain to match his crooked stick. Although not many copies of *The Clincher* have survived, there are still people in Glasgow who can look back and laugh, recalling the exclusive headlines produced by Petrie's silver cell, such as that on the death of Lord Overtoun, the chemical manufacturer:

> "Consternation in Heaven — Lord Overtoun
> fails to arrive!"

(Note: At one time this same Lord Overtoun had given out that he had discovered a way to manufacture gold. He managed to convince a number of prominent businessmen of the feasibility of such a process, with the result that they provided vast amounts of cash to support his highly secret experiments. When nothing came of them — at least, not gold — the said prominent businessmen preferred to keep the matter hushed up rather than be seen for the greedy fools they were.)

22 May 1968

"It is not the Tiber, it is the Clyde in Glasgow which is foaming with blood," claimed Mr Thomas Galbraith, Conservative MP for Glasgow Hillhead. He was, of course, referring to yet another "crime wave", and the Scottish Office was under attack in the Commons for its handling or otherwise of the crisis. Esmond Wright (Conservative, Pollock) described Glasgow as a "crime laboratory", a puzzling image, suggesting gangs in white coats wielding Bunsen burners and clipboards. Returning to the watery metaphor, Archbishop Scanlon had two days previously launched (the imagery is catching) an attack on the "wave of lawlessness" in Glasgow.

It is strange how outbreaks of good behaviour fail to merit equivalent attention.

---

23 May 1651

The postie calls:

The Magistrates, Council and
Community of Glasgow,
Glasgow,
N.B.

Dear Loyal Subjects,
In respect of our request of 9th inst., we have to acknowledge receipt of £100. We don't want to appear ungrateful, but you really find out who your friends are in a civil war. We'll send you a postcard from France.

> Yours aye,
>
> Carolus Rex (II).

(To begin with, the city fathers pled poverty, but were eventually persuaded to stump up the full £500, and also 5,000 merks in lieu of a force of a hundred men they should have raised. In July following, they actually raised 200, and kitted them out in full. They are said to have contributed £5,000 worth of cheese to feed the Royalist troops. Of course all of this had to be paid for by the unhappy citizens of Glasgow, who disloyally mobbed and assaulted their provost. Just when matters appeared to have reached a head, Charles took ship for the Continent.)

From the *West End News*, printed in Hillhead, Glasgow:

On Monday morning of 24th May, Bill Skinner died of heart illness at Garnavel General Hospital at the age of 67. He was the last of a distinguished line, being descended from the Rev. James Skinner, author of *The Reel of Tullochgorum* and *The Yowie wi' the Crookit Horn*, and Archbishop Skinner, Episcopalian Primate of Scotland and friend of Robert Burns. Bill's father was a robust, impressive, rather feckless man who lumberjacked and bummed his way across America at the turn of the century before ending his days in the Town Clerk's office of Glasgow Corporation. He also dissipated what was left of the family fortune because Bill, on leaving school, entered the shipyards as a marker-off, and retired from there in the 1940s with a heart illness. Thereafter he worked as a part-time laboratory assistant in a private college which crammed people for the university entrance exam and when that closed in the mid-sixties, he lived frugally on his National Insurance pension.

He never married, spending most of his life with his widowed mother in their home in Otago Street, in what is surely the last all-gas tenement flat in Glasgow. He had no children and his only living relation is a distant cousin in America.

These are the bare statistical bones of Skinner's life, and one could be excused for thinking them bleak. The living reality was wonderfully different. Bill filled his life with such various imaginative activities — political, artistic, scientific, alchemical — that he became a source of delight and satisfaction to an unusually wide circle of friends. He was a member of the Andersonian Society, the Connolly Association, the CND, an American scientific correspondence society, and the Scottish-USSR Friendship Society.

His Otago Street home had a small laboratory

where he did research into Particle compression and the Origins of Life, printing (at his own expense) a small pamphlet setting out his own views on these subjects. Anyone who cared to make an appointment would be shown over the small museum he had constructed in his mother's front parlour, with its fossils, pressed plants, the headphones powered by body electricity, the transparent seagull's skull and his exhibition of paintings. On average he produced two paintings a year: clear-edged, mysteriously coloured little works of a symbolic-abstractionist type with names like "Scotia Aspires", "Tyro Wisard Town" and "Death of Death". I once heard him grow highly indignant with a critic who called him a Primitive. He thought this was a slur on his meticulous technique. Even in his last years, when badly crippled with arthritis, he produced, with the help of friends, two editions of the magazine *Anvil Sparks*, in which he wrote science, art and political notes, advertised the exhibitions of friends, and serialised the career of Henry Dwining, the alchemist in Scott's novel *The Fair Maid of Perth*, a character with whom he felt great sympathy.

Before illness confined him to the house he was an alert, quick, small boyish man with nutcracker nose and chin, and a mop of pale nicotine-coloured hair. Apparently it had once been bright red. When this faded he tried reviving the colour with a concoction of his own, but without much success. His pubs were the State Bar, the Blythswood Bar and the Pewter Pot before they were modernised. His favourite drinks were vodka with lime and High-Ho, another invention of his which he distilled from pharmaceutical alcohol. It was only brought out for Hogmanay, and a small glass of it diluted by three parts of water to one and flung in the fire could still produce dangerous explosions. He was cheerful, utterly independent, had many friends of both sexes and all ages, and not one enemy. He *succeeded* in life.

Some time in 1940, when working in the yards, he became a founder of a political party which drew its

SOME
PROGRESSIVE
THEORIES AND DISCOVERIES
ON ORIGINS

W. K. SKINNER

Bill Skinner

members mainly from the Communist, Labour and Nationalist blocs. At the end of his life he was its only member, and he advanced its principles by fixing (with immense caution) small stickers to trees and lamp-posts in the quieter parts of the city near his home. The slogan on these stickers makes a good epitaph, and can be printed in full:

SCOTTISH
SOCIALIST
REPUBLIC

———

NEUTRALITY

Just to the left of "neutrality" is a small thistle.

---

25 May 1968

"Reverend Jack Glass of the Zion Sovereign Grace Baptist Church, Glasgow, will be at the next General Assembly of the Church of Scotland to protest the cause of the Scottish Covenant whether he is invited or not." So said Ian Paisley, Moderator of the Free Presbyterian Church of Ulster, when he ordained the budding ecclesiastical terrorist at a service in Glasgow last night. The newly reverend Glass, said Mr Paisley, might have to endure suffering and even imprisonment for his beliefs, but this had always been the case with prophets.

Mr Paisley spoke truer than he knew. Jack Glass, a born-again Christian at the age of 11, has proved tireless in his struggle with the Scottish tentacle of the Romish octopus. His crusades have taken him not only to the General Assembly in Edinburgh but also to Rome, to the very lair of the Beast, where he has had to endure being moved on by the Vatican polis no less than four times. At the canonisation of John Ogilvie (see 22nd February) he was to be seen in St Peter's Square carrying a banner with the curious message "No Pope Here"

---

26 May 1868

The scare that swept British cities in the wake of Fenian bomb attacks was particularly acute in Glasgow, which otherwise was settling down to enjoy the fruits of the Reform Act. On 16th January 1868, the Fenian leader Michael Barret was arrested for discharging a firearm in Glasgow Green. It was later found that he had caused a bomb explosion in London. He was executed on 26th May 1868.

27 May 1808

The first Gorbals Police Act was passed, dividing the not-yet-notorious barony into 12 wards, each with its own commissioner. Interestingly, these commissioners, who had the powers of constables, were to be chosen by the householders of Gorbals, perhaps not so much an early example of community involvement as a recognition that it was the propertied classes and their property that the police were to serve and protect. By the same Act, Glasgow maintained its influence with the power to appoint the fiscal and court officers, as well as providing three baillies to be *ex officio* commissioners.

28 May 1656

The death this year of Andrew Gray at the age of 22 years robbed Glasgow of one of its brightest young preachers. One of his sermons was called "Precious Remedies against Satan's Devices". While he offered really only one Precious Remedy ("to embrace Christ"), Gray identified five Devices of Satan. These were:

(1) to make Christians misinterpret sermons, scripture and providence;

(2) to generate a spirit of discouragement;

(3) to kill their convictions;

(4) to darken the freedom of the gospel for them;

(5) to make them fall asleep.

BAILLIE HUNKERS AND THE BEAR
(A Cautionary Tale)

I. At the Jiggin'

An Italian called Antonio Dollori arrived in Glasgow along with his dancing bear, whose name is not recorded. "Anty Dolly", as he soon became known, was putting the bear through its paces in a particularly filthy part of the city, the Old Vennel, before a large and admiring crowd.

II. Enter Trouble

There was at that time in Glasgow a certain magistrate who, because of his obsequious bearing in the presence of his social superiors, was known universally as Baillie Hunkers. It happened that while the said ursine ballet was in progress, the Baillie was picking his way through the Old Vennel heading for a civic banquet, fortified no doubt against the stench and ordure of those noisome wynds by the expectation of a great deal of claret to come.

III. The Convergence of the Twain

On seeing the Baillie approach, the crowd dispersed. But Anty Dolly and his bear did not, or at any rate did not fast enough for his satisfaction, for, losing his patience, he drew his rapier and sank it into the beast's rump. With a roar (probably) the bear snapped the rope which was restraining it and embraced the rash Baillie in a grip of hairy iron. The crowd, which had not gone very far, reformed.

IV. The Last Waltz

Fortunately, the bear's owner still had enough control over it to prevent any serious harm to Baillie Bunkers. What might have been a terminal assault became (grotesque! improbable!) a sort of *pas de deux*. Round and round they went, the bear and the Baillie, while the mob gawped helplessly, round and round until, their dance floor being all

bemerded and slippery underpaw, they lost their
balance and crashed into one of the several deepish
puddles that glinted with deceptive purity in the
morning light.

V. Rescue

Meanwhile a group of local bakers, ever a sound
breed, had appeared on the scene. Seizing their
opportunity, they managed to prise the bear's
forearms apart with barrel staves and free the
Baillie, who was unhurt but in "a bit of a state"
according to eyewitnesses.

VI. Flight

The Italian, realising that something very terrible
had happened, made himself scarce.

VII. A Fair Trial?

Obviously such an atrocity could not simply be
forgotten. A gross insult had been perpetrated on
one of the City Fathers; his dignity had been fatally
assailed, and that while he was going about his
duties *for the tounis gude*; further, there was no
saying what would happen if this sort of thing went
unpunished. Accordingly, the bear, who was being
held prisoner outside the Tolbooth by the town
officers and a detachment of the Blues, was
arraigned before the Council for trial. What
followed was a mockery of Scottish justice. The
panel was neither represented nor allowed to
conduct its own defence. Nor was it advised of its
rights of appeal, or trial before a jury of its peers. It
was sentenced to be executed, the pelt afterwards to
be hung in the town hall as an Example to Others.

VIII. Death of a Bear

That same day, the condemned bear was escorted
to the Butts on the east of the city, and shot. It took
several volleys of musket fire to dispatch it.

IX. The Malefactor's Concealment discovered — apprehension and trial — ingenious form of punishment — animal-loving Glasgow populace shows its big, warm heart — Italian national not stoned to death.

A few days later, Antonio Dollori was captured in the Cathkin Hills above Rutherglen, where he had been hiding out since his escape. He was tried in Glasgow and sentenced to spend one hour in the "jougs", with the skin of his dead partner draped over his shoulders. This latter sophistication upset him more than anything, and he wept throughout. No one threw anything at him, not even jeers. They could see he could not bear being pelted. In fact, they were all sorry for him and more than a bit ashamed.

X. Moralitas

And so they should have been.

---

30 May 1609

Early visitors to Glasgow leave us in no doubt that it was a delightful place. On this date, a Count of the Holy Roman Empire who was visiting Britain arrived with his party in Glasgow. He describes it in his diary as "a famous archiepiscopal and commercial town. It lies beautifully and has fine trees and a handsome bridge of eight arches over the river Clyde."

In 1650, Cromwell said of it, "The Town of Glasgow, though not so big, nor so rich, yet to all seems a much sweeter Place and more delightful than Edinburgh".

Rey, the naturalist, in 1661 called it "fair, large and well built cross-wise, somewhat like unto Oxford, the streets very broad and pleasant"; and an anonymous description of the period was, "The nonesuch of Scotland, where an English florist may pick up a posy".

An intelligent English traveller of 1704 found it "a more regular built and a cleaner town, and has more good streets in it than Edenburgh has, and the buildings are as handsome as those at Edenburgh, or are rather before them".

In 1727, the English spy Daniel Defoe called Glasgow "one of the cleanliest, most beautiful and best built cities in Great Britain".

A native and an early historian of the city, John McUre, Keeper of the Regality Register of Sasines, found the place as acceptable to the nostrils as to the eyes: "The City is surrounded with Cornfields, Kitchen and Flower gardens, and beautiful Orchyards abounding with Fruits of all sorts, which by Reason of the open and large Streets send furth a pleasant and odiferous smell. . . ."

Most of us remember, vaguely, how James Watt hit on the idea of the steam engine from watching kettles boil. Nonsense. What happened, in his own words, was this:

31 May 1765

> "I had gone to take a walk on a fine Sabbath afternoon, early in 1765. I had entered the Green by the gate at the foot of Charlotte Street, and had passed the old washing house. I was thinking upon the engine at the time, and had gone as far as the herd's house, when the idea came into my mind that, as steam was an elastic body, it would rush into a vacuum, and if a communication were made between the cylinder and an exhausted vessel, it would rush into it, and might be condensed without cooling the cylinder . . . I had not walked further than the golf house when the whole thing was arranged in my mind."

1 June
1982

On a blazing hot spring day in Glasgow, a Papal helicopter appeared over Bellahouston Park and landed among about a quarter of a million of the faithful who had been awaiting it for up to 12 hours.

It was the culmination of a most extraordinary feat of organisation on a vast scale, involving, among others, 6,000 police, 7,000 stewards, a flotilla of ambulances and a small army of priests. Certain things tend to happen when you get a vast number of people together; several hundred required treatment for ailments ranging from sunstroke to blisters, three elderly men had heart attacks, two women went into labour. To prepare the stage for the drama, the 59 trees in the park had, after weeks of amazingly acerbic controversy, been removed — not felled, but gently extracted and stored for eventual replanting.

All this was forgotten in the excitement of the visit, which went off without a major hitch. Pope John Paul Mark-II was given a rapturous welcome that included choirs, a pibroch, a folk band, and the presentation of various symbolic gifts to remind him of Glasgow. We can't remember exactly what they were, but they probably included a can of Superlager, a pie supper and a piece of turf from Celtic Park. Mass was celebrated *en masse* and *al fresco*, and the Pope talked about peace and brotherhood, both of which he was in favour of. When he left, the crowds sang "Glasgow Belongs to Me" and "Will Ye No Come Back Again?" before making their various ways home, exhausted but cheerful. Everyone agreed it had been a great day, and that he was a very nice man and a nice Pope.

Apart, that is, from the 1,800 Loyalists who demonstrated with the Rev. Ian Paisley in George Square against the visit. Around 26 arrests were made. Any other day this might have been news, but for once at any rate Paisley's thunder was well and truly stolen.

---

2 June
1837

Rab Steel, the infamous Marrying Provost of Rutherglen, took up his office this year, remaining provost until 1843. He was a tollkeeper in the burgh when the Scots law allowed any secular witness to legalise a wedding. He was noted for his deep distaste for any sort of lengthy or verbose ritual — at sermons he would dangle a large "turnip" watch in front of the offending preacher when he considered his time was up — and the marriage ceremonies he conducted were masterly examples of workmanlike concision. These were held at the toll itself, and there was no need for the couple to go inside. Rab Steel simply stuck his head out the window, asked them if they wanted to get married, and with a brief "A' richt", the solemn vows were sealed.

Cleland, in his *New Statistical Account*, notes that "Rutherglen had a questionable notoriety as to marriages" and was "the Gretna Green of Lanarkshire". (Milngavie, he adds, was also pretty bad for this sort of thing.) The procedure he complains of was quite ingenious. The intending couple would present themselves to the magistrate, and admit they had been married without banns being proclaimed and by an unauthorised person whose name they couldn't quite recall, somehow. Thus they made themselves liable to fining and imprisonment. The magistrate then fined them an understood amount, remitted the imprisonment and gave them an extract of acknowledgement of the marriage, which was thereafter binding. So everyone was happy.

The following is an account, dated as of today, from a Glasgow shoemaker to one of his clients, a Madam Elizabeth Moor:

3 June 1819

closing up Madam Moor	11d.
mending Miss Plowden	2d.
tapping and binding Miss Hambleton	11d.
turning, closing up and corking Madam Moor	9d.
turn over plase brought up	2s. 9d.
welting a pes into Madam Moor	2d.
stitching a bust into ditto	1d.
heeling Miss Plowden	6d.

repairing Madam Moor's soul	4d.
peesing and bottoming Miss Plowden	11d.
brought up	4s. 9d.
heeling and corking Madam Moor	2s. 11d.
stitching and making water tight ditto	6d.
tupping Madam Moor	2d.
lining, binding and laying a piece into do. . .	4d.
	8s. 8d.

Eight shillings and eightpence for all this! Where nowadays is such value for money to be found? Or such personal attention in the best traditions of craftsmanship and service to the customer? In this our age of self-service and the hypermarket trolley, we can only pause, and wonder.

---

4 June 1832

After a stormy passage through the House of Lords, the Reform Bill was finally passed. Since its introduction by Lord John Russel on 1st March the previous year, it had seemed touch and go whether it would make the statute book, and the battle against vested interests was a long and fierce one. Although it scraped through the second reading in the Commons, it was rejected in committee, Parliament was dissolved, and it was again introduced, only to be thrown out by the Lords. Glasgow was to the forefront in the demands for reform and its Town Council and prominent citizens petitioned both Parliament and the King. Following the bill's penultimate rejection by the House of Lords and the resignation of that Parliament, 70,000 assembled on Glasgow Green, and sent an address to the King urging him to take the necessary measures for passing the Bill.

The Act granted franchise to urban householders paying rent of £10 or more, so Glasgow now had an electorate of 7,024. She was also entitled to send *two* members to Parliament.

The following is the text of the memorial at Townhead to three of Glasgow's martyrs of the Covenanting persuasion who

"THO' DEAD YET SPEAKETH"

"Behind this stone, lyes James Nisbet, who suffered Martyrdom at this place, June 5th, 1684. Also James Lawson and Alexander Wood, who suffered Martyrdom October 24th, 1684. For their adherence to the Word of God, and Scotland's covenanted work of reformation.

"Here lye martyrs three
　　Of memory
Who for the Covenant did die
　　And witness is
'Gainst all these nations' perjury.

"Against the covenanted cause
　　Of Christ their royal King
The British Rulers made such laws
　　Declar'd was Satan's reign.

"As *Britain* lyes in guilt you see,
'Tis asked O reader, art thou free?"

Well, art thou? On the wall of the north transept of Glasgow Cathedral is a memorial to nine other victims of the "Killing Times" in the city. The note of subtle enquiry that ends the previous inscription gives way here to something more threatening:

"Here lies the corps of ROBERT BUNTON, JOHN HART, ROBERT SCOT, MATTHEW PATOUN, JOHN RICHMOND, JAMES JOHNSTON, ARCHIBALD STEWART, JAMES WINNING, JOHN MAIN who suffered at the cross of Glasgow for their testimony to the covenants and work of reformation, because they durst not own the authority of the then tyrants, destroying the same, betwixt 1666 and 1688.
　　"Years sixty-six and eighty-four
　　Did send their souls home into glore,
　　Whose bodies here enterred ly,
　　Then sacrificed to tyranny,
　　To Covenants and Reformation
　　'Cause they adhered in their station.
　　These nine, with others in this yard,
　　Whose heads and bodies were not spared,
　　Their testimonies, foes to bury,
　　Caused beat the drum then in great fury.

They'll know at resurrection day
To murder sancts was no sweet play!"

In other words,"*Ah'll* get ye!"

---

6 June
1814

The advances made in medical science in the early 19th century owed more than we might care to think to those who had already passed on before. The dear departed. Cadavers. The proper study of anatomy required the dissection of the same, in as fresh a state as possible. Hitherto, anatomists had relied on two main sources: executed criminals, and bodies from Ireland (there was a contemporary story going round about a whole cargo of Irish corpses discovered rotting in a ship at Broomielaw Quay). But now, demand was outstripping the supply. New sources had to be found. The professors were prepared to pay good money for bodies, and weren't too particular about their provenance. "It fell off a lorry" would have done nicely, if they'd had lorries.

Everyone knows about Burke and Hare, the Laurel and Hardy of the Edinburgh underworld, who perfected various techniques for turning spare people into saleable corpses. But they were decent straightforward murderers. They never went so far as to rob a grave in the course of their career. That is to say, they were not "resurrectionists", and "resurrection" or "shusielifting" was the game.

There is no doubt that it was quite common in Glasgow, as in Edinburgh, though the degree of collective paranoia it gave rise to was disproportionate. It was a most *popular* crime, in the sense that it might involve anyone in the community, one corpse being as good as another in the democracy of the dissecting room. And resurrectionists made excellent news, or at least rumour, combining as they did the irresistible appeals of blasphemy, high adventure and the macabre.

On 6th June 1814, Dr Granville Sharp Pattison of Glasgow College, his lecturer on surgery Andrew Russell, and two students, Robert Munro and John McLean, appeared before the High Court of the

Justiciary in Edinburgh. The charge was that they had violated the grave of Mrs McAllister in the Ramshorn Churchyard, Glasgow, and taken her body to their dissecting rooms.

The story was as follows. Certain "shusielifters" had been at work in Ramshorn churchyard and had made rather too much noise. The police were alerted, and the resurrectionists were seen to make off in the direction of the College. By the following day, the news had spread, causing general hysteria. Mrs Mc Allister's grave was found to be empty. The Glasgow mob were not stupid. They knew she had not popped out to the shops for a pint of milk and a paper. They put two and two together, and marched on the College.

They were in the middle of smashing the anatomy professor's windows when the police arrived, armed with a warrant to search for the errant body. This they proceeded to do, after restraining the crowd. When they called on Pattison's rooms in College Street, they found the doctor and his assistants, who invited them to search freely. Having found nothing, they were making their way back when they remembered a large tub of water they'd failed to investigate. They returned, emptied it, and discovered dismembered parts of a female body. A dentist identified the teeth as those of the late Mrs McAllister, a relative the fingers. Pattison and company were arrested.

At the trial, the first in which dental evidence was given, the defence counsel was able to point out some inconsistencies in the prosecution's case, in particular in the productions. Mrs McAllister had been a married woman with children, yet the pelvis found in the tub was that of a virgin. A cynic might have supposed that a quick substitute had been made before the police arrived. At any rate, it was enough to get the defendants acquitted.

The law may have been satisfied — popular opinion was definitely not. Dr Pattison was pressurised into resigning his post at the College. He emigrated to America, where it must be said he made a great name for himself in his chosen field.

7 June
1863

In a publication entitled *The Moral Statistics of Glasgow in 1863, Practically applied by a Sabbath School Teacher*, the following figures are given:

"Contrast between the offerings of Glasgow to Bacchus and Belial, and to Jesus Christ:

To cash yearly offered by professedly
    Christian Glasgow to Bacchus £1,184,412
To cash yearly offered by professedly
    Christian Glasgow to Belial £819,183
To sums raised in support of churches,
    sabbath schools, education, orphans,
    benevolent societies, refuges etc. etc. £347,389 9s. 9d.

"Hear, Oh Heavens! and give ear, Oh earth!—six parts given to the devil, and one part to Jesus Christ!—six times more to Hell than to Heaven! by the commercial capital of the most religious nation in the world, by the city whose glorious motto is 'Let Glasgow Flourish by the preaching of the Word' . . . etc., etc."

Modern economists are unable to say what effect inflation would have on these figures.

---

8 June
1928

Oscar Slater's belated appeal against a conviction 19 years previously for murder was upheld at the High Court in Edinburgh on the grounds of misdirection by the judge presiding at his trial, Lord Guthrie. Slater was a German Jew, his real name was Oscar Joseph Leschziner and he had only been in Glasgow about a month when the murder was committed (see 21st December 1908). Evidence against Slater was less than slight. A diamond crescent brooch had been stolen from the house and Slater was known to have tried to sell a pawn ticket for a similar item of jewellery. In spite of the fact that the police knew that Slater had pawned his brooch five days before the murder they had Slater extradited from New York. They also allowed three eyewitnesses to see Slater before he was formally identified, and omitted to call as a witness a man who may have been able to provide Slater with an alibi. A large part of the prosecution's time was devoted to an attack on Slater's moral character. He was sentenced to death but was reprieved two days before his hanging and given a life's penal servitude. Shortly after these questions were asked in Parliament by Sir Edward Marshall Hall, KC., Sir Arthur Conan Doyle published a book in which he expressed serious doubts about the case. Five years after Slater's trial, a police officer, Detective Lieutenant John Thomson Trench, went to see a lawyer, Mr David Cook, to whom he made statements about what he believed to be the truth of the matter. These statements formed the basis of an enquiry by the Sheriff of Lanarkshire, but the only consequence of this was the dismissal of Detective Trench (see 14th September 1914). Another 15 years passed before Slater's appeal was allowed. He was paid £6,000 for his trouble and curiously stayed on in Scotland until his death in 1948.

How did the youth of Glasgow get its kicks before Evostik? A clue is provided in today's report of a young man convicted at the Central Juvenile Court of "maliciously breaking an electric fuse box". Apparently it was a popular pastime, particularly in the South Side for some obscure reason, to rub a fuse box with a hammer, thereby getting a mild electric shock.

9 June 1949

A Commission of the Privy Council convicted one Kate Campbell of witchcraft, along with four other women and three men. She was sentenced to be taken to the Gallowgreen of Paisley, "there to be first worried and then publicly burnt". This was done.

10 June 1697

Kate Campbell was a serving maid. After being reproached by her mistress for the theft of a glass of milk, she was supposed to have put a spell on her mistress's daughter, Kirsty Shaw, wishing that the Devil might "harle Kirsty's soule thro' the bottomless pit". As a result, Kirsty took a fit, and was speechless for eight days. She was examined by a Paisley doctor. For three days, we are told, she kept vomiting out an amazing assortment of objects:

hair, hot cinders, pieces of candlestick three to four inches long, and the bones of various sorts of animals and fowls, of all sizes. Then she stopped, quite suddenly, and experienced no further manifestations of the curse.

The affair was widely publicised, and the name of Kirsty Shaw became well known. She married a minister, who soon died, and in her widowhood devoted herself to the preparing of thread, which she bleached on her own window sill. A friend sold it for her in Bath, where it went down well with the ladies of fashion. Another friend indulged in some industrial espionage on her behalf, travelling to Holland and peeking into a Dutch twining mill. She was thus able to open Paisley's first thread factory. It was from these bizarre beginnings Paisley's great textile industry sprung.

---

11 June 1965

On the occasion of a lunchtime concert in George Square, the audience, mainly teenage girls, rioted and mobbed the group in question, the Beatstalkers. These popular artists had to flee into the City Chambers for sanctuary, leaving behind such trophies as shoelaces, ties, buttons, and bits of hair. When the screaming girls failed to disperse after the Riot Act was read, a volley of musket fire was directed over their heads and a detachment of dragoons charged with drawn sabres. Actually, this latter part is not strictly true, but judging from the way they went on, one or two Glasgow councillors probably wished it was. In the event, no arrests were made, but the incident cast a cloud over plans for future concerts.

Ah, the Beatstalkers — where are they now?

---

12 June 1641

The magistrates of Glasgow ordained the City Treasurer to pay one James Colquhoun "fyfe dollars (or £1 sterling) for drawing the portrait of the toun to be sent to Holland". This must have been Glasgow's first map, or at least topographical illustration. We would like to think the Dutch were impressed, but with the likes of Ruisdael, Cuyp, Vermeer and Van de Velde around at the time, perhaps they weren't.

The city fathers of the seventeenth century were extremely canny about venturing into the world of fine arts. In 1670, to brighten up the interior of the Town Hall at the same time as demonstrating their civic loyalty to the crown, they sought to purchase portraits of Charles I and Charles II, "as also ane carpett". At the end of the day, they settled for just Charles II, who set them back £25 sterling.

---

13 June 1750

The Anderston Club, which first met on this date, was undoubtedly the most *intellectual* of the social clubs that flourished in Glasgow around this time. That is not saying very much in itself (see 11th January and 5th May), but considering its founder member was the eminent mathematics professor, John Simpson, and it numbered among its members Adam Smith, Robert Foulis and Dr Moore, its potential as a "think tank" was not negligible. The convivial thinkers met at 2 p.m. each Saturday in John Sharpe's tavern in Anderston where, over a jar or two, they would discuss the deep matters of the day. The exchange of ideas involved must have had some effect on these gentlemen's worthy contributions to the Enlightenment, always assuming they remembered anything next morning. In fairness, it must be recorded that 18th-century Edinburgh had its genius too, so much so in fact that it earned the description "the Glasgow of the East".

---

14 June 1630

For centuries, Lee House in Lanark, home of the Lockhart family, contained a strange charm widely held to be effective against disease, whether in man or beast. Known as the "Lee Penny", it was in the form of a silver disc with a stone inset. Sir Simon Lockhart was said to have come by it as part of the ransom of a Saracen chief he had captured in Palestine. He had been there on crusade with Sir

James Douglas who, as every schoolboy knows, was companioned by the romantic, if festering, cordate organ of the Bruce.

This, then, was the talisman which, dipped in water several times ("thrie dips and a sweil" was the prescription) had healing virtues famous throughout Scotland. Not only in Scotland: in June of 1630, when the plague was raging in Newcastle, the town applied for a loan of the "Penny", and lodged the immense sum of £6,000 as security for its safe return. When it arrived, the plague vanished, presumably having run its course. The Corporation of Newcastle was so impressed it offered to swop it for the £6,000, but its owners would not part with it.

Some years later, the Synod of Glasgow had to investigate a complaint made against Sir John Lockhart of Lee "anent the superstitious using of ane stone set in silver for the curing of diseased cattel".

The investigating authorities had a problem. Not only was the charm's owner an important nobleman, it is obvious that they themselves believed in its powers. They managed to resolve the dilemma and exempt the accused Lockhart from sorcery by the following judgement:

> "The Assemblie having enquirit of the maner of using thereof and particularlie understoode, by examinatioun of the said Laird of Lie, and otherwise that the custom is onlie to cast the stene in sume water, and give the diseasit cattel thereof to drink, and yt the same is dene wtout using onie words, such as charmers and sorcerers use in their unlawful practices, and considering that in nature there are mony thinges seen to work strange effects, qu'rof no humane witt cane give a reason, it having pleasit God to give unto stones and herbes special virtues for the healing of mony infirmities in man and beast . . . advises the brethren to surcease their proces, as qu'rin they perceive no ground of offence; and admonishes the said Laird of Lie, in the using of the said stone, to take heed that it be usit hereafter wt the least scandal that possiblie maye bie."

---

15 June 1819

The *Glasgow Courier* noted the death of the Reverend James Steuart at the age of forty-four, after a long and distinguished career as minister, first in St Andrew's Church and latterly in Anderston Old Church, in whose graveyard his respectable bones were laid.

James Steuart had the distinction of being the only Glasgow meenister to be the son of Bonnie Prince Charlie.

CLIFF HANLEY WRITES:

On this date, a few years back, a chartered accountant manqué saw the light of day, or fancied he had, in the elegant purlieux of Dennistoun in the high-toned East End of Glasgow. The city has never been quite, or even nearly, the same.

Leaping from double-entry rubbish into journalism, Jack House invented his own kind of journalism. He has been gratefully copied and imitated by a couple of generation of scribblers. As well as discovering the true magic that lies behind every grimy facade in his native city, his writings fought stalwartly for the city itself.

He has defended it not only against onslaughts from neanderthal outlanders, but from successive waves of City Fathers whose vision of a greater Glasgow was to complete the demolition that the Luftwaffe abandoned.

This genial bon vivant's genius has been in giving Glaswegians back a sense of identity and pride. There is a long and tedious queue of people who would like the title of Mister Glasgow. House is the man who never sought trumpery titles. He is himself entire, and he is the great Glaswegian by simple virtue of his unquenchable affection for the finest and daftest city in the world.

Zachary Boyd, enditer of sacred verse, minister of the Barony Church and benefactor of Glasgow University, of whom more elsewhere (see 2nd March and 26th October) met Charles I at Holyrood in the course of that monarch's Scottish visit. It is strange to have to relate that this fierce

Covenanter-to-be and scourge of Kings and Princes was highly impressed by Charles, and addressed a most extravagant panegyric to him in Latin.

18 June 1826

The practice of distinguishing between the deserving poor and the other sort, which currently enjoys such Parliamentary encouragement, has, of course, a long history. The distinction is drawn with delicacy and tact on the occasion of a new church being opened in Govan: "A collection was made for the industrious poor amounting to £24 10s. 0d., after deducting the average collection for the poor."

19 June 1951

The 500th anniversary celebrations of the founding of the University of Glasgow were attended by over 200 representatives of global academe. The then Chancellor and Rector, Boyd Orr and John McCormack, presided.

20 June 1806

An Act of Parliament was passed today instigating the Glasgow, Paisley and Ardrossan Canal. Its main purpose was to carry merchandise from the harbour and docks at Ardrossan (recently erected by the Earl of Eglinton) to Glasgow and Paisley, and to bring coal and other goods to the harbour by return. The Glasgow terminus was Eglinton Street. The canal was begun at Glasgow, and was of modest dimensions, only about four-and-a-half feet deep and, as it did not have any locks, had to follow a somewhat tortuous route to keep level. It got as far as Johnston before the money ran out. Despite extra borrowing, it became increasingly unlikely that it would ever reach Ardrossan. So a railway was constructed instead from Ardrossan to Kilwinning.

The Paisley Canal had a disastrous opening in 1810. As the boat was about to set off on the return journey to Glasgow with its passengers, a further crowd of Paisley passengers clambered aboard. The boat became top heavy and capsized, with considerable loss of life.

The canal was never a financial success. The Glasgow and South-Western Railway bought it in 1869, closed it, and opened the Paisley Canal Line over its grave.

For an institution that has flourished so spectacularly over the last hundred years or so, the theatre in Glasgow had some inauspicious beginnings.

The first effort was a primitive structure built this year against the wall of the old Bishop's Palace. The annalist Cleland describes it bluntly as a "timber shed". Modest though it was, opinion ran so high against it among the puritanical citizens that theatre-goers required a military escort. Just one year after it opened, the minister George Whitfield preached a sermon against it in the nearby "Hie Kirk" Yard, denouncing it as "the Devil's House". The inspired congregation promptly rose and tore it down. That night the Devil had to sleep rough.

Another attempt was made in 1764, subscribed to by a few brave individuals. They sought and failed to obtain the patronage of the city magistrates, who were unwilling to commit themselves to so unpopular a venture. No one would dare sell them any land for it. Eventually, however, they got their hands on some ground in the suburbs, in Grahamston, and opened in spring that year. On the first night, a disorderly mob set fire to the stage, burning machinery, scenery and other fittings. The damage was made good, and the theatre limped on with indifferent success until it was completely burned down in the winter of 1780.

In 1782, a comedian called Jackson built a theatre in Dunlop Street. Tastes were changing along with the growth of population and porsperity, and the philistine venom of the puritans was by now slightly diluted. The Dunlop Street building succeeded in not being burned down, but was eclipsed in 1805 by the much grander Queen Street Theatre.

This was a really palatial affair, the most expensive and superb outside of London. The cost was over £18,500, raised by subscription. Alas, it was not a success. It passed through the hands of several lessees, none of whom managed to make a go of it, and was sold for a mere £5,000 which barely discharged the debts it had accumulated.

In 1829 it demonstrated a respect for tradition by burning down.

---

22 June 1679

The defeat of the Covenanting army by the forces of Charles II's son the Duke of Monmouth put an end to the rebellion in the south-west of Scotland once and for all.

Since the Restoration, Glasgow and the surrounding areas, largely sympathetic to the cause of the Covenant, had suffered repeated attempts to enforce episcopalianism and suppress the illegal conventicles. Matters came to a head in 1679 with the murder of James Sharp, Archbishop of St Andrews, by a handful of zealots.

In an attempt to quell disaffection in the western shires, the Duke of Lauderdale, Charles's Commissioner in Scotland, assembled an army of around 5,000 Highland troopers, and turned it loose in the area. Many of the "Highland Host" were encamped in Glasgow on what later became known as Garnethill. There are many tales, not all reliable, of the outrages committed by these uninvited guests on the property and persons of the good citizens of Glasgow. It does appear that the Highlanders looked on the venture as more of a grand raid on the Lowlands than a military exercise in law and order. The Highland Host was disbanded after only two months. According to tradition, when the Highlanders were leaving Glasgow, a crowd of College students barred their way over Glasgow Bridge and refused to let them past until they had disgorged some of the souvenirs they had plundered, which suggests that both their numbers and ferocity have been hugely exaggerated.

On 1st June that year, Viscount Claverhouse ("Bonnie Dundee"), in command of a troop of Life Guards, surprised a well-armed conventicle at Drumclog, about 13 miles south of Glasgow. His Dragoons being outnumbered, he was forced to fall back on the city, which he prepared to defend.

Claverhouse had around one hundred men at his disposal, the Covenanters several thousand. Barricades were hastily set up, and men posted at the windows and street closes. The Covenanters split their forces, one body attacking through the Gallowgate, and the other through the College Vennel. But the assault was badly led and badly synchronised. After some bitter street fighting, they were forced to withdraw, leaving eight of their number dead on the streets. Thus ended the second "Battle of the Butts".

It is said that Claverhouse would not allow the dead Covenanters burial, but had them left on the street for the dogs. If so, he had some personal cause for revenge. His kinsman, Cornet Graham, had been killed at Drumclog. The Covenanters, mistaking him for Claverhouse himself, had mutilated his body.

Despite their failure to take Glasgow, the morale of the Covenanters was high, thanks more to injections of religious fervour from their ministers than to any realistic appraisal of their long-term chances. They rallied on Hamilton Hill south of the Clyde and by 22nd June their numbers had swollen to eight, or some say ten, thousand. But by this time there was a full-sized Government army ready for them.

The aftermath of Bothwell Brig was one of bloody repression and reprisal. The Covenant was provided with all the martyrs it could have wished for (see 5th June, 12th November, 7th December).

Furious at the imposition of the Malt Tax (amounting to 3d. on each barrel of beer) a mob

23 June 1725

attacked Shawfield House, elegant home of Glasgow's sole MP, Mr Daniel Campbell, who had treacherously voted in favour of the Bill. He was also suspected of having leaked secrets of the tobacco trade to the English.

A detachment of the military under the command of Captain Bashell failed to suppress the riot, but opened fire, killing two persons. They were ordered to withdraw towards Dumbarton, during which action a further nine rioters were shot and killed.

The city was then occupied by a force under General Wade and the Lord Advocate, Duncan Forbes of Culloden. Forbes further ordered the arrest of the Provost and Magistrates of the city, who were held in custody for a day. Captain Bashell got away with it — the Government intervened to prevent his being tried for murder.

Campbell successfully sued his own city and constituency for damages of £6,000. He was also awarded £3,000 costs. Part of this sum was raised by — a special tax on ale and beer in the city.

---

24 June 1450

King James II granted a charter of Regality in 1450 to Bishop Turnbull, giving to him and his successors in the church free regality over the city, barony and lands known as the Bishop's Forest:

> "The woods, plains, moors, marshes, ways, paths, waters, ponds, streams, meadows, grazings, pastures, grounds, mills . . . hawkings, huntings, fishings, watercourses, peat, turf, coals, stone quarries, stone and lime . . . heath, broom . . . with free forest and warren."

Believe it or not, this was Glasgow.

In return, Turnbull was required every 24th June on the feast of the Nativity of John the Baptist, or Midsummer's Day in the old style, to render to the King the tribute of "a red rose, at Glasgow, and the offering of devout prayers only. . . ." A charming ceremony no doubt, and one worthy of revival. Surely the Council and Interflora could put their heads together and arrange an annual dandelion, say, for EIIR?

The Alkali Act of 1863 was the first Government legislation to deal with gaseous pollution of the atmosphere. An inspector appointed under the Act found that of Glasgow contained more hydro-chloric sulphurous and sulphuric acid, more ammonia and more nitrogenous matter, more carbonic acid and less oxygen than any other large town in the United Kingdom.

A Glasgow chemist, writing a short time later, described the air, under certain winds from the east and north-east, where the chemical works were, as "positively unfit for respiration".

25 June 1863

Glasgow's Kingston Bridge was ceremonially opened. Costing £11.5 million, it was the longest in any British city, and the third longest of its type in the world.

26 June 1970

James Maxton, ILP Member for Glasgow Bridgeton (1922-46), spoke in the House of Commons on the cuts in the Scottish Health Estimates. It was an impassioned speech, and at one stage he called the Government and its supporters "murderers". Several other Clydeside MPs supported him, and were ejected along with him by the Sergeant at Arms. Their behaviour was *un-parliamentary* — just because people might die as a result of the actions of individuals in government is no reason why those responsible should be called bad names.

27 June 1923

One year minus a day from the laying of its concrete foundations, the giant factory chimney which became known as "Tennant's Stalk" was completed.

Designed to carry off the poisonous fumes from the St Rollox bleach and chemical works in the north-east of the city, it was $435\frac{1}{2}$ feet high, three times the height of Nelson's Column and the highest structure of its kind in the world. It dealt

28 June 1842

each day with the waste products of 120 tons of coal from the world's largest chemical works. Soaring high over lesser lums, this was without a doubt the most outstanding and malodorous landmark Glasgow has ever projected.

There is a story that Tennant as an old man had a dispute with the city fathers as to whether his stalk should be demolished, and at the same time had just married a young wife. When he won his battle to keep his lum, his wife simultaneously presented him with a baby. *The Clincher* (see 21st May) published an account of both events in his broadsheet newspaper under the single headline: "Tennant's Stalk Still Stands".

---

29 June 1928

Trial of the protagonists of the "Battle of Albert Bridge". This not untypical confrontation between two gangs, the South Side Stickers and the Calton Entry, had indeed something in it of more than a casual skirmish. It was planned in advance as a tournament between two picked teams of champions, five-a-side. The weapons were swords and daggers. After the first few passes in the lists, the rest joined in for a *grande melée*, throwing stones and bottles. One boy was stabbed to death. The warriors were all between 12 and 15 years of age.

---

30 June 1857

On this date began the celebrated trial of Madelaine Smith, accused of murdering her lover L'Angelier. So much has been written about it, we offer only the following observations:

(1) A close study of Madelaine Smith's earlobes and the distance between her eyes reveals beyond the shadow of a doubt that she maybe did it.

(2) Yes, the upper middle class of Glasgow *was* a whited sepulchre, a can of worms under a teacosy. What vices did these sober church-goers not pursue? The very wally of their

closes breathed abominations, their antimacassars blushed with the memory of a thousand unspeakable Gomorrahs. It goes without saying that every dunny in India Street concealed a dago paramour with a ladder.

(3) The legal verdict of Not Proven is incompatible with the logical Law of the Excluded Middle. Therefore, the law is an ass.

(4) Everyone has his or her own favourite way of making cocoa. Some put in one heaped teaspoonful, some three level ones. Some use hot milk, some milk and water. Some take no sugar, some two lumps, some three. Arsenic as a seasoning, though, is downright eccentric, at best.

1 July 1703

"The Session, with consent of the Magistrates, direct a box to be placed at the Hie Kirk-yard, and a man to ring a bell at burials to raise money given for seeing the Kirks up the way. They are only to drink part of it — drinking the whole is an auld gaw in their backs."

We are not quite sure what this is all about, but we feel the message is vaguely clear.

---

2 July 1943

An anonymous river-user reported to the *Glasgow Herald* that he had seen a seal swimming up the River Clyde around Milton.

Three years later, in the autumn of 1946, James Cowan ("Peter Prowler") saw a minnow in the Molendinar.

---

3 July 1883

Today was the date fixed for the launch of the new steamship *Daphne* at Linthouse shipyard. Two hundred men and boys were on board, finishing off the interior, as she was launched. All seemed to be going according to plan, but once she reached the middle of the river, the *Daphne* capsized. One hundred and forty-six were drowned, and it was three weeks before the ship could be raised and the last of the bodies recovered.

---

4 July 1700

In the eyes, or rather ears, of the pre-secession Church of Scotland of the early 1700s, those who employed bad language were not fit to attend the service of Holy Communion, a delight reserved for the godly. One minister declared: "I debar from these tables all who used any kind of minced oaths, such as 'losh', 'gosh', 'teth' and 'lovenenty'. As Communion took place in the open air and lasted from nine in the morning until late in the afternoon, or even night-time, depending on the number of communicants, debarment may have been a mixed anathema.

Another example of the kirk's language hang-ups was that they considered the words of the

Psalms too sacred to be used outside of actual worship. When the congregation was merely practicing, they had to substitute other words to the metre. "The Cameronian Cat", still remembered, was one such example; there are many others. We have to imagine choirs of the devout intoning in all solemnity words like the following:

(to the Psalm tune *Desert*)
> *Oh Paisley is a bonnie toun,*
> *And stands upon a hill;*
> *And by it rins the river Cart*
> *That ca's Jock Stirling's mill.*

(or to *Bangor*)
> *The high, high notes o' Bangor's tune*
> *Are very hard to raise,*
> *And trying hard to reach them gars*
> *The lassies burst their stays.*

Lovenenty!

A tinsmith in Glasgow was sentenced to 60 days imprisonment for stealing the brass door handles from a printer's premises. "The crime of stealing door handles has been very frequent of late," warns the *Glasgow Herald*.

5 July 1849

The original date for the beginning of the Glasgow Fair, instituted by William the Lion (or William the Big Softie as he was thence known). It was appointed to be held annually for eight full days from the octaves of Sts Peter and Paul. The sixth of the month was "Fair E'en", when the fair was proclaimed.

6 July

This custom lasted into the 18th century, when the Town Council ordained it should commence on the first Monday of July, and continue only to the end of the week. The reason for the change was that the Sabbath kept getting in the way, which was unseemly. Gradually, and without further official decision being taken, this changed to the second

Monday of July, and the full term we enjoy today. It has been speculated that this was due to a climatic change, whereby the rainy season (the word "fair" is from an un-Glaswegian source meaning "wet") began a week later.

Launch of a ludicrous ship, the *Livadia*, at the shipyard of John Elder & Co., Govan. It was a "water palace" ordered by seven-foot Grand Duke Alexis for his seasick-prone father, Tsar Alexander. Plans were provided by the Russian chief naval designer, Admiral Ivan Popoff.

It was to be of 7,200 tons, 230 feet long and 152 feet wide at its broadest part. The draught was to be only 6 feet. It was in effect a huge saucer.

Despite the shipyard men's grave misgivings the hull was completed by the launching date.

The Grand Duke Alexis and numerous Russian and British aristocrats attended the launch which was watched also by some 40,000 citizens on each bank of the Clyde. At the four-hour civic banquet after the launch the Grand Duke praised Glasgow as "the centre of the intelligence of England".

Two months later the sumptuously fitted out *Livadia* sailed for London. From there the Grand Duke with his huge retinue of aristocratic guests and their servants set off in the craft on its maiden voyage to Sevastopol.

Storms lashed its scheduled route and for five weeks nothing was heard of the saucer-ship. Then six weeks after leaving London it limped into Fuengirola, near Malaga.

Men and women staggered ashore pale and ill-looking. Some had to be carried to the nearest hotel. They had a sorry tale to tell.

In the Bay of Biscay the ship had been tossed about like a cork, completely out of control. Tons of water kept crashing into the crew's quarters and the luxurious staterooms and dining halls. For over a month passengers and crew were soaked to the skin and in a state of collapse from seasickness.

After a week at Fuengirola the *Livadia* resumed

its voyage to Sevastopol. Most of the passengers had rejoined her and were relieved to note the Mediterranean was calm. But within two hours a storm blew up and seasickness was again the order of the day and night. Eventually the ship reached Sevastopol.

The farce ended in tragedy. The Tsar was preparing to visit his water palace when, on 18th March 1881, he was assassinated by an anarchist bomb.

The *Livadia* never put to sea again. She was stripped of her luxurious fittings and her three engines were installed in three old Russian cargo vessels. She lay rotting on the beach at Sevastopol until 1927 when she was broken up.

The wretched Admiral Popoff was sacked from his post as chief designer and died a broken man.

Plans for an astounding form of transport were announced to the world on 22nd September 1921: the George Bennie Railplane System of Transport, a form of overhead railway. Bennie, a Scottish engineer inventor, built this during the next nine years and it was opened to international acclaim on 8th July 1930. His vehicle consisted of a plushly furnished passenger carriage, cigar-shaped and powered by airscrew propellers at either end. Suspended from stanchions which could straddle a working railway line, at a time when nearly every British town was linked by these, the monorail would have cost almost nothing in the way of land acquisition if the railway companies had become shareholders. It was hoped that speeds of up to 200 m.p.h. might be achieved.

Unfortunately the inventor could find no financial backers in the depressed economy of the 'thirties. It may have been due to the scant quarter mile of track which hardly allowed his machine to show its paces. Bennie sank into terrible debt and was declared bankrupt in 1937. His elegant passenger torpedo with its art-deco easy chairs and tables hung from its track above a railway siding on the road between Glasgow and Milngavie for another two decades before being pulled down. Bennie died in Epsom the following year.

9 July 1797

Death of the great and historical Edmund Burke, whose connection with Glasgow, though minor, is flattering. Having been elected Rector of the University (the title "Lord Rector", by the way, is a nonsense) he visited the city in April 1784 to be installed in office. On rising to deliver his inaugural address, he professed himself to be quite overcome. For once (he said) he found himself at fault, as he had never before addressed so learned a body.

It must be remembered that his previous experience was largely confined to Parliament.

10 July 1589

Just because kirk attendance was compulsory was no reason why it should be tolerable, particularly if you belonged to that sex whose contribution to the Fall of Man and all his subsequent miseries was so fondly and frequently recalled by the patriarchs of the reformed church. Vessels of sin and corruption were they all and, it seems, sadly inferior in their powers of concentration. So it was ordained that "no woman, married or unmarried, come within the kirk doors to preachings or prayers with their plaids about their heads, neither lie down in the kirk on their face in time of prayer, sleeping that way; with certification that their plaids shall be drawn down or they roused by the beddel (beadle)".

The previous year, the session had instructed that certain ash trees growing in the churchyard be felled to make pews — for the males in the congregation only, of course. Women had to bring their own stools, or sit on the floor.

11 July 1690

Date of the Battle of the Boyne, or rather of two battles: the one that is fought over again each year in the imagination of Orangemen, and the real one.

Every good Glaswegian Son of the Citrus knows

how William III, "King Billy", that noble champion of the Protestant cause, arrives in Ireland to quell the papist rebels. Sword in hand and mounted on a milk-white steed, he crosses the Boyne River at the head of his loyal army, driving the Catholics of James II before him in disarray. Thus he wins the great victory that ensures the integrity of the Protestant ascendancy for ever and ever.

The reality is more complex and less dramatic. William's real concern was to frustrate Louis XIV of France's designs on the Netherlands. It is unlikely that he cared very much about Ireland and the Irish, whether Protestant or Catholic. He himself would much rather have fought Louis on the Continent, but Parliament insisted he retake Ireland and put a stop to the Jacobite return bid. So it was on Irish soil that his Dutch troops met Louis' mostly Irish mercenaries under James II. The victory was not a particularly decisive one (that came a year later, at Aughrim) although James's precipitate flight from the field — and over to France — was a notably symbolic one.

One person who was quite satisfied with the outcome was the Pope, who had supported William's conquest all along and had a mass said in Rome for his victory. Regarding the white horse and pointing sword of Orange iconography, we have to say it seems likely that King Billy rode a brown one that day and had his sword arm in a sling.

Legend is much more enduring than accuracy. It is the heroic legend that will be recalled tomorrow on the twelfth, when Glasgow's Orangemen take to the streets with flutes, drums and piano accordions to celebrate a spectacular irrelevance.

Today is Fair Friday — a day unique to Glasgow. It shifts every year, being always the second Friday in July. This is the day when the boozers are packed out with normally meek clerks, each of them deluded that they are Dylan Thomas on a New

12 July 1985

York bender. By half-past one the streets are awash with heavily tipsy building workers, still in their overalls but acting like Bright Young Things in the Astor Bar. On Fair Friday a wife can expect the fabled drunken beast of a Glaswegian to come home late for his tea and fall asleep before it can be served up.

This too is the day when the rain starts. The thin drizzle of the average Fair Friday heralds the annual Glaswegian monsoons, for as decent Calvinists, Glaswegians choose the wettest time of the year to take holidays in. The good Calvinist in us also chose places of abject misery such as the Clyde Coast resorts to have cheerless fun in. These are the places where thin-lipped landladies with boundless contempt for the working classes can poison their proletarian guests with sausages clearly made out of snake meat, and tea thin enough to read a magazine through. The only sign of contentment on the coupons of the Clyde Coast locals is when they see the keelies going home.

This is not as the Glasgow literati (Ha!) would have it. According to this gang, the Glasgow Fair Fortnight is practically Mardi Gras in Rio with Fred Astaire and Ginger Rogers in attendance. "Jings!" they write, "whit a stushie it wis at the Ferr! there we were at St Enoch's, skipping excitedly in oor wee black sannies, a bottle of exciting shoogarally water in oor exciting wee pockets. . . ." Anybody, outside of Molly Weir, who ever actually went "doon the watter" knows the foregoing to be salivating drivel.

---

13 July 1793

"By the Lord Provost and Magistrates of the City of Glasgow: Whereas certain information has been given that within these few days several MAD DOGS have been seen in the city and neighbourhood, which have bit several other dogs . . . the inhabitants of the city are therefore hereby strictly prohibited and discharged from allowing their dogs to go loose through the streets for ONE MONTH after tomorrow. All persons contravening this order will be fined FIVE SHILLINGS."

These days, Glasgow dogs are daft only in a non-rabid sense. Glaswegians like dogs well enough, but don't usually go overboard about their welfare or groom them for Crufts. "The dug" has become a kind of Scottish and Glaswegian abstraction, like "the wife" or "the drink". It should be noted that your average five-foot Glaswegian weakling gains immense reflected machismo from walking a bear-sized Alsatian on a steel chain.

On Saturday, 13th July 1811, Sir William Forbes and Co. of the Paisley Union Bank had brought an unusually large sum of money from Edinburgh to be deposited in their Glasgow branch in Ingram Street. That same day — it was Fair weekend — the bank was locked up as usual, and the key of the safe taken to the manager's house, again the normal practice. This was the prelude to one of the most cool and daring robberies carried out in Glasgow, and itself only the first of a bizarre sequence of events.

On Monday morning when the bank was opened up, everything was in order, with the exception of the safe, which was quite empty. The bank had been completely cleaned out. About £50,000 was missing — nearly £1 million at today's value.

The owners and managers of the Paisley Union Bank were unflappable, level-headed business-men. They panicked. A reward of 500 guineas for information was promptly advertised in two Glasgow papers.

This had results. On the Sunday, three men had been seen leaping over the wall outside the bank, and behaving in an altogether suspicious manner. Three men of identical description had left in a post-chaise to Airdrie. The hunt was on. It should not have been a difficult trail to follow, as the robbers wined and dined themselves handsomely at every stop, paying each time with £20 Paisley Union notes. Nevertheless, after being chased to Edinburgh, they vanished. An intensive search of the capital was carried out, but they had escaped to England.

With the assistance of two Bow Street officers, they were at last traced to London. by this time, their identities had been discovered: Huffey White, James Moffat or M'Coul and Harry French, all well known to the London police. Huffey White was picked up, but not with any of the stolen money. So the bank made a deal with him to recover his share, and he walked free. The man French was never heard of again, and there was speculation that one of the others had poisoned him for his share.

M'Coul was eventually caught. He denied everything, but he was identified, and on 10th April 1812 brought to Glasgow by mail coach to stand trial. However, owing to a technical flaw in the warrant, he had to be released. Before further proceedings could be taken, he went underground.

Had M'Coul stayed hidden, that would be the end of the story. Unfortunately for him, he was recognised while trying to change Paisley Union banknotes. Although he was not arrested on the spot, he made the almost unbelievable blunder of raising a legal action for recovery of the very notes he'd been attempting to "launder". From then on his downfall was assured. A civil court having found in the bank's favour, he was quickly arrested and brought before a criminal one. There a witness positively identified him as one of the men he'd seen on that Fair Sunday. He was found guilty of robbery and sentenced to death. After three stays of execution had been granted, M'Coul cheated the gallows by taking arsenic in his cell.

---

15 July
1297

Although William Wallace in the course of his war of liberation had several encounters with the English in the Strathclyde area, whether or not he fought them on that steep part of the High Street of Glasgow known as the "Bell o' the Brae" has been a matter of dispute. Not only does the English historian Holinshed fail to record any such encounter, neither do the Scots Buchanan, Lindsay or Robertson. Our sole authority is the poet Blin Hari (*anglice* "Henry the Minstrel"), author of the epic of Wallace's life and deeds. Hari was, on form, a very fine poet, but had at times a rather casual attitude towards history. For example, he has the hero (to whom he attributes giant height and super-powers) invading and conquering England, whose besotted queen is soon writhing at his feet moaning, "Take me, take me" or stanzas to that effect. Nevertheless, his account of the Battle of the Bell o' the Brae is free of such excesses, and a very plausible affair. Glaswegians prefer to regard it as fact.

One evening, Wallace and around three hundred of his men rode from Ayr to Glasgow, crossing the one wooden bridge over the Clyde, "Glasgow bryg, that byggit was of tre". He split his force into two; one, under his uncle Auchinleck's command, made a detour. His own men marched up the "playne streyt", which must have been the High Street, towards Bishop's Castle where the English were garrisoned. He attacked directly, the English made a sally, battle was joined. At a crucial moment, Auchinleck made a flanking movement, appearing from the Drygait to the north-east and splitting the English force.

Their disorder turned to rout, as they were chased across open ground towards Bothwell, whose castle was at that time the Clydesdale headquarters of the army of occupation. Blin Hari describes it with characteristic economy:

> "Out of the gait the byschope Beik thai lede,
> For thar thaim thocht it was no tyme to bide,
> By the Frer Kyrk, til a wode fast besyde.
> In that forest, forsuth, thai tarryest nocht;
> On fresche horss to Bothwell sone thai socht.
> Wallace followed with worthie men and wicht."

At 5.30 a.m., the first atomic bomb, built at Los Alamos, was exploded there in secret. Twenty-one days later, a similar bomb was dropped on the city of Hiroshima. If, dear reader, you entertain the

16 July 1945

faintest shadow of a notion that these facts have no relevance to Glasgow, then we are indeed lost.

---

17 July 1968

Chief Constable Sir James Robertson accepts an invitation from four gang leaders to be a trustee of the Easterhouse Youth Centre Project. It is the culmination of a remarkable week, and a chain of events set in motion by none other than the entertainer Frankie Vaughan, him of the cane, the boater and the requests for moonlight.

Seven days previously, after speaking to leaders of the four main Easterhouse gangs, the Drummie, the Pak, the Provy Rebels and the Torran Toi, Frankie "Real Mental" Vaughan spoke to the press. He assured them that on the night of the following Sunday they would surrender their weapons — swords, bayonets, sledgehammers and meat cleavers. In return, they asked for help to organise a youth centre.

Many had their doubts about the genuineness of the offer, but on 15th March the *Glasgow Herald* reported that the police had collected a number of weapons from the "neutral ground" opposite St Benedict's Hall, Easterhouse. The police had reported a particularly quiet Fair Holiday weekend and, while some were scornful, others considered it a success.

Publicity led to growing support. The Minister of Sport, Denis Howell, promised financial backing and ex-boxer Peter Keenan, now a sports promoter, pledged assistance. But some, like the immaculately reactionary (or in political terms "Progressive") Baillie James Anderson continued to be un-impressed.

In the end, Easterhouse got its premises, known as the "Easterhouse Project". It was far from being a panacea for the area's problems, and could not possibly live up to the inflated emphasis placed on it by the media, but it had a place in a larger scheme of reform for this much barbarised outpost of Glasgow.

Common as muck they were, the salmon from the limpid Clyde. To underline the fact, the noble fish were advertised in the Glasgow market at one penny the pound.

The burdensome crown of Scotland had scarcely been balanced on the head of the fourth James when word came of a rebellion by a number of the western nobles, led by the Earl of Lennox and his son, Matthew Stewart. They were dissatisfied with the division of the spoils following the demise of the gay but gloomy James III.

The new king acted decisively to crush the revolt, using Glasgow as his base of operations. On 18th July, he accompanied the big guns of the capital, including probably Mons Meg, on the road to Glasgow. Considering the massive weight of the former and the miry surface of the latter, this can have been no small operation, but they reached their destination eventually and were drawn through the streets of Glasgow in triumph. James, with a new silk standard made up, mustered his troops on Glasgow Muir, east of the Gallowgate, and marched off to take on the rebel strongholds of Crookston, Dumbarton and Duchal Castles.

The psychological effect of the presence of Mons Meg and her marrows seems to have been enough— they had scarcely opened their mouths before the castles surrendered and the rebellion crumbled.

"Only fancy a little man, scarcely five feet in height, with a Punch-like nose, with a hump on his back, a protuberance on his breast and a halt in his gait, donned in a long scarlet coat nearly reaching to the ground, blue breeches, white stockings, shoes with large buckles, and a cocked hat perched on his head, and you have before you the comic author, the witty bellman, the Rabelais of Scottish ploughmen, herds and handicraftsmen."

Dugald Graham, described here by the social historian Strang, died on this date aged 55 or 56. About his early life little is known. It seems he was born near Stirling. His first appearance in Glasgow was in the wake of the '45 Rising. He had followed the Jacobite army from the outset, though as a packman, not a combatant.

On 29th September 1746, only five months after the Battle of Culloden, an advertisement appeared in the *Glasgow Courant* for:

> "A full, particular and true Account of the late Rebellion in the Year 1745 and 1746, beginning with the Pretender embarking for Scotland, and then an Account of every Battle, Seige and Skirmish that has happened in Scotland or England.
> "To which is added several Addresses and Epistles to the Pope, Pagans, Poets and the Pretender: all in Metre. Price Four Pence."

It went on to add: "The like has not been seen in Scotland since the Days of Sir David Lindsay", a puzzling claim, as Lyndsay never attempted anything remotely similar.

Nor, it must be said, did anyone else. The author was none other than the little packman. The book was an immediate hit, and went to three editions. Sir Walter Scott was impressed, though not by the poetry, which was villainous. He wrote, "It really contains more traits and circumstances of manner worth preserving."

Dugald was appointed to the post of Glasgow's bellman, wielder of the "Skellat Bell". It was said that his Jacobite connections were an obstacle to this and that he revised his "History" to bring it more in line with the whiggish attitudes of the magistrates. But this is unlikely, as his treatment of the rebels actually becomes more sympathetic in the later editions.

Aside from his epic, Dugald Graham was a prolific writer, publisher and seller of chapbooks of his own devising, containing tales usually bawdy, scandalous or picaresque: sometimes all three. He used to compose directly onto his printer's frame, presumably backwards. The stories are uneven, but some deserve rescuing from obscurity. Their titles give some idea of their flavour: *The Colman's Courtship; Comical Transactions of Lothian Tom* (no connection with our hero of 5th December); *The History of John Cheap the Chapman; Leper the Taylor; The History of the Haveral Wives; The Comical and Witty Jokes of John Falkirk; The Scots Piper's Queries* or *John Falkirk's Cariches; The Comical Sayings of Pady from Cork; Simple John and his Twelve Misfortunes; The Ancient and Modern History of Buckhaven* (a harvest of hilarity), and a terrible slander of the great Renascence writer, *The Witty and Entertaining Exploits of George Buchanan.* For the teuchter point of view, there is nothing to beat *John Highlandman's Remarks on the City of Glasgow.*

---

21 July 1744

Death of James Macrae, an example of the poor local boy made very good indeed. The son of a Glasgow washerwoman, he sought (and found) his fortune in the East, in Siam and India, becoming Governor of Madras. He returned to Scotland sorely encumbered with filched gemstones and was shortly elevated to the dignity of Burgess of the City. In 1734, he presented Glasgow with its first equestrian statue; a bronze one of King William III, or Billy to his friends. This stood originally at Glasgow Cross, outside the Tontine Hotel, and became a great source of pride to the Lords of the Plainstanes.

A peculiar, and probably unique, feature of the horse was its tail, which depended from a ball-and-socket joint. It was thus cleverly enabled to creak fluently in a strong wind. No patent was applied for. John McUre, Glasgow's first historian, was particularly inspired by the qualities of the four-legged part:

Methinks the steed doth spread with corps the plain,
Tears up the turf, and pulls the curbing rein,
Exalts his thunder neck and lofty crest
To force through ranks and files his stately breast:
His nostrils glow, sonorous wars he hears,
He leapeth, jumpeth, pricketh up his ears,
Hoofs up the turf, spreads havoc all around . . .

and waggeth his tail of course.

After a century and a half the statue was removed to Cathedral Square, where it now stands. The four cannon which guarded the corners of its pedestal and which were said to have seen action at the Battle of the Boyne (see 11th July) have since gone, presumably to decorate mantelpieces in Bridgeton.

---

22 July 1837

Recession, commercial panic sweeping the country, a fall in the price of manufactured goods, a consequent fall in wages — in short, the hungry 'thirties. The 1830s, that is. The first to respond to the desperate state of affairs were the cotton spinners in and around Glasgow, who went on strike in July 1837, followed by the colliers and iron miners of Lanarkshire.

As trade unions in those days were unable to provide any maintenance during a strike, there were soon around 80,000 starving workers demonstrating in the streets of Glasgow. With only around 280 of a police force, the authorities were more than a little worried. Then a new hand, suspected of being a blackleg, was shot dead in the street (on 22nd July). A reward of £500 was offered for information leading to his killers, and two informers emerged ... but here we leave off until 29th July, when a tale of suspense, skulduggery and swashbuckling bravado unfolds. Look out for Sheriff "Lone Star" Alison in his leading role as the fastest strikebuster in the Gallowgate.

---

23 July 1823

Two days ago, a number of Glasgow men took the law into their own hands and demonstrated how much more jealous they were of their rights and privileges than their 20th-century descendants.

For as long as anyone remembered, the footpath along the Clyde from Glasgow to Carmyle had been a public facility, a popular place for strolling or dalliance. When a huge stone wall appeared, reaching right down to the water's edge and completely cutting off the walkway, people were outraged.

It was Thomas Harvie, the proprietor of Westburn, who had walled off his property in this high-handed fashion. Harvie, who had started out as a humble carter, had made a fortune in the whisky trade, with "Harvie's Dram Shops" all over the city. His wealth had gone to his head. He tended to put on airs and graces. And he turned a deaf ear to the public outcry over "Harvie's Dyke".

At last, some citizens decided on direct action. A crowd, composed mainly of weavers from Bridgeton and Parkhead, took pickaxes and crowbars to the wall and destroyed it. When the Inniskillin Dragoons appeared on the scene there were scuffles, a number of people were arrested and imprisoned, and a number got very wet.

Harvie showed his stubbornness by having the wall rebuilt as before. However, legal processes were got under way, supported by public inscription. After long litigation, the House of Lords decided in favour of the right of Glasgow's citizens to go roamin' in the gloamin', or, indeed, whenever.

An anonymous letter from Glasgow to the Lord President of the Court of Session threatened to "tear him limb from limb and feed his bowels to the cats". This, the writer suggested, would be letting him off lightly.

24 July 1767

The occasion for the outburst was the so-called "Douglas Cause" which was stirring up such high feelings throughout the country, and the substance of it was the claim of one Archibald Stewart to be the son (and, more important, heir) of Lady Jane Douglas, of the vast estates. Popular opinion favoured the pretender, and when the Court of Session found against him, was raised to a pitch of fury.

Scandalised and insulted by the letter, the Court of Session demanded that the Magistrates and Council of Glasgow do everything in their power to bring its perpetrator to justice. However, despite advertisements in the Glasgow papers offering £100 — an unprecedented amount then — the culprit was never discovered.

---

25 July 1983

Crossing Paisley Road West, a man was struck by a passing taxi, whose wing mirror he knocked off in the act of falling down. An observant police officer charged him with vandalism. At the trial a 17-year-old girl, who had seen the incident, said she was surprised the man had been charged as it had appeared to her that the driver was to blame. The mirror, she explained, was accidentally struck by the man's flailing arm as he fell. The Procurator Fiscal asked if she knew the man? She replied that, prior to the accident, she had never seen him.

"Do you know the meaning of the word PERJURY?" thundered the Fiscal.

The witness burst into tears. The man was acquitted.

Scots law is, of course, second to none in the meticulous fairness with which it pursues that elusive unicorn, Truth. And Glasgow Sheriff Court, until recently the busiest of its type in Europe, is the place to see it in operation at its best advantage.

---

26 July 1790

Eve of the opening of the Firth and Clyde Canal from sea to sea. The following day, a hogshead of water from the Forth was poured ceremoniously into the Clyde at Bowling.

For a long time, the short distance between the estuaries and the lack of any serious obstruction had made this connection not only plausible, but obvious. The Romans, who knew a thing or two about getting quickly from one place to another, thought so, and built the Antonine wall on virtually the route the canal would follow.

The canal was completed in stages. In 1768, an Act of Parliament authorised its construction between Grangemouth and Dalmuir, with branches to Glasgow and Bo'ness. In 1773, it was opened from Grangemouth to Kirkintilloch, and four years later had entered Glasgow's boundary.

While it proved an enormous financial success, its proprietors displayed a disappointing lack of foresight on one occasion at least. In 1802, the *Charlotte Dundas*, the first practical steamboat ever built, was launched on the canal at Grangemouth. She was built for towing purposes, with an engine designed by James Watt. Her trials were a success, but the proprietors, fearing, quite needlessly, that her wash would damage the canal banks, refused to adopt her. The honour of being the first to introduce steam navigation fell to Robert Fulton on the Hudson in 1807, five year's before Bell's *Comet*.

---

27 July 1777

Thomas Campbell, poet, born in George Street, Glasgow, into a family of distressed merchants. He attended the Old College in High Street, where he made a name for himself with his facility with the classics, his undergraduate japes, and something called *The Origin of Evil*. But his first big hit was the long poem *The Pleasures of Hope*, published in 1799. This swept him to a sort of vertiginous glory it is difficult to understand today, considering the unrelentingly third-rate quality of his verse. Superlatives were heaped upon him by his contemporaries, who seemed in no doubt they had a real genius on their hands. For this darling of the Muses, Glasgow was obviously not good enough, and he moved to Edinburgh. In 1827 he returned to his native city to be installed as Rector of his alma mater. His *Lines on revisiting Cathcart* were very regular. He wrote a number of larger poems, with magnetic titles like *Gertrude of Wyoming*, as well as the better known ballads *Ye Mariners of England, The Battle of the Baltic* and *Hohenlinden*. (He was actually an eye-witness of that last fracas, though you'd never know it from the poem.) As with Sir Henry Newbolt after him, generations of schoolboys have found in such martial verse a wholesome alternative to self-abuse.

Even today, not all anthologies have been purged of him. Thomas Campbell began decomposing in June of 1844, and continued the process amid strange company in Westminster Abbey.

Murder isn't what it used to be. Orwell said it, De Quincey said it, and we concur. To be sure, in this century we have seen some spectacular examples of the genre, and hardly a day goes by without a new record being set in scale or horror. But scale and horror aren't everything. The social role of murder has changed. While it's still good press copy, particularly if lurid enough and a Beast or a clergyman is involved, it has lost its status as a true folk art. We believe the principal reason for this is the demise of the public hanging, that culmination of the criminal and judicial procedures that in its awesome symmetry so satisfied the public's aesthetic sense. An eye for an eye, and a good day out for the kids.

There is a 50 per cent chance that the foregoing paragraph is nonsense.

Glasgow's public hangings were latterly carried out in Jail Square (now Jocelyn Square), between the High Court and the Green. The last one was that of Edward William Pritchard, on 28th July 1865. He was an English doctor who had come to Glasgow to practise medicine and seduce all the women he could — a dapper philanderer. Unfortunately he was married, a circumstance that placed intolerable restraints on a liaison he'd formed with his Highland maid. So he poisoned his wife, slowly, so as to make it seem a wasting illness. His mother-in-law, who had begun to suspect something, was disposed of more hastily. The two deaths were traced to Pritchard, who was duly tried and sentenced. His feigned distress at his wife's death and his general presence of mind earned him the nickname "The Human Crocodile". Nowadays we'd call him a psychopath.

About 30,000 gathered to see him hanged. Pritchard, ever the dandy, wore his best suit and a new pair of boots, and was meticulously groomed. He was, one might say, turned off well turned out, as befits such an historic occasion.

For more of the lowdown on the homicidal heartland of the city, we recommend Jack House's book *Square Mile of Murder*. (This is *not* a history of Glasgow music halls.)

Three days after a reward was issued to discover the murderers of a young apprentice during the cotton spinners' strike (see 22nd July), two men arranged a meeting with Sheriff Alison in the Old College in High Street. There, under cover of darkness and secrecy, they told him of a plot by the strike committee to murder blacklegs and employers. One had already been dealt with; next on the list was a manufacturer called Mr Arthur. Alison learned that the next meeting of the strike committee would be held on Saturday evening, 29th July, in the Black Boy Tavern, Gallowgate.

That night, Sheriff Alison, along with the Procurator Fiscal and the principal Sheriff Officer, met up with Police Superintendent Miller and 20 constables at the entrance to the Black Boy close. Four constables were left to guard the close mouth, 12 were stationed in front of the tavern, and four at the back. All had orders to sieze anyone attempting to pass. Sheriff Alison and the others entered the tavern and, by means of a ladder and trapdoor, an upstairs room, where they found all 16 members of the strike committee seated round a table. Still unobserved, the Sheriff retreated, and brought eight of the policemen into the room below. Then he went back upstairs.

Entering the room, he crossed over and stood under the solitary gas light to prevent it being extinguished. The men were completely taken by surprise, and seemed frozen in panic. Superintendent Miller called each of them by name, and beckoned him out. One by one they were arrested without offering any resistance. Either Sheriff Alison and his posse were an overwhelmingly authoritative as well as a heroic bunch, or the strike committee were not the cut-throat desperados they were later made out to be in court. Take your pick.

All those arrested were acquitted of murder, but sentenced to seven years' transportation on other charges. The Monday following their arrest, the cotton spinners met on Glasgow Green and voted to return to work. (See also 8th January.)

---

30 July 1870

The City of Glasgow Union Railway Company acquired the University buildings in Glasgow's High Street, along with 26.5 acres of land, all at a purchase price of £100,000. The University had already gone west (see 4th April).

It was the railway company's original intention to keep the front part of the building as offices, but in 1885 the whole structure was demolished to make way for the High Street Station. Frank Wordsall, in his architectural tragedy *The City That Disappeared*, describes the old college buildings as one of the two finest examples of 17th-century architecture in Scotland, the other being Heriot's Hospital in Edinburgh. The original Hunterian Museum, designed as a "classical temple" and opened 80 years previously, was torn down along with it.

---

31 July 1740

It was recorded that all the ministers in Glasgow were absent, being "at the goat's whey". That is to say, they were enduring a health holiday which involved retreating to the country and drinking nothing but the uncoagulated parts of goats' milk. This therapy, while never achieving the popularity of visits to spas and mineral wells, enjoyed a brief vogue before educated people decided it was better to stay at home drinking claret in the library, a process known as the Enlightenment.

Glasgow was far and ahead the first place in Britain to show appreciation of Lord Nelson's victorious behaviour by erecting a monument to him. No sooner had the stricken hero made his controversial request to Hardy than public subscriptions were being enthusiastically collected for the 143-foot obelisk in Glasgow Green.

There is an enduring story regarding the monument's inscription. Someone suggested it should read simply "Glasgow to Nelson", whereupon a thrifty bailie proposed they could have it as a milestone as well by making it read "Glasgow to Nelson (i.e. 'Neilston', as pronounced), six miles".

1 August 1806

Professor S. G. Checkland in his book *The Upas Tree*, a study of Glasgow between the years 1875 and 1975, devotes much attention to the reshaping of the city that has taken place since the 'fifties, the overspill policy, the new towns, the planning of new public housing schemes and so on. The tone of writing is neutral, but if anything Mr Checkland tries to look on the bright side, not always successfully. "The rebuilding of Glasgow has not been the outcome of blind brutalism," he assures us. The suggestion that it was done with open eyes fills us with even more dismay, if possible.

Many of the planners responsible came from the south and were quite ignorant of the climatic conditions prevailing so far north of London. No doubt they did their best. Checkland tells us how they were attracted by "the challenge of remaking a major city". Splendid! We would hate to think their fat contracts had anything to do with it.

2 August 1960

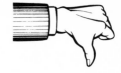

At today's meeting, Glasgow Corporation voted to lift restrictions on public houses in schemes. Henceforth, applications for licences in council areas would be considered in the same way as any others. Only six voted against the motion, including the "progressive" Councillor James Anderson.

3 August 1967

4 August 1834

Shortly after its introduction, a catastrophe overtook the prototype steam carriage intended as a public transport service between Glasgow and Paisley. On reaching the Halfway House on Paisley Road, its boiler exploded. Several passengers were killed, and others seriously injured. The contraption, which used to proceed with a disconcerting "snorting noise", had been viewed with great suspicion by both communities, who preferred the slower but safer stagecoach, or even canal boat (but see 20th June).

Even today, travel between Glasgow and Paisley is not without its hazards, as our Paisley sources, mostly unemployed yarn-spinners, inform us. Apparently, it is a common experience of Paisley rustics when visiting the big city to have rather too much to drink and fall asleep on the train home. Thus they are spirited past their station and, by the miracle of the Trans-Clyde Network, delivered to one of the colourful resorts down the Clyde Coast. This process is known as "doing the buffers". Sometimes it happens that the traveller is so overtired that either he fails to wake up even then, or falls asleep again on the return journey, thereby reacquainting himself with the delights of Glasgow's Central Station. This is the "double buffers". "Triple buffers" are said to be not unknown.

It is a tough game, and sobriety means instant disqualification.

5 August 1810

At about 4.15 this Sunday afternoon, Nelson's obelisk in Glasgow Green was struck by a bolt of lightning. The top 20 feet was torn open by "the effects of the destructive Fluid", as the *Scots Magazine* described it, and stones were left hanging in such a dangerous and threatening way that it had to be cordoned off by the military for the protection of the curious throng. The *Scots Magazine*'s report ends by recommending the use in future of "Thunder Rods" or lightning conductors. Benjamin Franklin had said as much in his visit to

the city in 1760, but only the College heeded his advice. However, once the monument was repaired, the authorities decided to assist Divine Providence by installing a Thunder Rod.

Nelson's monument was not the only casualty of this storm. The Royal Infirmary was enveloped in a lightning flash, and in a house in Rottenrow utensils were melted and humans singed and discomfited.

This Monday, Euphemia W—, keyholder and counter assistant at a haberdasher's establishment in the Candleriggs, opened her master's shop at 8.30 a.m., her usual hour. No sooner had she got off her coat to begin the day's business than George T—, recently her escort during Sunday walks on Glasgow Green, forced his way into the shop. He held her at the point of a double-barrelled sporting piece and accused her of various treacheries, culminating by claiming that he had seen her the previous day in dalliance with another gentleman on the very paths where once she had favoured him with her smiles and conversation.

No denial by Euphemia could placate the maddened swain who now raised his fearsome armament and discharged the first barrel into her person, and then, in a fit of remorse and self-loathing, dashed into the street and loosed off the remaining barrel into his own mouth.

But the star-crossed lover's double slaying was doomed from the outset. For the villain who supplied the shotgun had also supplied George with cartridges of too small a bore for the barrels. With this result — that Euphemia was amply protected by her whalebone stays in which the shot, discharging with insufficient force, all lodged, while George escaped with little more injury than a singed tongue.

He was charged with unlawful possession of fire-arms and attempted murder. And also — perhaps to remind him that life is not without its little ironies —attempted suicide, in 1888 held by the law a most grievous offence.

7 August
1942

Today's *Glasgow Herald* reports that, un-employment having virtually disappeared, there is little now for the Community Service Council to do. It was founded in 1935 to deal with the social effects of unemployment, as the bland phrase has it. Clubs set up for the unemployed are being closed as their leases expire. The short-term social benefits of global warfare are truly breathtaking.

---

8 August
(Late
Bronze Age)

Shipbuilding on the Upper Clyde is at its peak. The ring of bronze adze on oak echoes along the swampy yards as yet another of the legendary firth-going dugouts takes shape — vessels dour and un-compromising as the men who build them. Vessels, too, commanding the very latest in modern technology: independently crafted tailboards with rudder-holes, tapered bows, fully integrated paddle rests. Vessels that prove that today, as ever, the proud trademark "Clyde Built" stands for Reliability.

---

9 August
1815

The Glasgow Periodical Publishing Friendly Society was established as of today's date, in recognition of a recent and revolutionary develop-ment in both book publishing and readership. A large number of book societies had sprung up offering books by instalment, and sending agents round all the main Scottish towns, rather in the manner of the circulating libraries. The effect, particularly on working-class readers, was to open up vast new possibilities. Books that before were way beyond their means were, by this method, suddenly accessible. They leapt at the opportunity.

The actual range of writing available must have been limited. The societies insisted on a strongly moral tone being maintained — no "inflammatory or immoral" book was to be produced — and in effect about two-thirds of those sold were religious works. Cleland in his *Annals* estimated that by 1816 about 200,000 large family bibles had been sold in

Glasgow by this method and "several million" other books.

The *Glasgow Herald* reports the erection of the Cleland Testimonial, a tribute to James Cleland, Glasgow's Superintendent of Public Works and historian and statistician of the city. His *Annals* are a priceless source of information, and made Glasgow the best documented Scottish city of the day. The tribute did not take the form of a plaque or statue, but something equally handsome and considerably more useful: two tenement buildings designed by David Hamilton.

Hugh MacDiarmid, born Christopher Grieve on this date, did not have many good words to spare for Glasgow. In the handful of poems, not his best, where he refers to the city or makes it his subject, it is the Glasgow of the prewar slums he invokes, a touchstone of squalor and ignorance, or that of the *Glasgow Herald*, small-minded and irredeemably bourgeois.

Having said this, as with most statements about MacDiarmid, we have to allow for its opposite. His poem *In the Slums of Glasgow* shows this same environment, not as something smothering and stupefying, but a spiritual window through which the "seamless garment" of all living experience is discerned. And his essay *The Dour Drinkers of Glasgow* is a celebration, albeit a perverse one.

The latter was written in 1952, and it's interesting to look at in the light of later developments. The outlawing of sexual discrimination, more liberal licensing arrangements and a general tidying up have made those dingy all-male bevvy shops he so ghoulishly relishes the exception rather than the rule in most areas of the city. Yet this is really irrelevant, for reading the piece you gradually realise that it is not about Glasgow drinkers or Glasgow pubs at all, even those of the 1950s. There is nothing in it of the specific, of the concrete image or detail that would reveal The Grapes, Cockburn's, Munn's Vaults, The Quarter Gill, The Mally Arms, Betty's Bar in all their complex simplicities. And even the atmosphere and attitudes described seem more east coast, working-class Edinburgh, say, or even the borders. In fact, it's just MacDiarmid having an entertaining wee abstract ramble to himself.

In the poem *Glasgow*, he really goes to town. The city is a vampire, a corpse, a hag ".... whose soul-gelding ugliness would chill/To eternal chastity a cantharidised satyr". The old heartwarming cliché is denied, that it's the people who really "are" Glasgow — instead, Glasgow is the houses that own and feed on the people. The poem ends with a plea to:

> "Open Glasgow up! Open it up. It is time
> It was made sun-conscious. Give every house
> Ceilings and roofs of iridescent glass, windows for
> walls,
> Let great steel-framed windows bring the blaze
> Of the sky into every room. . . ."

Some buildings something like this have been erected, but they seem to be all banks or shopping centres.

How much has changed? In 1934 MacDiarmid published a poem that began "All buildings in Glasgow are grey . . .".

Far from it. The old hag has given up smoking and gone to the beauty parlour. A good scrub and a facelift, and instead of the sooty wrinkles and the blackheads, it's all blushes and peaches-and-cream. Sandstone glows — honey-coloured or clean grey; brindled like a tabby or ruddy in the sunlight ("a rose-red city, under all the grime"). What matter if careless cleaning may have left the surfaces porous and defenceless against the elements? What if hundreds upon hundreds of homes in the neo-slumlands of the schemes are virtually uninhabitable because of dampness and water-penetration? What if the relevance of the whole exercise to homelessness, unemployment and poverty may be distinctly remote? The tourists will love it, all those miles-better tenements, those smiling facades.

Facades. The poem goes on "All the buildings in Glasgow are grey/ With cruelty and meanness of spirit" and is about John MacLean. He has not been the last political prisoner to see the inside of Barlinnie. A city, too, can smile and smile and be a villain.

Joseph Lister's theories of antisepsis were put to the test for the first time today in the treatment of a compound fracture case at Glasgow Royal Infirmary. The outcome was completely satisfactory. Further successes followed, patiently recorded by Lister, and the results published between March and July 1867.

Lister had come to Scotland after training at London's University College Medical School. In 1860 he was promoted to the Regius Chair of Surgery at Glasgow University. There, through the chemistry professor, Thomas Anderson, he heard about Pasteur's discovery of the micro-organisms responsible for fermentation. Lister had the idea of using carbolic acid dressings and sprays to combat infection in the operating theatre. For several years, with no assistance, minimal equipment and at his own expense, he experimented to achieve an efficient carbolic dressing.

Despite the instant success of his methods and their enthusiastic adoption in Germany and France, he met some local opposition. The management of the Royal Infirmary was sceptical about the need for antisepsis, claiming the high death rate in cases where it was not used could be explained by the temporary overcrowding of the hospital with fever cases. But the argument of the statistics won out. Between 1870 and 1890 almost twice as many operations were performed in the Royal Infirmary, and the post-operative mortality rate was halved. Later, William McEwen, also working in the Royal, would extend Lister's methods into the field of asepsis. Antisepsis and asepsis combined made

12 August 1865

hospitals vastly safer places. Consequently, their reputations in the community rose, and fewer people fled screaming from treatment.

---

13 August (1849)

From the *Glasgow Herald:*

> "We have just received a New Song . . . called 'We'll row thee o'er the Clyde'. The poetry, which is apropos to Her Majesty's visit, is from the fluent pen of Mr Andrew Park. The music is without a name, but it suits the character and stamina *(sic)* of the lines."

Queen Victoria reached Glasgow on the following day, along with Prince Albert. It was the first royal visit to the city since that of James VI (apart from Prince Charlie and a few thousand gatecrashers in 1745).

Despite the poet's offer, the Queen was not rowed o'er the Clyde, but driven across it via Jamaica Bridge, under a huge triumphal arch of stone. This, with typical Victorian prodigality in such matters, was demolished as soon as it had served its purpose.

Queen Victoria is supposed to have said that, having visited the second city of her Empire once, she had no desire to repeat the experience. Cheeky old baggage.

---

14 August 1872

Fountain: (noun) a spring of water; an artificial jet of water; structure for such a jet.

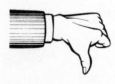

But not, apparently, in Glasgow's public parks, where every one of them is condemned to perpetual drouth. The Stewart Fountain in Kelvingrove Park is a notable example. Erected on 14th August 1872, ironically to commemorate the efforts of Provost Stewart in bringing about the city's Loch Katrine water supply, it was once the park's lively centre, with kids and jets of water playing reciprocally around it. Now it resembles nothing more than a dusty and decayed folly, and the nearest thing you'll find to a fountain in Kelvingrove is the sprinkler on the duckpond. Of course, the inevitable excuses are trotted out regarding the crippling expense of restoring and maintaining an operational fountain, but they sound hollow when you consider the history of the nearby skateboard rink. Opened proudly at the height of the craze, it was obsolete within a couple of years. It has now been filled in and landscaped. God knows what that venture cost.

Glasgow's other great fountain is the huge Doulton Fountain in Glasgow Green, which Doak and McLaren Young describe in *Glasgow at a Glance* as "the most amazing piece of earthenware ever made". Composed entirely of terracotta, it was built by the London firm of Doulton of Lambeth for the 1888 International Exhibition in Kelvingrove Park. Afterwards it was presented to the city, and re-erected in the Green in 1890. Ugly enough if you don't adore Victoriana, it is certainly impressive. It is, naturally, as arid as the Stewart Fountain, and in an even worse state of repair.

A fountain without water is not a fountain — city fathers please take note.

The Romantic composer Felix Mendelssohn called on Glasgow in the course of his Scottish visit. Although his stay was brief and his impressions of the place unrecorded in prose, we need only listen to the so-called "Scottish" Symphony to be profoundly aware of Glasgow's impact on him. Only the most cloth-eared bigot could fail to discern in the slow movement the sombre rhythms of our grey and massy tenements. So blatant is the association, that we have no hesitation in proposing that henceforth Symphony No. 3 be known by its proper title, the "Glaswegian".

15 August 1829

After Montrose had defeated the Covenanters at the Battle of Kilsyth (15th August) just outside Glasgow, the city fathers of Glasgow decided that, while their sympathies were almost wholly with the losers, they had better play safe. They invited the

16 August 1645

victorious Marquis to enjoy the city's hospitality. He accepted, was feted for two days, and departed, taking with him £50,000 Scots he'd borrowed. This was never repaid, hardly surprising in the light of later events.

A mere month later, Montrose was defeated at Philiphaugh, and this time it was David Leslie, commanding the Covenanting forces, who visited Glasgow in triumph. He was scathing about the city's treatment of Montrose, and to underline his displeasure relieved the Council of £20,000 Scots, saying this would pay for the interest on Montrose's money. It was tough being a city in the middle of a civil war.

Anxious to demonstrate its real allegiance now it was becoming obvious which side would prevail, Glasgow executed a number of Royalist prisoners (see 21st October).

---

17 August 1950

Pope Pius XII issues his decree *Humani Generis* against the growing menace of Existentialism. This has been particularly rife among young intellectuals in Glasgow who, in an attempt to distinguish between essence and existence, stay up late at night drinking jazz and listening to coffee. Other heresies too have reared their heads, including the anaconda of linguistic philosophy. Taking as their axiom Wittgenstein's famous premise "Glasgow ist alle, was der Fallt ist" ("It is all Glasgow's fault") bands of young writers in the city have taken to wearing black and not washing.

---

18 August 1670

Glasgow University has traditionaly been jealous of its own rights of jurisdiction, and resentful of outside interference in college affairs. Since earliest times, its faculty courts had assumed the task of disciplining students for the usual undergraduate pranks of rioting, assault, arson and so on, boys, after all, being boys. Once, though, they undertook to try a charge of murder.

On 18th August 1670, Robert Bortane, a student

at the college, appeared before the Rector, Dean of Faculty and three regent assessors, accused of killing Jonnet Wright in her house "by the shoot of ane gun". The prosecution sought the death penalty.

The accused having pled "not guilty", a jury of 15 was empanelled. Having serious doubts about the right of the University to try such a serious criminal case, the jurers, before agreeing to participate, tried to obtain a guarantee that they would in no way be held responsible for the proceedings if there was any comeback. As it happened, they returned a "not guilty" verdict. But it is intriguing to speculate just how the University would have disposed of the case had the verdict gone the other way.

The Humane Society of Glasgow, founded in 1790, has done so much good work over the years fishing punters out of the Clyde that we are loth to disinter anything which might bring it into the least semblance of ridicule. It is only in the certainty that they no longer apply that we mention the "Directions for the Recovery of Drowned Persons" from the Society's early years.

19 August 1790

The first part of the document is unremarkable. It advises that the drowned, or par-drowned, body be taken to the nearest house, public or otherwise, and kept warm with a good fire and hot baths. Idly curious spectators are to be discouraged. But with Direction No. 6, the lifesavers get down to business:

> "It will be proper for one of the assistants, with a pair of bellows of the common size, applying the pipe a little way up one nostril, to blow with some force, in order to introduce air into the lungs; at the same time the other nostril and mouth are to be closed by another assistant, while a third person gently presses the chest with his hands after the lungs are observed to be inflated. By pursuing this process, the noxious and stagnant vapours will be expelled, and natural breathing imitated."

It adds that if the nozzle of the bellows proves too large for the circumference of the nostril, the mouth may be used. Nostrils are to be preferred however.

Direction No. 7 introduces refinements such as

rubbing the body with salt and flannel, or sprinkling it with rum, gin or whisky, applying a warming pan, or heated tiles covered with flannel, or hot bricks to the palms and soles of the feet. "Fomentations of hot brandy or whisky may be efficaciously applied to the pit of the stomach, loins etc." Meanwhile, the nostrils could be tickled with a feather and snuff.

By this time the corpse is probably ready to give up and come alive for the sake of peace. If it persists in stubborn inanimation, Direction No. 8 is to be brought into force:

> "Tobacco fumes should be thrown up the fundament; if a fumigator is not at hand, a common pipe will answer. The operation should be frequently performed, as it is of importance. . . ."

As well as this, the body should be "shaken well every ten minutes". If there are signs of life(!) it is to be rewarded with spoonfuls of warm liquid, such as brandy — orally. Finally, electricity might be "by the judicious and skilful". The above methods are to be employed "with vigour" for three hours or more.

It is obvious that the Humane Society's function in the beginning was one of deterrence. The risk of falling into its hands must have kept citizens away from the river in droves.

---

20 August 1872

Death of William Miller, Glasgow's "Laureate of the Nursery". His infantile laurels (surely among the tenderest shoots of that honour'd bay) stem from a collection published in 1863, *Scottish Nursery Songs*. Dedicated "to Scottish mothers", it appended the pious hope that its contents would find immortality via their wee maternal memories. In one of these songs at least, this hope has surely been fulfilled. Who among us has not had implanted in him the image of the ageless "Wee Willie Winkie", rinnin up and doun at all hours in a state of undress, bawling and shouting and behaving in a disorderly manner to the disturbance of the lieges, and thereby causing a breach of the peace. He is the lovable archetype of juvenile delinquents everywhere, and probably a pioneer of solvent abuse.

---

21 August 1803

William and Dorothy Wordsworth have a real treat in store for them tomorrow, the highspot of their Scottish tour — Glasgow. They arrive by hackney coach, a rarity in these parts, and put up at the Saracen's Head Inn (see 10th November). Dorothy found it "quiet and tolerably cheap" and dirtier than English inns.

What inspiration, if any, the Lakeland poet drew from his Glasgow experience remains a matter for future research. It could be the biggest thing since *Yarrow Unvisited.*

> (Customer: Where's it nou, the glory and the dream?
> Barman: Sorry, we're just oot of stock.
> William writes furiously in the background.)

Local bards were duly honoured and impressed by the great man's presence:

> *Wee Wullie Wordsworth's kent*
> *Fur pomes aboot the hills.*
> *Forbye he hisnae seen*
> *Ma hingin windae-sills. . . .*

---

22 August 1949

An obituary in today's press notes the passing on 20th August of Alexander Somerville, revealing him to be the donor of the St Mungo Prize. This consists of a cash award plus a gold medal, given every three years to the person deemed to have been the city's greatest ornament or benefactor. To date, the recipients were Sir Patrick Dollan (the flamboyant and flexible Provost), Dr T. J. Honeyman (the art gallery supremo of *soi disant* audacity) and Sir William Burrell (the millionaire magpie).

Aside from the St Mungo Prize, Somerville is credited with another civic boon, namely the invention of the square-toed shoe, enabling Glasgow drinkers to stand nearer the bar.

23 August
1301

While in Glasgow on business, Edward I of England lodged in the Convent of the Dominicans (the Black Friars) in the High Street. Although his visit was in connection with a particularly worldly strategy for bringing the western shires of Scotland under his domination, the *Malleus Scotorum* did not neglect to perform his religious observances at St Mungo's shrine. The records show several offerings made; on this date seven shillings to St Bartholomew.

24 August
1560

The citizens of Glasgow, at that time around 4,500, went to bed for the last time as members of a Papish state. By the next evening, the Church of Scotland had been established by law, and they were a Protestant community. Public authorities had been told to "pass to the several kirks and tak down the haill images thereof and bring furth to the kirkyayrds thereof and burn them opinly. And sichyk cast down the altairs and purge the kyrk of all kynd of monuments of idolatyre".

Glasgow's Council enthusiastically set about applying these instructions to the Cathedral. The great pile, with its 32 separate altars, was gutted, and furnished enough bonfires to warm the heart of the most frigid reformer.

The Corporation was left with a vast shell on its hands, unfitted for any sort of worship whatever. The reparation and maintenance of the "hie kirk" as they henceforth called it, was to be an almost intolerable burden on its inheritors for years to come.

25 August
1881

The recently formed Volunteers from the Glasgow area took part in the notorious "Wet Review" before Queen Victoria at Holyrood. About 40,000 paraded in torrential rain. Eventually, the crowds of spectators could stand it no longer and broke up, with the result that the battalions and brigades bringing up the rear had to fight their way through a dense, soggy throng. Several of the men died as a result of their ordeal, and the health of others was seriously impaired. Most of the Volunteers, however, survived to be potted by Boers in a drier clime.

Dr William Porteus, mentioned in this month's Burgh Records, was a Glasgow minister appointed in 1782 to prevent alien paupers from settling in the city and thus qualifying for civic charity. So successful was he that he earned the title "Buff the Beggars". However, we are happy to relate he was at least equally zealous in looking after the interests of the deserving (i.e. Glaswegian) poor. He was also the originator of Sunday Schools in Glasgow.

26 August 1784

Today's *Glasgow Herald* was even more rivetting than usual:

> "There is nothing in our domestic intelligence which can furnish material even for a passing remark. The foreign intelligence is of little importance. . . ."

The complacency of Pax Britannica!

27 August 1849

> "On Sunday, 28th August 1587, William Cunningham when going up by the wynd heid with his son Umphra (Humphry?) and some other person abused Mr Wemyss the minister of the Hie Kirk (i.e. the Cathedral) and in coming doun from the kirk the father and son attacked Mr Wemyss with a quhinger (sword) and a pistolet, called him a liar, and struck him on the head and breast, which made him retire. Mr Wemyss in fear of his life cast his goun over his arm and drew his quhinger in his defence. The Cunninghams attempted to draw their pistolets but were prevented by the Parson of Renfrew, who coming down the Rattenrow at the time, and seeing the scuffle, drew his quhinger and defeated the Cunninghams, who were sentenced to ask pardon of God, of the Magistrates, and of Mr Wemyss, first at the Wynd heid, and then before the Congregation."

28 August 1587

At least the bold ministers would have a good text for next Sunday's sermon: "I came not to send peace, but a quhinger . . ." (Matthew Ch. X v. 34).

29 August
142

Scene: Antonine's Wall, Duntocher. A damp, chill mist is creeping over the fenny moors. The solitary Roman soldier pacing up and down the earthworks draws his cloak about him and curses, in Latin. The Wild Boar emblem on his *scutum* proclaims him a legionary of the 20th, one of those who'd just built the sodding wall, he reflects, all sodding 37 miles of it. He is on punishment duty, having been caught red-handed carving graffiti with his *gladius* on the walls of Balmuidy Fort, things like "ANTONINVS PIVS IMPERATOR MASTVRBAT" and "LOLLIVS VRBICVS DECADENS ILLEGITI-MVSQUE EST". He has been given two weeks wall-patrol for insubordination, plus 16 months for bad grammar.

A figure emerges from the Caledonian fog. It is a Barbarian. The two regard each other suspiciously for several seconds.

Barbarian (pulling out a battered phrase-book): SALVE!

Legionary (also pulling out phrasebook): Ciamar-a-tha-thu?

Barbarian: Tha gu math — er, NON MALUS... er (searches frantically through phrase-book) . . . VENI, VIDI . . . er . . .

Legionary ?? (also searches through phrase-book): Càit a bheil Seumas? Tha Seumas air an loch. Nach do dh'fhag Màiri an taigh? Is feàrr leam fion na uisge. Cha mhisd thu agrìob a ghabhail.

Barbarian: ??

Conversation fades to glum silence. Suddenly, as if inspired, the Barbarian reaches into his elk-skin carrier-bag and pulls out a rude earthenware flask. This he offers to the Roman, who accepts it gingerly. They drink together. Half an hour later, they are propped up against a distance-slab singing "Morag of Dunvegan" over and over again, in Latin.

---

30 August
1820

Shouts of "Murder!" from the huge crowd of 20,000 accompanied the most unpopular and unjust execution ever witnessed at Glasgow Green.

Only the greatest show of military force to have attended a Glasgow execution allowed the sentence to be carried through. The victim was hanged, the executioner struck off his head and, holding it up to the crowd, cried, "Behold the head of a traitor!"

The "traitor" was James "Pearlie" Wilson, a 60-year-old weaver from Strathaven. He was by all accounts the mildest and most inoffensive of men, well respected in his community and, incidentally, the inventer of the "pearl" stitch in knitting. Throughout his life he had made no secret of his radical convictions, but when he was approached that April to join in the radical rising that was to sweep the country he was aghast at the idea, and lent his support only with the greatest reluctance. In fact, as was made evident at his trial and in his final letter to his wife, he was virtually forced to march with the rebels, who felt that as a grand old man of the movement he would lend authority to their cause. But march he did, carrying an old flag with the slogan "Scotland Free or a Desert" and "armed" with a rusty broken-tipped sword with a hole bored through the blade which had served as a bow for his stocking frame. Such were the "overt acts of treason" that were to hang him.

After the collapse of the rising, Wilson was the first of his group to be arrested, captured in the graveyard near his home in Strathaven. He was brought to Glasgow and arraigned before an English court of *Oyer and Terminer*. The charge was High Treason. Perhaps the jurists did not imagine that the death penalty could possibly be applied in this case, or they would not have returned a "guilty" verdict. At any rate, despite their unanimous recommendation of mercy, he was sentenced to be hanged, drawn and quartered. This last refinement was, from fear of the crowd's wrath, eschewed.

Two other weavers, John Baird and Andrew Hardie (an ancestor of Keir Hardie) were sentenced to death as ringleaders, and suffered a similar fate to Wilson's at Stirling on 8th September that year. Their bodies were buried in Stirling and guarded by the military, but later exhumed and reinterred in Glasgow's Sighthill cemetery. A tombstone was erected there by public subscription; it still stands, but it, like the cause they suffered for, in a bad state of repair.

As for "Pearlie" Wilson's remains, they were secretly removed from their shallow grave in the Cathedral yard, and brought home to Strathaven, to a martyr's reception.

Most of the other captured rebels suffered transportation to New South Wales (see 2nd January). The petitions of Peter Mackenzie and others eventually secured a free pardon for the survivors.

---

31 August 1967

Glasgow Parks Committee tentatively suggested that consideration be given to removing the statues from George Square, landscaping the acre, and using it for concerts and bands. The Cenotaph would remain, of course, but traffic might profitably be banned from the area.

The proposal never came to anything. Both dwellers in and visitors to Glasgow are used to having the statues together in the one place, where they make their impact as a team. They are "The Statues in George Square", a corporate entity, comprising Prince Albert, James Watt, Robert Burns, Sir Walter Scott, Sir Thomas Moore, Lord Clyde, Thomas Campbell, Thomas Graham, James Oswald, MP, Gladstone, Robert Peel and Queen Victoria (the thirteenth, of David Livingstone, was unlucky enough to be moved to Cathedral Square).

Local superstition has it that each full moon, on the stroke of midnight, the statues come to life, climb down from their pedestals and queue for taxis outside Queen Street Station.

Was there a dry eye among the crowds lining the route of the last Glasgow tram on its last run? Hard to believe. It was a Number 9, from Dalmuir West to Auchenshuggle, and the final representative of a mode of getting from one place to another which managed to engender and maintain an extra-ordinary affection in the hearts of Glaswegians. The trams and the service they gave are still talked about with a sort of awe. Actually, although this was the date of the *official* last run, they kept some going for three more days to give the grieving public a chance of a final shoogle along the rails.

1 September 1962

A. C. Bradley, who died on this date, was perhaps the most illustrious critic of English literature of his day and prime mover of a particular and influential school of Shakespearean criticism. After being educated at Cheltenham and Oxford and teaching at Liverpool University, he was elected to the chair of English Language and Literature at Glasgow, where he held sway from 1890 to 1900.

Without going into detail about his approach to Shakespearean criticism, far from fashionable today, we may state its central axiom as being the reality of Shakespeare's human creations and the treatment of them as fully realised persons rather than phenomenal aspects of character and behaviour within the text. Rewarding — compelling, too — as this approach may have been, it tended to soar away from what Shakespeare actually wrote into speculation of the most subjective kind. Bradley would probably claim that Shakespeare was a special case, that the nature of his genius merited and even demanded such a treatment. But it is hard to deny his method was based on a form of pathetic fallacy.

2 September 1935

A committee set up by Glasgow's magistrates to look into the running of the Grammar School (established in 1450, long before the University) recommended an extension of the course from four

3 September 1803

years to five. They also recommended increasing the wages from 7s. 6d. per quarter to 10s. 6d.

---

4 September 1775

Wrongdoers in 18th-century Gorbals were liable to a cruel and unusual punishment. They could be banished to Glasgow.

On this day in 1775, James McAteer, a smith in Gorbals, and his wife, Jean Stevenson, were convicted of "keeping a disreputable house, entertaining people of bad character therein, of cursing, swearing, making noise, alarming and disturbing neighbours" etc. etc. The sentence: "At 12 o'clock on the 16th of September to be banished . . . from the village and Barony of Gorbals during the whole of their natural lives".

This was the last sentence of banishment from the Gorbals. Glasgow, having become increasingly annoyed at having extra malefactors unloaded on it, called the legality of the practice into question; after all, Glasgow had acquired baronial rights over Gorbals as early as 1647.

---

5 September 1818

Glasgow's first gas lighting was turned on at James Hamilton's grocery store in 128 Trongate, marking the debut of the Gas Lighting Co. in the city. In 1816, the Town Council had given it a cautious welcome, taking £500 worth of shares in it.

---

6 September 1605

Exile is indeed bitter, and all the more so when a native of Glasgow is afflicted. The Burgh Records of today's date tell how one John McCleland, having been banished from the city, returned and was arrested. The magistrates were all for hanging him, but hit a snag: the city at the time did not employ a hangman, and no one was willing to take on the job. This was hardly surprising, as the hangman tended to be a vilified pariah, who received no money for his services but a handful of grain from each bag produced in the public market.

The solution was an elegant one. McCleland's

sentence would be remitted if he took on the job of public hangman. He could hardly refuse. So, banished or not, 1606 found him still hanging around. But the appointment was so unpopular that the Town Council had to pass a special enactment penalising anyone who annoyed him to the tune of £5 Scots (8s. 4d. sterling).

Alexander Graham Bell's new invention called the "telephone" was first publicly demonstrated in Glasgow by Sir William Thomson (later Lord Kelvin — see 28th December) at a meeting of the British Association. The expression "Hullawrerr" is supposed to have derived from early "telephone" conversation.

7 September 1876

The coronation of King William and Queen Adelaide was marked in Glasgow by a huge demonstration in Glasgow Green in favour of Reform. A crowd marched with bands and banners to the Green shouting, "The Bill, the Bill and nothing but the Bill!" Probably this was the peak of solidarity of purpose ever achieved in Glasgow, the community being united on the Reform issue as never before, or since.

8 September 1831

A French manuscript relating to the Battle of Flodden, fought on this date, lists the names of the Scottish nobles who fell there. One entry is for "le Doyer (Dean) de Glasco". This was, in fact, the Provost, Sir John Stewart of Mynto, who led a large force of Glasgow men to that disastrous encounter. He was one of a family that had a predominant influence in Glasgow for nearly two centuries.

The first of them to settle in the city was Sir Thomas Stewart, who became Provost as early as 1472. No fewer than five of his descendants were to hold the same office — consecutively. One of them, his great-grandson, Sir Matthew Stewart, was Provost twice, and a great Royalist and

9 September 1513

Episcopalian. Around 1580, during his first provostship, he is supposed to have caused much offence by dragging a Presbyterian minister from the pulpit of the Cathedral by force. If God is not mocked, neither are the Elect. A curse was widely believed to have attached itself to his descendants as a direct result of the outrage. Certainly, none flourished as he had done. The family fortunes of the Stewarts of Mynto went into decline, but a fairly comfortable decline as declines go.

---

10 September 1462

Among the incorporated members of Glasgow University appears the name of "the venerable Master Robert Henryson, licentiate in arts, and bachelor in degrees". It is not certain that Henryson actually studied at Glasgow — in fact, he probably reached student age before its foundation — and the enrolment may have been an honorary one. The University would indeed have been honoured by any connection with the humble "Schulemaister of Dunfermling" and author of *The Testament of Cresseid, Orpheus and Eurydice*, the *Fables* and many other poems. Considering the University also had among its numbers the makars Walter Kennedy and Mark Alexander Boyd, and the extra-ordinary polymath George Buchanan, we are forced to the conclusion that the history of its arts faculty at any rate has been one of headlong decline since the 17th century.

---

11 September 1790

The sloop *Mary McEwen* arrived at Grangemouth two days ago, having travelled to Greenock via the Forth and Clyde Canal, the first vessel to travel from sea to sea since it opened (see also 26th July).

---

12 September 1832

The first interment in Glasgow's Necropolis was that of Mr Joseph Levi, who was buried in the Jewish Cemetery. This was a small corner of ground at the end of the park near the Molendinar Burn, and had been purchased by the chief of the synagogue in 1830 for the bargain sum of 100 guineas.

The first Christian interment was of an Elizabeth Miles, in February the following year, although the cemetery had still not been formally opened for business. (See also 12th March.)

---

13 September 1755

Mr Smeaton, the celebrated engineer appointed by the city to survey the River Clyde, reported that the river at the Pointhouse Ford, about two miles below Glasgow, was only 1 foot 3 inches deep at low water, and 3 feet 8 inches at high. A walkover for wellies, but bad news for the Cunard Line, neither of which, it must be admitted, was yet a twinkle in its inventor's eye. Smeaton's suggestion, to erect a weir and lock, thereby securing a depth of $4\frac{1}{2}$ feet, was accepted, but not acted upon. Fortunately for the Clyde.

In 1768, a further survey by the English engineer Golborne of Chester, and confirmed the following year by James Watt, revealed a depth of 2 feet at Kilpatrick. Golborne's proposal for deepening the river was to "assist Nature" by narrowing the channel several miles below the city. By January 1775, he had erected 117 jetties from the banks, at differing distances apart, causing the channel to scour itself deeper. Vessels drawing more than 6 feet were now able to come up the Broomielaw at high tide. Golborne had succeeded in deepening the Clyde by 10 inches more than his contract had promised, for which he was voted a £15,000 bonus by the delighted city fathers.

The Clyde never looked back, even as a figure of speech. By 1821, vessels drawing 13 feet 6 inches could come up the Broomielaw. By 1847 the river there was 18 feet at its highest, and never fell below 9 or 10 feet.

---

14 September 1914

Detective Lieutenant John Thomson Trench was dismissed with ignominy from the City of Glasgow Police Force (see 8th June 1928). Trench was the policeman who had doubts about the guilt of Oscar Slater. He spoke of these doubts to a lawyer who communicated them to the then Secretary of State for Scotland. Trench was found guilty of divulging information to a person outside the police service. If Trench had doubts about the Slater case then he cannot have been the only one, as he had not himself worked on the case. But he was the only policeman with enough conscience to speak out and he must be honoured for that. Trench died on 13th May 1919, nearly ten years before Slater's innocence was finally proved. On the 19th of August 1969 there was a motion put to a meeting of Glasgow magistrates by Baillie John Young that the Lord Advocate and the Secretary of State for Scotland should hold an independent inquiry into Trench's dismissal. The magistrates advised him that they were not legally competent to reopen the case.

In his history of the Glasgow police force, Inspector Douglas Grant comments that the Slater case did nothing to enhance the reputation of that body. He also asks the question "did the magistrates of 1914 act harshly in dismissing Detective Lieutenant Trench?" but does not attempt an answer.

15 September 1811

Heads were ducked and breaths held as Halley's Comet buzzed Glasgow (and other places) at a distance of only 142,500,000 miles. Glasgow's Observatory, erected the previous year, duly observed and took particulars. Bell's paddle steamer, the *Comet*, inspired by this heavenly visitation, was launched in June of the following year.

This little boat was built of wood and by, appropriately enough, a John Wood. Henry Bell was responsible for the design. during the building, Bell was constantly vexed by the jibes and jeers levelled at him, but when it was launched it made five knots against the wind and became the first paying passenger steamer in Europe. It had a single cylinder vertical engine, driving two paddles on either side. In 1819 it was lengthened from 43.5 feet to 62.5 feet and was given a new engine by Anderson and Campbell, who also reduced the number of paddles to one on each side.

The *Comet*'s career ended on 13th December 1820, when she was wrecked near Craignish on a return journey to Glasgow.

Although, sadly for historians, the City of Glasgow did not reply to the Poor Law Commission's questions on the matter, some interesting statistics emerged around that time concerning pawn shops and in particular the "wee pawns".

16 September 1843

Licenced brokers were required to limit their interest to 15-20 per cent, itself a substantial rate, but the "wee pawns", which operated illicitly under the pretence of "sales", sometimes charged interest of 300 per cent and more. The latter were by far the more numerous. Police Superintendent Miller of Glasgow explained:

> "There are 30 licenced pawnbrokers and upwards of 200 small unlicenced brokers within the royalty, besides about 300 dealers in old clothes etc., who have no shops, and reside in various places. . . ."

When we hear that the loans from the *licenced* brokers amounted to around £11,000 per month (about £1 per year per adult) the scale of operation of these "wee pawns" must have been immense. There was a regular market in forfeited pledges, mostly old clothes, which found their way to Ireland and even to America, to the slaves on the cotton plantations. J. G. Lockhart had observed one such cargo in 1825, when he was travelling to Ireland with Sir Walter Scott:

> "The steamboat (he writes) was lumbered with a cargo offensive enough to the eye and nostrils, but still more disagreeable from the anticipations and reflections it could not fail to suggest. Hardly had our carriage been lashed on the deck before it disappeared from our view among mountainous packages of old clothes; the cast off raiment of the Scotch beggars was on its way to a land

where begging is the staple of life. The captain assured us that he had navigated nearly 40 years between the west of Scotland and the sister island, and that his freights from the Clyde were very commonly of that description."

Thirty years after this was written, the Rev. A. K. McCallum addressed the Statistical Section of the British Association on the subject of juvenile delinquency. The Rev. McCallum, who was governor of Glasgow's "House of Refuge", singled out the "wee pawns" as a major "source of evil", alongside Depraved Parental Influence, Corrupting Associates and Shows and Minor Theatres (the worst of all). After being needlessly informed that "wee" is Scottish for "little", he is reported in the Society's journal as saying:

"They are the favourite haunts of the beggar, the thief, the drunkard, and the juvenile delinquent, from the universal nature of the articles they receive. That the young person was confirmed in his nefarious traffic from the facilities afforded by these places for the disposal of his booty. That the whole system of pawnbroking houses should be thoroughly revised, and a severe penalty inflicted on anyone who received articles from YOUNG *persons under any pretence whatsoever.*"

We would like to write more on this fascinating subject, but unfortunately we are obliged to go out and pawn the typewriter.

---

17 September 1771

The novelist Tobias Smollett was born into a Dunbartonshire family, and educated at Dumbarton School. In 1735 he came to Glasgow to study medicine at the University, and became apprenticed to Dr John Gordon, who had his apothecary's shop at the corner of Princes Street and the Saltmarket. He worked there for four years, during which time he also lived poorly in a garret, got into trouble with women and completed his first, untypical, literary production: the *Regicide*, a blank-verse tragedy (or blank verse-tragedy) about the death of James I of Scotland. Then, it seems, he got fed up and packed his bags for London, where he arrived with little to declare but his *Regicide* and his wit.

Although he visited Glasgow again, he was effectively lost to Scotland, but many of the settings and characters of his novels, in particular *Roderick Random*, are based on his Glasgow experience.

He died on this date, aged 51 years.

---

18 September 1818

Mozart's *Don Giovanni* played to a packed house at the Theatre Royal in Queen Street. The reason for all the excitement was that, for the first time, the great crystal chandeliers were to be illuminated by "sparkling gas". Even ladies, who were rather supposed to avoid the theatre, attended in considerable numbers. It was indeed the dawn of a new era. A sort of Dawn-Geo-Fanny-by-Gaslight? (See also 5th September.)

---

19 September 1845

A House of Lords Committee met this year to consider a Bill proposed by the Gorbals magistrate Andrew Gemmill, to allow a new company to supply his part of the city with fresh water from a reservoir at Barrhead. This scheme was opposed by the Glasgow Waterworks Company, which pumped its fluid out of the Clyde at Dalmarnock. There is a romantic notion nowadays that most Victorians pursued private gain through the channels of public spirit and moral rectitude. The following extract from the report indicates that they were, on average, as anti-socially demented by their greed for profit as ourselves.

> (The counsel for the Gorbals company is questioning the secretary of the Glasgow Waterworks Company, Mr Mackain.)
> *Counsel:* Am I right in supposing that in your opinion the water supplied is *pure in quality* and that Glasgow has been better supplied than any town in the Empire?
> *Mackain:* I think it is.
> *Counsel:* So that to use your own words, considering the magnitude whether in quantity and purity of water, Glasgow is the best supplied city in the Empire.
> *Mackain:* It is.

Counsel: That is your opinion at the present moment?
Mackain: It is decidedly my opinion.
(Mr Dobbie, Glasgow Commissioner of Police is sworn in.)
Counsel: Do you know the quality of the water which has been supplied by the Glasgow company?
Mr Dobbie: Muddy!
Counsel: Have you ever found any small animals in it?
Mr Dobbie: I have, on more than one occasion.
Counsel: What sort?
Mr Dobbie: Little animals — centipedes or something of that kind.
Counsel: Little fish?
Mr Dobbie: No, not fish, but animals with a great many feet.

Further evidence showed that waterpipes were sometimes blocked by eels up to 20 inches in length, and that the water left thick deposits of mud and chopped straw at the bottom of kettles.

The Gorbals Water Company Bill was passed by the Lords. The Glasgow Water Company revenues were so reduced that it started closing down standpipes which supplied the poorest parts of the city, parts where people had to queue in big crowds for water and the company had difficulty collecting rates, especially in times of high unemployment. (In 1834 the Corporation had rejected a proposal to amalgamate the city waterworks, because this would reduce competition.) (See entry for 14th October.)

---

20 September 1967

The last of the great ocean liners was launched today at John Brown's shipyard in Clydebank by the present monarch, who also chose her name.

That this was *Queen Elizabeth II* was probably less a calculated insult to the independence of the Scottish nation during Gloriana's reign, than a harmless piece of arrogant insensitivity. Nevertheless, in the light of later events, one could be forgiven for seeing it as a bad omen.

Trouble dogged the *QE2*, as she became known, from the outset. During her fitting-out, all sorts of materials and fittings kept vanishing mysteriously. Rumour has it that the standard of interior decor in

Clydeside houses improved enormously around this time. Then her maiden voyage, scheduled for January 1969, had to be humiliatingly postponed because of turbine troubles. Once she did get under way, she made 28.5 knots and lost £500,000 per annum. In 1972, she was the victim of a bomb hoax in mid-voyage. Arab terrorists threatened to blow her up in 1973 as she steamed towards Israel (it later transpired that the dashing Colonel Gaddafi of Libya had expressed a keen interest in torpedoing her at the same time). In 1976 her engine room caught fire. In 1978 she suffered extensive storm damage. She was not a lucky ship.

In fact she was a 67,000-ton anachronism. Ironically, her publicity tended to stress this, being along the lines of "book your passage now, while you still have the chance".

---

21 September 1705

In an Act in favour of the City of Glasgow, Parliament referred back to a previous Act of 1693 which had touched on the delicate matter of the civic debt. Glasgow had been granted the authority to raise the sum by taxing whisky at 2d. the pint, and given 13 years to do it. By 1705, time being almost up and no settlement in sight, a further 16 years' grace was granted.

---

22 September 1576

While it is possible to admire Andrew Melville, the hard man of the Presbyterian Reformation, human sympathy on his behalf is less likely to gush forth. Yet his own account of some of his tribulations at Glasgow University make one feel almost sorry for him.

Melville became Principal of the University when it was in a state of almost total decay following the Reformation. It was he more than any other who rescued it, persuading James VII to endow it with a new charter, the *Nova Erectio* that gave it a new constitution and source of revenue. As a teacher too, Melville was a great personal success, and after

two years, they were clamouring to get into his classes.

Not all of his students were well disposed towards him. In his autobiography he tells how he was Regent to one Mark Alexander Boyd, "a youthe of grait spreit and ingyne, but verie cummersom and refractar". Young Boyd, a relative of Lord Boyd, the Regent Morton's friend, was "besought to be well conditioned, and he should find nathing in me bot special courtessie and affectione", but if he caused any trouble ". . . als meik as I seimed, he would find me scharper nor onie he haid delt with".

For the first six months all went well, until Melville was called away to Edinburgh. He left his students work to get on with and warned them to be on their best behaviour. Alas, on his return, he learned that Alexander had been extremely naughty indeed, ". . . . deleated in grait faultes, namlie, absenting himself from the kirk and pleying the loun on the Sabbathe". Melville remonstrated with him. Boyd was not a whit abashed, in fact, downright cheeky and rebellious. When Melville had chastised him, he resorted to a ruse to get his own back:

> "He sittes doun in a nuk fra my sight, and whill I was teatching my lessone, he takes his pen and ink horn, and striks him selff on the face an nease (nose) till effusion of blood; he ryves (tears) his buik, and dightes (wipes) his nease with the leaves thairof, and drawes the bluid athort his face, and spots his clothes with the samying; and incontinent (immediately) after the lessone rinnes out of the College, and away and compleans to his frends he was sa misusit crewalie be me."

No one was taken in, and Boyd stayed away from the College for a while. About a month later, on a summer evening after supper, Melville was coming out of the Castle with two companions, when he saw Boyd and Alexander Cunningham, nephew of Lord Boyd, lying in ambush for him. The pair attacked Melville. Here the narrative becomes slightly confusing, as Melville refers to both young men as "Alexander", but it seems that Boyd was captured by Melville's companions, while Melville himself overpowered Cunningham, who had come at him with a drawn sword.

The upshot was a confrontation between the faction of the Boyds and Cunninghams on the one hand, and the University and magistrates on the other. Cunningham refused to apologise and ask forgiveness, and it was rumoured his family and in-laws were going to burn down the College and kill the masters. It was only when the King himself had commanded his penitence on pain of imprisonment that he turned up, and then it was in the company of Lord Boyd, Lord Glencairn and four or five hundred other supporters. The College held firm in the face of this menacing array, and the decree was duly adhered to. Boyd's associate made homage "bear-heidit and bear-futed" to Melville's immense satisfaction.

Obviously, Mark Boyd was a spoilt, arrogant and rather ludicrous young man. In some ways, though, it was a pity he and Melville didn't hit it off, for they were both notable Latin poets. Of Boyd's vernacular poetry, only one sonnet has come down to us, yet it is in itself sufficient to rank him with the finest of the Makars. We leap at the opportunity of quoting it here, and suggest that on the strength of it he be forgiven his youthful foolishness:

> *"Fra bank to bank, fra wood to wood I rin,*
> *Ourhailit with my feeble fantasie;*
> *Like til a leaf that fallis from a tree,*
> *Or til a reed ourblawin wi the win.*
> *Twa gods guides me; the ane of them is blin,*
> *Yea and a bairn brocht up in vanitie;*
> *The next a wife ingenrit of the sea,*
> *And lichter nor a dauphin with her fin.*

> *Unhappy is the man for evermair*
> *That tills the sand and sawis in the air;*
> *But twice unhappier is he, I lairn,*
> *That feedis in his hairt a mad desire,*
> *And followis on a woman throw the fire,*
> *Led by a blin and teachit by a bairn."*

23 September

The autumnal equinox. A great silence falls over Glasgow pubs this evening, as conversation among the regulars splutters and dies. An essential bulwark of phatic communication has been taken from them. Still, tomorrow they will be able to mutter once more, with flawless accuracy, "Aye, the nights are fair drawin' in."

24 September 1668

It was never a foregone conclusion that the city of Glasgow would dominate the Clyde in the way it so triumphantly did. The occasional obtuseness of some of its rivals on the littorals must have contributed to a degree. In 1668, an offer was made to the Town Council of Dumbarton to construct harbour works. They declined, because they felt "the influx of mariners would tend to raise the price of butter and eggs to the inhabitants".

In that same year, a Crown Charter was granted for the erection of a harbour at Port Glasgow, which also achieved the first graving dock in Scotland. Twenty-six years later, a quay was constructed on the Broomielaw, and Glasgow became its own port.

25 September 1695

John Glass is born, in later life to give his name to the "Glassites", a dissenting religious movement known in England as the "Sandemanians" or perhaps "Sandemaniacs".

In 1719 he was ordained minister in Dundee and, after declaring his opposition to the national churches in his *Testament of the King of Martyre* (published in 1727) he was deposed. He proceeded to establish congregations in the major Scottish cities based on his conception of the primitive Christian Church. The movement came to Glasgow around 1760 where, although his congregations might number about 200, the actual membership was nearer 40. They met for worship in No. 136 George Street.

Among the intricate taboos which they held they specified abstinence from the "eating of blood" and "things strangled", and enjoyed endless internal debate on the precise nature of such doctrine. That John Glass has the same name as the 20th-century dissenter (see 25th May) is a pure coincidence, though a nice one.

---

26 September 1844

Death of the Glasgow poet Sandy Rodger. He was the author of the bucolic *Muckin' o' Geordie's Byre* and the very polite *Behave Yourself Before Folk*. The epitaph on his Necropolitan tomb describes him as "gifted with feeling, humour and fancy", while admitting
> "What tho' with Burns thou couldst not vie
> In diving deep and soaring high. . . ."

Sandy Rodger did some of his diving and soaring in *Whistlebinkie*, an anthology that also included William Motherwell, doyen of neo-viking Paisley balladeers, and William Miller, the "Laureate of the Nursery" (see 20th August). It contains some of the most overrated, complacent, trivial, sentimental, derivative, dull, inconsequential, clumsy, couthy, prettified, pretentious, insular, inflated, dilettantesque and unnecessary versifying of the post-Burnsian folk-miasma.

Sandy Rodger was perhaps the best of them and, poetry apart, was an enthusiastic radical reformer. He was imprisoned for a time on suspicion of high treason following the rising of 1820.

---

27 September 1983

A mentally retarded man was brought from Carstairs mental hospital to Glasgow Sheriff Court, on petition. If dealt with according to rule, he would have been kept in solitary confinement before his court appearance. The turnkeys were told that he could not read. He was placed in a cell with several other prisoners. The petition sheet, with the list of charges, was handed to him. He asked a fellow prisoner to read it to him. The list contained, amongst other offences, a charge of raping a six-year-old girl. As far as the other prisoners were concerned he was guilty. He was beaten up and suffered a broken leg and a fractured skull.

There were no newspaper reports or public enquiry into this incident. Why should there be? Who, in modern Britain, thinks it important that a mentally retarded illiterate accused of child rape should have a fair trial?

---

28 September 1847

The trial was nearing its conclusion at the Justiciary Court in Glasgow of Alexander Bannatyne, a grain and provisions merchant in Hope Street. He had been charged with adulterating oatmeal purchased from him by the Highland Relief Committee for sufferers from the famine in the north. The jury found that he had adulterated the meal with such materials as bran and sawdust, defrauding the committee of many thousands of pounds, and with such results for the starving Highlanders as can be imagined. The scandal had been exposed by Peter McKenzie, campaigning editor of the *Reformer's Gazette*.

In delivering their verdict, the jury recommended "utmost leniency" on the extraordinary grounds that lots of merchants were doing the same sort of thing throughout the country.

Bannatyne was sentenced to four months' imprisonment in the Bridewell, and a fine of £300. But he had influential friends. Some of these had the ear of the Home Secretary, who quashed the sentence. Bannatyne's fine was remitted, and he walked free.

---

29 September 349m BC

It was like any other afternoon in the later Paleozoic. The swamps of Glasgow Green lay stagnant under a sky heavy, low, humid and warm. A thick yellow fog of microspores hovered over the Calton. In the dark pools of Turnbull Street, *fusiline foraminifera* abounded. There too might be discerned the occasional *placoderm* plashing through the *trilobite*-haunted shallows, while all around towered the mighty carboniferous forest —

Glasgow Green in the late Carboniferous Era, viewed from the site of Glasgow High Court of Justice, Stockwell Street. A indicates the spot near the public drying green where James Watt will conceive the separate steam condensation chamber; B the future site of the Nelson Monument, erected by public subscription to celebrate the establishment of British naval supremacy after the Battle of Trafalgar.

ferny *odontopteris* and *sphenopteris*, tall *sigillaria* and tufted *lepidodendrons* (easily recognisable by their characteristic lozenge-shaped leaf scars).

All of a sudden, the immemorial silence was violated. One hundred-foot giant at the corner of Greenhead Street and King's Drive creaked, leant and toppled (narrowly missing a scuttling *eoscarpius dunlopi*) to fall with a splash into the oozy mire. The oozy mire closed over it and it became coal, though not immediately. 349,001,868 years later, the Corporation of the City of Glasgow decided it should be dug up, that is, they decided to lease Glasgow Green for mining. This, they believed, would produce the revenue to pay off the £100,000 debt they had incurred for property in the west of the city, including the West End Park. The resulting subsidence was to be filled in with the city's garbage.

The attitude of the east-enders to this proposal was unequivocal. They understood that they were expected to subsidise the parks of the rich in return for a rubbish dump and were suitably outraged. Moreover, Glasgow Green, the ancient "lungs of Glasgow", the "playground of Glasgow" (*palestram de Glasgow lusariam*), was theirs, they felt, an inalienable public facility. The matter was dropped, then resurrected several times, but nothing came of it.

---

30 September 1768

The construction of Glasgow's *first* second bridge gets under way. Known variously as Glasgow Bridge, Jamaica Bridge or Broomielaw Bridge, it was designed by William Wylie and was opened for traffic four years later, had seven arches and was 500 feet long by 30 feet wide. The steepness of its ascents and descents was notorious, and a real problem for horse-drawn traffic. Moreover, it became just too limited for the city's booming commerce. Another bridge, designed by Thomas Telford and 60 feet in width, was completed in 1836. This in turn was superseded by the present bridge, opened in 1899 and an impressive 80 feet wide.

Glasgow boasts the first Temperance Society to be set up in Britain. On this day, the first pledge was made at Gairbraid by one Lilian Graham, daughter of Mary Hill, who was a lady before she was a district, and a hill only by coincidence. (For later developments see 5th November.)

The year of 1878 had been to all appearances a flourishing one for the City of Glasgow Bank. Since it began business in 1839, it had become popular with both the wealthy and tradesmen classes alike, and had by now 33 branches throughout the country. It had recently declared a dividend of 12 per cent. It was with astonishment and disbelief, then, that Glaswegians read in their morning newspapers that the "City" bank had closed its doors. Although some other banks continued to accept its cheques, panic was widespread.

Within a few days an investigation by a number of firms had revealed a story of blatant fraud and duplicity. The bank, in short, had lost over £6 million. It had issued notes on 28th September to the value of £604,196 with only £336,464 in bullion to back them up. Shareholders had been grossly misled as to both amounts lent in credit and those held in security. Gold reserves were found to be short, and a completely fictitious amount of around £7 million credited on the balance sheets.

The directors, manager and secretary were arrested and tried on 20th January 1879 for fraud (charges against the secretary were dropped). One of the directors, Potter, and Stronach the manager, were each sentenced to 18 months' imprisonment; the two other directors received eight months.

The bank went into voluntary liquidation. There was a terrible mess left behind. A relief fund was set up to help the shareholders who had been victims of the crash, and it managed to raise about £400,000 from the community. But the following winter was a black one. Scarcely a day passed without a failure. Trade ground to a halt. Schemes were started to counter the massive unemployment that resulted, and about 12,666 applicants were granted emergency relief.

---

3 October 1749

The great Major-General James Wolfe has been stationed in Glasgow since March, in the comfortable surroundings of Camlachie Mansion. Shortly after his arrival, he wrote to a friend giving his impressions of the people. The men he found to be "civil, designing and treacherous", the women "coarse, cold and cunning".

Three episodes in Wolfe's career have become legendary. First, his attempt to stop Cumberland's troopers from butchering wounded Highlanders after the Battle of Culloden; second, his claim that he would rather have written the *Elegy in a Country Churchyard* than gone off to capture Quebec; and third, his assurance that the troops he was using in that adventure being Scottish Highlanders, it would be no great matter if they fell.

"Civil, designing and treacherous?" "Coarse, cold and cunning?" It is difficult not to suppose that *both* Wolfe's parents were Glaswegian.

---

4 October 1883

Recruiting began on this date for the Boys' Brigade in a Free Church Mission Hall in Glasgow. After three nights, 59 boys, aged between 12 and 17 years, had enrolled. It was a modest beginning for a movement that was to grow and grow, and attain worldwide influence.

The man who started it all was a Glasgow Sunday School teacher called William Alexander Smith. He was born in Thurso in 1884, and moved to Glasgow to stay with relatives at 14 years of age. Here he attended a private school, and enjoyed a thoroughly middle-class upbringing.

Smith's Victorian contemporaries found it perfectly possible, desirable even, to combine militarism with Christian piety. Young Smith was no exception. The Volunteer movement was particularly strong in Glasgow and the West of Scotland around that time, and in 1874 Smith enlisted in the 1st Lanark Rifle Volunteers, a force of West End businessmen. He rose slowly through its ranks, and was an honorary colonel until his death.

On the religious side, he was influenced by those 19th-century Billy Grahams, the evangelists Moody and Sankey, who preached in Glasgow to gatherings of 5,000 and over. For healthy outdoor activities for boys there was the precedent of the Woodcraft Indians, the American youth movement started by Ernest Thompson Seton, author of *Woodmyth and Fable*, *Romances of the Wild* and so on. (Unlike its British equivalents, this was founded on essentially left-wing theories.)

These, then, were the main elements that combined to give Smith the idea of the Boys' Brigade, its object:

> "The advancement of Christ's kingdom among Boys and the promotion of habits of Reverence, Discipline, Self-respect and all that tends towards a true Christian manliness."

The word "obedience" was added in 1893. The crest was an anchor engraved with the motto "Sure and Stedfast" (*sic*). It spread like wildfire, or the plague, whichever lasts longer. By the end of the century, true Christian manliness (or boyliness) was firmly established in Glasgow, and seeping throughout Scotland and England. Glasgow had 91 companies, London 83, and there were others in Liverpool, Dublin, Manchester (or Boychester), Edinburgh and Belfast. Jewish and Catholic versions appeared. The movement spread to Australia, Canada and the USA. Last year it celebrated its centenary in Glasgow.

The Boys' Brigade was in no small measure responsible for the formation of the Boy Scout movement, whose founder, Baden-Powell, was an associate of Smith's and involved in many of the BB's functions. In 1902 he was appointed their vice-president, and in 1906 an early version of *Scouting for Boys* appeared in the Boys' Brigade *Gazette*. Despite its dubious and suggestive title, it seems to have evaded the censor. Scouting became part of the BB's curriculum, as well as marching and drilling in pillboxes, but there remained a difference of emphasis. Smith rejected Baden-Powell's idea of combining the two movements.

William A. Smith died of a cerebral haemorrhage in May 1914. He did not survive to see his ex-members from Glasgow who, full of Reverence, Discipline, Self-respect and Obedience, had enlisted in the 16th HLI (the "Boys' Brigade Battalion"), cut down in the Battle of the Somme. Over 550 were killed during three days of the slaughter.

---

5 October 1051

Supposed date of a Charter of Malcolm III, King of Scots, to the masons of Glasgow (although as he didn't ascend the throne until 1057, the scribe must have been nodding).

The masons had been complaining about unskilled and inferior workmen coming into the city to work on the Cathedral (that is, the old building, virtually a ruin at the time). Malcolm granted them leave to form an Incorporation within the city, a sort of closed shop, and promised "That the Incorporated Masons of Glasgow shall have a Lodge for ever at the City of Glasgow".

Well, they still have, though it's doubtful if many of the boys with the dust-free aprons and the funny handshakes would know what to do with a chisel.

---

6 October 1883

This was to be a great day of ceremony, pomp and circumstance for the City of Glasgow. The foundation stone for the new municipal buildings in George Square was to be laid — the municipal chambers which were to symbolise the wealth and importance of the Second City of the Empire. Religious ceremonies and a great trades and masonic procession were organised with meticulous detail, worked out weeks in advance.

As was customary, the carters led the procession, each of the trades following in their order. A firm from one of their newer trades—the photographers

— arranged to take part, and their advertisement reads as follows:

Look out for Instantaneous Photography
Represented by
GOODALL AND STEVEN
49 Jamaica Street

A well-known young lady in full ball costume will be photographed en route and her cartes presented to her Admirers and the Public.

The crowd were surprised and delighted to find that the "young lady" was no other than Old Malabar, the Glasgow juggler and well-known street character attired in all "her" finery. Old Malabar, alias Patrick Feeney, was an Irishman by birth and had learned his trade when apprenticed to a Chinese juggler in the streets of Dublin. He came to Glasgow as a young man, and made a precarious living from his juggling and conjuring acts. He was an expert with Chinese rings, but his main skill was in juggling with wooden and metal balls which he caught in a leather cup strapped to his forehead.

The trades procession of 6th October was virtually Malabar's last great public performance. He died the following month, penniless, in a lodging house in McPherson Street. Mrs Fell, the keeper of the Trongate waxworks judiciously paid his funeral expenses and laid claim to his juggling equipment, which with his death mask, was exhibited for decades thereafter. A. E. Pickard, the last owner of the waxworks, sold off the entire collection in 1944. The death mask disappeared, but the juggling equipment was purchased for the People's Palace, where the story of Old Malabar is still commemorated.

Some of Glasgow's early golfers, who played on the Laigh Green, part of Glasgow Green, were unsporting enough to bet openly on the noble game. Examples such as that of October 1810:

7 October 1810

"Five guineas and a bottle of rum against a drive for the monument (that is, Nelson's) to the trees beyond the farthest up hole, tee there and return drive";

or May 1809:

> "Marshall v. Craigie, that the latter breaks a club in a match with Adamson"

were not uncommon.

Golf, or *gowf*, was played in Glasgow from at least the early 17th century, and probably earlier. The Green was for centuries the venue. A writer of 1819 describes it:

> "In the neighbourhood of the Nelson Monument, we saw several elderly citizens playing at the old Scots game of golf, which is a kind of gigantic variety of billiards, the table being a certain space of the Green, sometimes of many hundred yards in extent; the holes situated here and there at great distances, and the balls, which were made very hard and stuffed with feathers, being swung to and fro in a terrific manner by means of long queues with elastic shafts . . . a fine healthful game. . . ."

It wasn't only elderly citizens who enjoyed it. The game was popular among the students of the early College, who, of course, played it in Latin. A golf ball was *pila claveria,* a driver *baculus*, a tee *statumen* and a bunker *fovea* (literally "goat", for some reason). And the phrase *in paludem* referred to that vexatious but all too common situation, "in the bog".

---

8 October 1844

Date of the inauguration of a bronze statue of an Iron Duke opposite Exchange Square. The Duke of Wellington's, next to King Billy's, is Glasgow's most wonderful equestrian statue. It was the work of Baron Marochetti, who was also responsible for the youthful mounted figures of Victoria and Albert in George Square.

---

9 October 1863

From the *Gazette:*

> "WONDERFUL ORGAN FOR SALE
> (By Private Bargain)
>
> "The wonderful organ of James Watt, the illustrious inventor of steam, made by his own hands for his own amusement in the city of Glasgow nearly 100 years ago, latterly in the possession of and duly authenticated by

the late Archibald McLellan Esq., one of the Magistrates of the city and Deacon Convener of the Trades House of Glasgow . . . etc."

James Watt was indeed a man of parts and more than one organ. In fact, he made three while in Glasgow, before his move to Birmingham in 1776. He enjoyed music and, though he didn't know one note from another, constructed several different musical instruments "with brains, sir". In his day, "Kists o' whistles", especially those of the church variety, tended to arouse strong feelings among the presbytery and the anti-prelatical mass of the populace. But Watt was ever a godless man (see 31st May).

Yesterday the first shipment of tea direct from India arrived at the Broomielaw. Tea was still a novelty to some Glaswegians, who had rather hazy notions as to its function. There are stories of it being added to stews, broth or porridge, with lamentable results.

10 October 1834

JACK HOUSE WRITES:

11 October

Cliff Hanley is a right bind. He shouldn't be allowed to compete with the rest of us ordinary mortals. He's like that Admirable Thingamyjig — you know the chap I mean, who could do everything.

However, I agree with those lovely Glasgow ladies who say it's nice to be nice, and I will now be nice to Cliff. He is a living example of the old Scots proverb that guid gear goes into sma' buik. Maybe Cliff would like it better as "Multum in parvo", unless that's Greek to him.

He is an expert on everything, including tap dancing, the proper use of words, cycling, recycling, the media, motor cars, the Scots, golf, Socialist Sunday Schools — the list is endless. And he wrote the words of *Scotland the Brave*.

Cliff is also a man of principle and that is why this day is important to him. When the Second World

War started he registered as a conscientious objector and in due course appeared before a CO tribunal.

There were all sorts of difficult questions, especially from a Professor of Theology. At the end Cliff was the only one of a large group who was accepted as a CO.

I've known and worked with Cliff Hanley for so many years that I can't bring myself to call him Clifford — the name you will see on his books nowadays. I still think of Cliff as a Wise Man of the East — the East End of Glasgow, that is. Edinburgh I consider Far East.

---

12 October 1845

Yesterday was cut the first of many sods for the Caledonian Railway's Glasgow to London line. Three years later, on the day before its public opening, the directors made a trial run from Glasgow. Near Beattock summit, at a point where the road and railway almost touched, they saw a sad sight — the down Mail, crawling by at 10 m.p.h. After 60 years it had given up in the face of overwhelming competition, and this was its last run.

Alas, some of the rail passengers had the bad taste to cheer. None of them would be likely to remember that Monday in July 1788 when the first mail coach from London drew up outside the Saracen's Head Inn (see 10th November) with great pomp and circumstance, an escort of horsemen and a fanfare of trumpets. However, whereas the mail took 42 hours for the journey, the Caledonian took under 16 hours. Ever since, the railways have proceeded on the extraordinary assumption that, whether by Flying Scotsmen or the truly terrifying Advanced Passenger Train, Glasgow folk just can't wait to get to London.

---

13 October 1812

Mr Stirling has lost a bottle of rum to the Club relative to the kind of fish at supper.

(Minutes of the Board of Green Cloth)

Loch Katrine, a very deep rock-and-forest girdled body of water in the lonely heart of the Trossachs, was the setting of Walter Scott's poem *The Lady of the Lake*. This made it Scotland's main tourist attraction for over a century. On the 14th October 1859, Queen Victoria crossed it by the steamer *Rob Roy* to the mouth of a tunnel where she turned a handle. Water started to flow through 17 miles of tunnel past Loch Chor and Ben Venue and Ben Lomond to Mugdockbank reservoir, just above Milngavie, from which it descended to the whole city.

This steady supply of pure water had been achieved by the Glasgow liberals against three sorts of opponent.

1. Shareholders of private water companies who said that a single municipal water supply would undermine their profits and the principle of free competiton.
2. Prosperous citizens, who thought it cheaper to rent pure water privately than pay rates to a community which would supply everyone.
3. The British Admiralty, who pointed out that part of Loch Katrine's overspill was a source of the River Forth, and a reduced flow might make the Firth of Forth silt up, thus depriving the Royal Navy of its most important dock and harbour north of the Humber.

The liberals, on the other side, declared:

1. That Glasgow's heavy industries now depended on sophistications of the James Watt steam engine, which needed large amounts of pure water. (While muddy water in a workman's tubes might make him sick, labour was cheap: but muddy water in an engine's tubes might make it break down, and machines were dear.)
2. That while diseases like typhus, typhoid and cholera always began among the overcrowded and poor, who seldom paid for their water, and were therefore perhaps being punished by God, the epidemics often spread to perfectly respectable households.

3.   That the Admiralty might be wrong.

So Glasgow became the industrial city with the best water supply in the United Kingdom. For many years steam pumps, hammers, mills and locomotives thrived on Clydeside. Glasgow escaped the 1866 cholera epidemic which attacked the rest of the country. And the Firth of Forth did not get too shallow for the British Navy.

Note: The Loch Katrine waterwork scheme, combining as it did a romance of Walter Scott with the romance of modern science, made a great impression upon the French romancer Jules Verne. His novel *The Child in the Cave* is about Scottish mining engineers who discover a vast cavern in the Trossachs beneath the bed of Loch Katrine. They at once start building a city there, lit by electricity and heated by gas, where people will live and work protected from the horrors of the Scottish climate. Unfortunately Loch Katrine empties itself into this industrial Utopia through an accidental fissure. The hero and heroine escape through a tunnel of volcanic origin finally to emerge a short distance from the summit of Arthur's Seat.

---

15 October 1784

From the *Edinburgh Advertiser:*

> "The Monkland Canal is now finished to Glasgow, and on Monday last, the first boat with coals arrived at the basin at Howgate head, which will greatly lower the price of coals there."

---

16 October 1589

The people of Glasgow have been using what they call "language" for a long time now, to the distress of those entrusted with the city's image. On this date, the Magistrates and Session passed an Act to curb the prevalence of "sweiring, banning and sclanderous flyting", by which terms we may recognise today's stairheid polemics, tending towards disorderly conduct and breach of the peace. Fines were imposed, and for those who could not afford them, the "joggs", that is to say, doing time *al fresco* in a metal choker. Interestingly, parents were to be liable for children's behaviour "because the barnis learnis of evill parentis to sweir at everie word, and also to ban". Too bloody right!

Glasgow Town Council decided it would not undertake the responsibility of repairing and maintaining the monument to John Knox, the celebrated 16th-century man of opinions. This was begun in 1825 in the Fir Park, the pleasant wooded hillock, owned by the Merchants' House, that would shortly become the Necropolis (see 12th September).

The monument, being a statue of Knox himself, large as life and twice as adamantine, glowers to this day from atop its stout Doric column. It casts a long shadow. Strangely, it is erected on a supposed site of pre-Christian sun worship (before the cult was superseded by the more practical one of rain worship). Perhaps, after all, Knox was just another solar myth.

17 October 1827

On this date, a mob gathered round a house in the High Street where a number of Catholics were understood to have assembled for worship. The worshippers escaped after being pelted with dirt and stones and several of the women having their caps and cloaks torn. The mob kept up the disturbance till nightfall, breaking every window in the house. Following this riot, Glasgow's Catholics took to worshipping in the house of the potter Robert Bagnall, which adjoined or was near his shop in the Gallowgate (see 9th February).

18 October 1778

Robert Pollock, the poet, was born on this date at North Moorhouse Farm, nearby the Kilmarnock Road. In his short life — he died of consumption in the correct fashion at the age of 29 — he contrived

19 October 1798

to write a rather ambitious verse epic. *The Course of Time* is a history of the world from its creation to its destruction, through mankind's pre-nuclear folly. No one could describe Pollock as a miniaturist. The pessimism and long-winded moralising of the poem seems to have suited the public taste of the time, for it enjoyed considerable success on publication. This has proved thoroughly ephemeral. Pollock died in September 1827. In 1900 a monument to him was unveiled near his birthplace. Inscribed on it is a verse tribute that begins: "Are you forgotten, Bard of Earn?"

We may answer for him — "Yes."

---

20 October 1792

Colin McLiver was born in a George Street tenement, son of a cabinetmaker from Mull. Under the name of Colin Campbell, he was to pursue an extraordinary military career involving quite a chunk of the known world.

At 16 years of age he was already an ensign, whatever that is. He retreated with Sir John Moore in Spain, and returned there for the replay. He served in Wellington's army, in the American wars, fought with Irish, Chinese and Sikhs. In fact, the man was just naturally belligerent. In the Crimean War, he distinguished himself at the Battle of Alma, and by sewing up Balaclava with a thin red line. In 1857 (by now a Major-General) he was put in charge of suppressing the Indian Mutiny, and set off to relieve Lucknow. He did so, putting it to the sack for good measure. In all these campaigns he was heroic to the point of monotony. No one knows where he went for his holidays.

Having collected about ten large cabinets full of medals and orders, Campbell was created a peer on 16th August 1858. Not having any obvious bit of land to attach to his title, they made him Lord Clyde of Clydesdale. He was elevated in statue form to the George Square pantheon.

Three Royalists, prisoners from the Battle of Philiphaugh, Sir Philip Nisbet, Sir William Rollock and Alexander Ogilvie, were brought before a Committee of the Estates in Glasgow. They had surrendered after a promise of mercy — a promise which in the prevailing mood of vengeance and bloodlust that prompted the slaughter of prisoners and even camp followers after that battle, was unlikely to be honoured. Their doom was pronounced:

> "Rollock to be on that afternoone, Ogilvie and Nisbet to be on the morne afternoone, execut at the Croce of Glasgow by straiking aff thair heads from thair bodies."

None of the three men had anything to do with Glasgow, but it was felt politic that the city should demonstrate its solidarity with the Covenanting cause. (See 16th August.)

When at last their friend Montrose was captured and butchered at Edinburgh, and his corpse was partitioned, Glasgow is said to have received his right leg ("Let them bestow on every airt a limb . . ."). As the meenister said, "The wark gangs bonnilie on".

21 October 1645

A fire damp explosion in one of William Dixon's collieries in High Blantyre claimed the lives of 230 miners. The city of Glasgow set up a relief fund for the widows and orphans which realised the sum of £48,246 19s. 3d.

22 October 1877

An application for a patent for the city's coat of arms was before the Lord Lyon King of Arms. It was granted on the 25th of this month. Earlier, the magistrates had expressed consternation on finding that Glasgow had no authentic arms, i.e. those authorised by the Lyon Court.

The man appointed to design the badge was Andrew McGeorge, a Glasgow lawyer. At a stroke he trimmed the motto down from "Let Glasgow

23 October 1866

Flourish by the Preaching of the Word" to the journalistically punchy "Let Glasgow Flourish". The diplomacy and tact with which McGeorge thus opened the way for developments material as well as spiritual cannot be too highly commended.

A further change was the removal of King Roderick and his Queen (protagonists in the St Mungo legends — see 13th January) as heraldic supporters and their replacement by "two drunken salmon" as contemporary cynics called them.

The ring-bearing salmon on the shield at any rate, although "naiant", or swimming, on his back is, in heraldic terms, "proper".

---

24 October 1522

The eve of John Knox's admission to Glasgow University, then under the Principalship of John Major. The latter, though less of a name to conjure with, had some scholarly standing in his day. His theology and philosophy blended Melville, Buchanan and Patrick Hamilton, and he was to be among the audience at Knox's first sermon in St Andrews in 1542.

Between 1524 and 1530, Major taught at the University of Paris, the Sorbonne, and the College of Montaigu, "that lousy college" Rabelais called it, meaning it literally. Indeed, it seems the great Rabelais knew Major around this time, and was not too impressed by him. In chapter 7 of *Pantagruel*, where he catalogues the extraordinary library of St Victor in Paris, Major is credited with a treatise on the art of pudding making (*De modo faciendi boudinos*). This may have been a reference to the practice, abhorred by Rabelais, of cramming in university teaching; our equivalent modern expression would be "the sausage factory".

Whether Major introduced this practice to Glasgow is arguable. Certainly, the University has battery-farmed some fine batches of dumplings since.

The day of execution of one Andrew Marshall, soldier of the 38th Regiment, sentenced on the 15th September for robbery and murder.

This was the first occasion on which it was incumbent on the city's magistrates to oversee an execution (an office previously the responsibility of the Sheriff). They were most disgruntled about this and the events of the day did nothing to improve their tempers.

The entourage arrived in due course at the gallows at Howgate-head, the prisoner in a horse-drawn cart. The rope was placed round his neck and the horse lashed to pull the cart from under him. At the crucial moment, however, the condemned man sprang up and seized hold of the gallows beam. His arms, it transpired, had been inadequately pinioned. He clung there, with extra-ordinary strength and persistence, considering that he had been kept on a diet of bread and water since the trial. The hangman had to belabour his head and arms with a stick, until he fell, and was satisfactorily strangled. His body was later hung in chains (the only recorded instance of this practice in Glasgow) but it was quickly and clandestinely removed by the offended inhabitants of the locality.

Following this the magistrates petitioned unsuccessfully to be relieved of the duty of presiding at executions.

Cromwell, who had arrived in Glasgow for the first time on Friday, 24th October, attended this Sunday a service at the Cathedral. There Zachary Boyd, minister of the Barony Parish, preached against him from Daniel VIII (comparing the he-goat of Daniel's vision with Cromwell). Cromwell's secretary was furious and suggested shooting Zachary on the spot. But Cromwell decided on a more fitting revenge. He invited the preacher to dinner. The meal was as scantily ascetic as possible, with three solid hours of prayers for dessert.

Cromwell had underestimated Zachary Boyd,

for he did not leave until three o'clock the next morning, apparently quite satisfied. (See also 2nd March and 17th June.)

27 October 1613

Glasgow Presbytery had to deal with some grave and distressing cases. This one involved George Semple, minister of Kilellan, who was accused by a Paisley bailie of a number of offences. These included possessing a book by Michael Scott "of unlawful airtes" and buying works by Albertus Magnus; also uttering "sundry unlawful conceits" and, to cap it all, his accuser *"hard tell that he made ballads and sonnets"*. The outcome of the trial is not known.

The errant minister's reading matter is of some interest: the Dominican Albert the Great, mentor of Thomas Aquinas, Aristotlean and inspiration of Francis Bacon and the Renaissance scientists. Michael Scott, one of the brightest ornaments of that glittering court of the Emperor Frederick II in Sicily. Court astrologer, astronomer, alchemist, experimental scientist, translater and interpreter of Aristotle, Averroês, Avicenna, he was an internationally respected polymath, one of the most important Scots of his day. It says something of the degree of civilisation of his native country that five centuries later it still thought of him as a warlock.

28 October 1773

Dr Samuel Johnson: "Sir, you lie!"
Adam Smith: "You are a son of a ——!"

Whore, presumably, though it's an academic point, as this unedifying exchange probably did not take place. Sir Walter Scott must take some of the blame for the rumour that Johnson met Adam Smith while visiting Glasgow in the course of the Highland jaunt. There is no evidence for it — Boswell makes no mention of such a meeting in his *Journal*, and it is unlikely he refrained from doing so out of sheer delicacy. It seems the two great men did have an altercation regarding David Hume, but that was earlier, before the philosopher's death.

Despite it, they appear to have held each other in mutual, if guarded, esteem.

However, after his overnight stay at the Saracen's Head, Johnson was visited by Professors Stevenson, Reid and Anderson and by the Foulis brothers (see 31st March). Boswell wasn't there to record the conversation, but it seems the Glasgow contingent at least held their own. Boswell describes the discomfiture of the Grand Cham afterwards (we quote from memory):

> "He came in a flutter to me, and desired I might come back again, for he could not bear these men. 'O ho! sir, (said I,) you are flying to me for refuge!' He never, in any situation, was at a loss for a ready repartee. He answered, with quick vivacity, 'Why don't you just fuck off, Boswell.' I was delighted with this flash bursting from the cloud which hung upon his mind, closed my letter directly, and joined the company."

---

29 October 1670

The fight to keep muck off the streets of Glasgow was a long and bitter one. On this date, the city magistrates fired an early salvo by ordering each citizen to clean the street in front of his house, and prohibiting filth from lying in the street for more than 48 hours (after which time, we suppose, it got a ticket).

In 1696, the Council passed an Act forbidding the throwing of excrement, dirt and urine from windows, or leaving the same in stairways, streets, lanes etc. It is gratifying to note that Glasgow was well ahead of the capital in this particular measure: each night, on the stroke of ten, for another 60 years, the "gardyloo" continued to fall from the Edinburgh lands like the gentle rain from heaven upon the place beneath.

Not that Glasgow was as wholehearted as it might have been. As late as 1776, there were only two men employed to clean the streets. By the end of the century, responsibility for this had fallen on the Chief Constable, or rather on his police and night watchmen (see 15th November).

In 1843, the Council took statutory powers to deal with watering, sweeping and cleaning the streets. The Police Board dealt with domestic refuse, originally contracted out, but in 1868 put under the control of the newly formed Cleansing Department.

Both human and horse dung had commercial value in the 19th century. The increasing population and the busy horse-drawn traffic ensured there was plenty of both around, to be collected in ashpits and sold as "urban manure". But after the invention of the water closet, there was proportionally less excrement in the ashpits, so a method of sorting the refuse had to be devised. This was pioneered by the St Rollox chemical works, extracted the shit for the farmers and dumped the rest. Until the demise of the horse traffic, "pan boys" armed with brush and shovel dodged in and out collecting horse dung, a very dangerous activity during the rush hour.

---

30 October 1886

During an F.A Cup match at Hampden Park between Preston North End and Queen's Park, Jimmy Ross, a Scots player with Preston, fouled the Queen's Park centre forward before a crowd of 15,000. The Queen's Park supporters immediately invaded the pitch, calling for blood. Ross had to be smuggled away to safety. This incident brought to a head the differences between the Football Association and the Scottish Football Association, and the following year (5th October 1887) the S.F.A. ordered all Scottish teams to withdraw from the F.A. Cup. the S.F.A. had stood out for amateurism much longer than its English counterpart, and though by 1893 professionalism had won out, the Scottish League was organised on its own national and proletarian lines.

---

31 October

Halloween, in the Christian calendar, and in earlier times the festival of *Samhuinn*, marking the entry of winter and the Celtic new year. F. Marion McNeill in *The Silver Bough* finds its origins in a pre-Christian cult of the dead, as a time for offering and sacrifices to ancestral spirits. Today, it's strictly for the kids.

Although in the matter of bonfires and fireworks it tends to run into and get confused with the Guy Fawkes celebrations, Halloween is still enthusiastically observed in Glasgow by "guising" in masks and fancy dress, and by parties with witches, turnip-lanterns, gnashing for treacle scones and dooking for apples. The significance of this last ritual has been long forgotten: the successful apple-dooker was supposed to gain the ability, during Halloween, to see into the future, in return for a wet face. Apples have a long association with Halloween, not least in Glasgow. Only last century, towards the end of each October, up to a dozen Jersey sloops would sail up the Clyde laden with apples from the Channel Islands. Children from the poorer parts of the city used to gather on the quay at the Broomielaw as they unloaded, to scramble for the apples that were thrown to them.

1 November 1889

Amid high winds the partly constructed facade of Templeton's carpet factory collapsed. Twenty-nine women and girls were killed while working in the temporary weaving sheds behind the structure.

The building had been commissioned from the architect William Leiper, after the previous one had burned down in 1886, with an estimated damage of £30,000. He was asked to design a building appropriate to the setting at the edge of Glasgow Green. He chose as his model the Doge's Palace in Venice, and the extraordinary ornamental brickwork facade is still known as the "Doge's (or *Dodge's*) Palace". Carpet weaving ceased there at the end of the 'seventies and it has become a business centre.

---

2 November

It is still three days to "Guy Fawkes", but the gangs have been out on the streets of Glasgow for at least a couple of weeks. Long past their bedtime, well-organised cells of infants are found blockading every pub entrance and accosting passers-by with "Penny for the guy, mister?" They don't mean a penny, of course — it's 10p at the very least, if you don't want an earful. As for the "guy", nine times out of ten it's a disgrace, either a teddy bear in an anorak sat in a cardboard box, or someone's baby brother stolen and shoved about in a pram.

Be firm with these young extortionists. Refuse to contribute a halfpenny until the 4th of the month. Never go out in groups of less than three.

---

3 November 1982

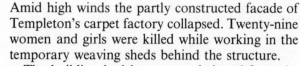

The new extension to Glasgow's Mitchell Library was formally opened by the Duchess of Gloucester or someone, on the site of the old St Andrew's Halls and abutting the North Street building. St Andrew's Halls, Glasgow's first concert halls, were designed by the architect James Sellars in the neo-classical "Greek" Thomson style. They were gutted by fire in 1962, and thereafter earmarked for the library's extension. The original facade, with its massive sculptural groups by John Mossman, has been preserved.

The Mitchell Library has a stock of over a million volumes, around 70,000 of which are on open access. With 50,000 square metres of floor space it is, in terms of area, Europe's largest public reference library.

Among its several specialities is the rich and extensive Glasgow Collection, without which this Diary would not have been possible. This last circumstance can only fortify nostalgia for the great days when it was a concert hall.

On this day a collier named Matthew Clydesdale was executed for murder. After dangling for the prescribed length of time, the body, as was customary, was delivered to the University's Anatomy Department, under the aegis of Dr James Jeffrey, "to be publicly dissected and anatomised".

4 November 1819

A large crowd attended, comprising lay members of the public as well as students. Much interest had been aroused by reports that a newly invented galvanic battery was to be tried out on the body. The murderer's corpse was duly arranged in a sitting posture on a chair, the handles of the instrument in his hands.

"Hardly had the battery been set working when the auditors observed the chest of the dead man to heave, and he rose to his feet. Some swooned for fear, others cheered at what was deemed to be a triumph of science. But the professor, *alarmed at this aspect of affairs*, put his lancet in the throat of the murderer and he dropped back into his seat." For a long time the community discussed whether or not the man was really dead when the battery was applied. "Probably not," said the chronicler. "There was in these days no long drop from the scaffold to break the spinal cord. It was simply a case of strangulation."

The facts in this account are disputed and there is an interesting correspondence/disputation in the *Glasgow Herald*, June/July 1983. The story was dramatised in Radio Clyde's "The Bell and the Tree" series, out of which arose the newspaper correspondence. However apocryphal the story may be it is not out of character with the times.

On 13th July 1983, 164 years later, the British Parliament seriously discussed a return to this gruesome state of affairs.

Mary Shelley's *Frankenstein* had been published only a year before this event.

---

5 November
1844

The newly formed Scottish Temperance League was bold enough to have its headquarters in Glasgow. Ten years later, the Glasgow Abstainers' Union was set up. The tactics adopted by the latter to wile sottish Glaswegians from their pubs included concerts, morning coffee stands, missionaries, seaside convalescent homes and penny savings banks. Pathetic, really. Another anti-drink conspiracy was the Scottish Prohibition Society for the Suppression of the Sale of Intoxicating Liquor by Legal Enactment, or SPSSSILLE, which was formed in 1856 and continued until 1858, when the Scottish Permissive Bill Association began. Nothing permissive about this: their aim was to prohibit *all* traffic in bevvy, although in this case by popular vote. In 1869, Scotland's first Lodge of the US-based Independent Order of Good Templars was established in Glasgow with similar objectives, and November 1870 saw the founding of a Band of Hope Union here.

And so on. The abstainers scored their greatest victory with the passing of the Temperance (Scotland) Act in 1913. This came into full force seven years later, and allowed each parish, burgh or ward to decide by vote whether or not to have pubs in the district, or to limit the number of licences granted. But it was all a waste of time. The names of all these associations are now no more than bogeymen such as one might invoke to frighten naughty children. The drinker in modern Glasgow has nothing to fear. Indeed, thanks to recent developments in the science of licensing extension, it is now possible, with minimal resort to the cocktail cabinet,* to drink virtually round the clock. Try it, and astonish your friends.

* Cocktail cabinet: polythene bag of the two-handled carrier type containing six cans of Tennent's Lager and a half-bottle of Grouse.

Ah, how things change! On this day Mr Hugh Wylie, merchant of Glasgow, was elected Dean of Guild in place of James Sommerville who, having been himself elected, had declined to serve and was fined £40. Sommerville in his turn had been chosen in place of one Peter Murdoch, who had also preferred to stump up the same not-inconsiderable sum rather than take the post.

The practice of fining those base enough to refuse the high dignity of public office was widespread in Glasgow around this time, the scale of fines being:

6 November 1776

for refusing to accept the office of

		Lord Provost	£50
,,	,,	bailie	£40
,,	,,	Dean of Guild	£40
,,	,,	councillor	£20
,,	,,	deacon-convener	nil

It was said that merchants known to be both wealthy and unwilling were (s)elected for office as a convenient means of boosting the city's revenue.

The Reverend James Clark, minister of the Tron Church, upon the occasion of a fast ordered by the Commission of the General Assembly to implore Divine deliverance from the impending calamity (the Treaty of Union with England), preached a fiery sermon from Ezra VIII, 21. He, moreover, reminded his congregation that prayers were not enough, that other matters must be assayed — *"Wherefore up and be valiant for the city of our God"*.

This was taken as a signal for general insurrec-

7 November 1707

tion, and the people took to the streets. The Provost, whose opposition to the Union was lukewarm, had to flee the city. When he returned, he escaped lynching only narrowly in the course of a second and more serious disturbance. This time the mob disarmed the regular guard and instituted their own. They stormed the Tolbooth and liberated the town's arms, consisting of 250 halberds. One ringleader by the name of Finlay ("a loose sort of fellow") set off with 45 men towards Edinburgh, intending to disperse the Parliament there. When they got to Kilsyth, it became evident that no further support would be forthcoming, and they returned to Glasgow. Although the threat of serious rebellion had dissolved, it took a troop of dragoons to recover the city.

---

8 November 1924

"The citizen of Glasgow," said a Medical Officer in 1905, "has less of the earth's surface than any other citizen of the realm." He could not have realised how much worse this was to become as the century wore on.

In November 1924, *Cancer of Empire*, by William Bolitho, was published. The title referred, of course, to the Dear Green Place itself, and it is a lurid account of the author's descent into the hell-pit that was Glasgow. Written at the time of the "Red Clydeside" scare, its exposure of poverty and suffering among working people was intended more to warn against the capital the "Reds" (sic) would make from it, than to assert the needs of these people as a matter of simple justice. "Revolution or Subsidy" was the conclusion of the horrified author. However, despite the rhetorical prose, the patronising attitudes and the amazing lack of identification with the humans he describes, Bolitho did not exaggerate the conditions, and his facts are substantially accurate.

Housing was the big problem. Two-thirds of the population of 1,081,983 lived in houses below Board of Health minimum standards. 40,591 families lived in one-roomed houses; 112,424 in a room and kitchen. There were 13,000 condemned houses, nearly all of them occupied.

A particularly shocking illustration of the degree of overcrowding — and the desperate attempts to contain it — was the system of "ticketed houses". These each had a painted disc on the door which stated the number of people permitted to live inside. This was calculated on the basis of 400 cubic feet per adult (half of this for children under ten). Municipal inspectors had access at all hours of the day and night to enforce the regulations. There were almost twenty thousand of these "ticketed" houses in Glasgow, most of them single rooms, and they accounted for between 10 per cent and 15 per cent of the population.

While damning the undoubted stupidity, short-sightedness and sheer vandalism involved in the "solutions" to Glasgow's housing problems, it is only fair to bear in mind the scale and urgency of the need. Stairhead camaraderie, warmth of community feeling, caring, helping and whatever aside, there were *no* good old days for Glasgow's working people.

A committee appointed by the Kirk Session reported that 1,270 paupers in Glasgow were being supported on the Session's funds, each being paid an average of 3 shillings 1 penny and $1\frac{1}{8}$ farthings.

Of course, that eighth of a farthing made all the difference.

9 November 1815

The Saracen Head Inn, Glasgow's first real hotel and its most famous by far, advertised for business on this date. It was established by Robert Tennent, founder of the Glasgow brewing dynasty that still gives us passable lager and weak, gassy keg beer. Glasgow Town Council were keen for the city to have something with a bit more class than the rough and ready taverns and inns she was used to, so they gave Tennent permission to take stones from the

10 November 1755

old Bishop's Castle in the High Street for the building.

The result was something more splendid than anything Glasgow had known. Tennent called it the Saracen Head after the famous London prototype, and proudly advertised it as being free of bugs. Its stables could hold 60 horses, its ballroom 100 dancers. "Senex" the historian recalls it at its most posh:

> "On the arrival of the Mail especially, all the idlers of the city crowded round it, and at the door stood two waiters (who were specially selected for their handsome appearance) with embroidered coats, red plush breeches, and powdered hair, to welcome the passengers to the comforts inside."

When the likes of circuit judges were in residence, the flunkeys became even more ornate, donning silk stockings.

"Things have changed greatly since the old times," quavers "Senex", and today nothing is left of the great inn but some relics such as the five-gallon punch bowl in the People's Palace (see 22nd January). Nearby, but not on, the site there is a pub called the Saracen Head (pronounced "Sorry Heid" in consideration of the effects a night there may have). The visitor will find a notable shortage of embroidered coats and red plush breeches among its bar staff, although times are changing fast. The pub has a notoriety that is really rather unearned — it is by no means the worst in the area — and features in a number of folktales. One concerns a total stranger who arrived in the city and went into the first pub he found. This happened to be the Saracen Head. Having heard so much about the friendliness and sociability of Glaswegians, he was delighted to have this confirmed by the buzz of conversation among the customers. It was some minutes before he realised they were all talking to themselves.

---

11 November 1715

On 15th November 1715, the first Glasgow newspaper, the *Glasgow Courant*, appeared "containing the occurrences at home and abroad" from the 11th of the month to the 14th, the day of the Battle of Sheriffmuir was more or less fought. Not only was it the first Glasgow newspaper, it was the first specifically municipal newspaper to be established in the community. It cost three halfpence (1d. to regular subscribers). It was published three times a week, on Tuesday, Thursday and Saturday. In the fourth number, the name was changed to *The West Country Intelligence.* It continued under that banner, but did not survive beyond 1729.

The *Glasgow Journal* of 1741 is the next we can be certain of. Its editor had a terrible time trying to decide a safe by plausible line to take on the Jacobite rising. Eventually he cracked up and resigned, though the paper survived a further 50 years or so.

A much more important newspaper made its debut in January of 1783, the *Glasgow Advertiser and Evening Intelligence*, later to become better known as the *Glasgow Herald.* It began its long life with a considerable scoop — the Treaty of Independence marking the end of the American war — but got progressively duller.

The *Herald* proudly celebrated its bicentenary in 1983 as the oldest national daily newspaper in the language. It has indeed come a long way, from John Mennon's little shop in the Saltmarket to its current niche in the Lonrho empire. In its time it has embraced the entire gamut of political opinion from right-wing conservative to right-wing liberal; now and again a powerful telescope is needed to locate its drift to starboard. In short, the *Glasgow Herald* has been, and continues to be, an *establishment* establishment.

We should add that it keeps winning prizes in the abstract and minimally controversial field of design and layout.

"When did you last see your father?" The painting and its title have entered the dimension of cliché: the defiant little Cavalier boy facing the brutal Round-

12 November 1680

head interrogators. But Cromwell's Commonwealth was benign compared to the reign of terror imposed by Royalists against the Glaswegian supporters of the Covenant.

John Spreull, a Glasgow apothecary, was asked that infamous question in the aftermath of the Battle of Rutland, in which his father had fought on the Covenanting side. Despite threats and imprisonment, he refused to reveal his whereabouts. He was released, but shortly afterwards cited for nonconformism. Though he managed to escape to Holland, his troubles were only beginning.

On returning to collect his family, he was seized and brought to trial in Glasgow on 12th November 1677. He was questioned about the risings at Drumclog and Bothwell Brig. Were they rebellions? Was the killing of Archbishop Sharp an act of murder? Spreull refused to define the risings as rebellions, and would make no comment regarding Sharp. It was decided to put him to the torture of the "Boot".

His foot was forced into the iron sock, and at each question, the hangman struck the crushing wedges with a mallet. Did he know of a plan to blow up the Abbey and the Duke of York? Who was in the plot? Would he now subscribe his confession? When he refused, his interrogators decided that the Boot they were using, a new model, was not doing the job effectively enough. The old Boot was called for, and Spreull was tortured a second time. Throughout his ordeal he bore himself with great fortitude. Afterwards he was carried off to prison on the back of a soldier.

On 10th December, Spreull was indicted for high treason, in that he took the rebels' part at Bothwell Brig and kept company with the Archbishop's murderers. The charges were found "not proven", but he was still not freed. On the February following, he was brought before the Privy Council to answer charges of attending conventicles. Having refused to deny this on oath, he was found guilty, fined £500 sterling and imprisoned on the Bass Rock.

He spent six years there, earning the nickname by which he is better known: Bass John.

Disgusting practices revealed in the course of an advertisement in the *Glasgow Mercury* for Pollockshaws races:

> ". . . a goose race. He that pulls off the head gets the goose. A cock race. He that catches the cock in his teeth and walks three paces with him gets the cock, and half a crown. Their hands must be tied behind their backs that try the race. . . ."

13 November 1754

Andrew Fairfoul was appointed by Charles II to the Archbishopric of Glasgow, in the face of widespread opposition from the majority of Scottish ministers, who did not want any bishops at all. Such was the distaste for episcopalianism that soon Fairfoul and his suffragens were complaining that they were "not being honoured" in Glasgow and the west of Scotland. In fact, none of the recently ordained ministers would acknowledge him. So the Privy Council called a meeting in the College Fore Hall to sort them out.

At this, the "Drunken Meeting" as it came to be known, everyone was allegedly steaming (with the sole exception of Sir James Lockhart of Lee who was also, by curious coincidence, the only dissenting voice there). On 1st October 1662, they passed an Act ordering conformity, and threatening those who didn't (hic!) toe the line with being (hic!) punished as frequenters of (hic!) conventicles, by God! (hic!)

Those responsible for this dastardly oppression were reputed to be in the habit of drinking the devil's health at the Cross of Ayr at midnight, a sure sign of episcopacy bordering on papishness. In the aftermath of the Drunken Meeting, 400 ministers were expelled, 14 from the Presbytery of Glasgow, thus ensuring a centre of popular resistance to the Stuart monarchy that was to last into the 18th century.

14 November 1661

15 November 1800

The Glasgow Police Act received royal assent on 30th June 1800, but the first mustering of police was on this day. The first Glasgow police force was granted temporary use of the Session House of the Tron Kirk and from there the two sergeants, six officers and 68 watchmen patrolled the city. The watchmen were also obliged to sweep the streets, call out the hours at night and announce the state of the weather.

The watchmen also sold the dung which they swept up and in the year 1803 this added the sum of £450 to the police accounts. Unfortunately, this practice was abandoned in 1804 and a good source of income was thus lost.

16 November 1852

Harriet Beecher Stowe, authoress of the immensely influential *Uncle Tom's Cabin*, visited Glasgow and addressed a public meeting in the City Halls on the subject of slavery. As a result, the campaign known as "Uncle Tom's Penny" was begun, the idea being that each person who read the book would donate one pence to the anti-slavery movement. It proved a popular cause, and in April the following year the Glasgow and Edinburgh Emancipation Societies presented Ms Stowe with £1,000 from the collection (representing, we calculate, exactly 24,000 readings).

Ms Stowe also visited the Highlands, in particular Dunrobin, seat of the Dukes of Sutherland. There she was lionised by the Duchess and her society cronies, who were terribly concerned about the poor slaves in America. Later, she wrote a book about her experiences, called *Sunny Memories*. It contained a spirited defence of her friend's benign policies of "Improvement" that had so assisted the mobility of thousands of Highland tenants.

Ms Stowe was born without the faculty of irony.

17 November 1812

Mr William Stirling bets a bottle of rum and 10 guineas with Mr James Monteith that Mr John Douglas does not charge anything for his trouble for

Mr Findlay in the late election. Mr Monteith bets
that he does make a charge for his troubles.
(Minutes of the Board of Green Cloth)

For three months Glasgow was host to the "Poet
and Tragedian" William Topaz McGonagall. He
gave three "entertainments" in the city. No objec-
tive account of them survives, but he writes that he
was treated "like a prince". Considering the treatment Glasgow audiences have dealt out to later and
rather better entertainers, this claim is astonishing.

But McGonagall's stay was not an unmitigated
triumph. In a letter to a friend — he had a friend —
he admitted he had not sold many poems, and went
on to complain of the din and the climate, saying "I
fear it will soon put an end to my existence". (In fact
he survived another 13 years.) McGonagall wrote a
poem about Glasgow, called "Glasgow". Despite
its obsession with statuary and the shattering
closing couplet, it is so full of good things that we
feel it deserves quoting in full:

18 November 1889

Beautiful city of Glasgow, with your streets so neat and clean,
Your stately mansions, and beautiful Green!
Likewise your beautiful bridges across the Clyde,
And on your bonnie banks I would like to reside.

Chorus
Then away to the West — to the beautiful West!
To the fair city of Glasgow that I like the best,
Where the river Clyde rolls on to the sea,
And the lark and the blackbird whistle with glee.[1]

'Tis beautiful to see the ships passing to and fro,
Laden with goods for the high and the low!
So let the beautiful city of Glasgow flourish,
And may the inhabitants always find food their bodies to
    nourish.

Chorus

The statue of the Prince of Orange is very grand,
Looking terror to his foe, with a truncheon[2] in his hand,
And well mounted on a noble steed, which stands in the
    Trongate,
And holding up its foreleg, I'm sure it looks first rate..[3]

Chorus

Then there's the Duke of Wellington's statue in Royal
    Exchange Square—
It is a beautiful statue I without fear declare,
Besides inspiring and most magnificent to view,
Because he made the French fly at the battle of Waterloo.

Chorus

And as for the statue of Sir Walter Scott that stands in
    George Square,
It is a handsome statue — few can with it compare,
And most elegant to be seen,
And close beside it stands the statue of Her Majesty the Queen.[4]

Chorus

Then there's the statue of Robert Burns in George Square,
And the treatment he received when living was very unfair;
Now, when he's dead, Scotland's sons for him do mourn,
But, alas! unto them he can never return.[5]

Chorus

Then as for Kelvin Grove, it is most lovely to be seen
With its beautiful flowers and trees so green,
And a magnificent water-fountain spouting up very high,
Where the people can quench their thirst when they feel dry.[6]

Chorus

Beautiful city of Glasgow, I now conclude my muse,
And to write in praise of thee my pen does not refuse;
And, without fear of contradiction,[7] I will venture to say
You are the second grandest city in Scotland at the present day.

Notes:
1 Not quite accurate—larks *trill*.
2 Strictly speaking, the baton of a field marshal, not a nightstick.
3 . . . whereas if it held up its *hind* leg, it would suggest a dug at a
   lamp-post.
4 Strangely, no mention is made of that of the Prince Consort.
   What *is* McGonagall suggesting?
5 It may not be totally farfetched to identify a certain personal
   bitterness on McGonagall's part surfacing in this stanza.
6 Not any longer (see 14th August).
7 He was a brave man.

---

19 November
1804

Robert Dreghorn died by his own hand. Last of a
merchant dynasty, he lived in an impressive
mansion in Clyde Street and had an income of
around £8,000 per annum. This meant that, at a
time when 10s. per week was a good wage, he had
about £10 per day. He was wealthy, but couldn't or

wouldn't believe it, and lived in perpetual fear of poverty. He was a miser who refused to contribute to the poor rates until the Court of Session ruled he had to. And "Bob Dragon", as he was better known, was supposed to be the ugliest man in Glasgow. Though tall, erect, and always modishly dressed, with long coat and cane, his face was disfigured by smallpox. This did not deter him from following any girl who took his fancy in the course of his daily promenades. If we are to believe contemporary accounts, all he did was pester what they called the fair sex and amass a reputation as an incorrigible lecher. Much entertainment was had of this sad and ultimately desperate person. The ugliest man in Glasgow these days is Kentigern McCodrum, of Dreichmuir Road, Drumlie (see illustration).

This disconcerting advertisement appeared today in the local press:

20 November 1808

> "LINEN RAGS. As the managers of the Glasgow Royal Infirmary find a great difficulty in obtaining a quantity of Linen Rags sufficient for the purposes of the Patients in the House, they respectfully inform the Public that a supply of OLD LINENS will be received with thanks at the Infirmary."

We in the 1980s may rest secure now that the Conservative Government, reaffirming its commitment to the Health Service, has issued a firm guarantee that the supply of old rags will be maintained at its present level. Certain areas of the Used Bandages and Communal Bedpan services, though, may have to be privatised to improve efficiency and cost-effectiveness.

One of the most important meetings of the Church's General Assembly began today in Glasgow Cathedral. When the Covenanting faction outvoted the Episcopalian bishops on the subject of the authority of Church Courts, the Marquis of Hamilton, acting on the King's authority, promptly

21 November 1638

declared the meeting over, and had a proclamation read at the Cross declaring all who remained at the Assembly guilty of high treason.

Nothing daunted, the Assembly continued in session until 20th December, during which time it excommunicated the bishops and renounced Episcopalianism in favour of the Presbyterian form of worship.

---

22 November 1882

The monthly report on the quality of Loch Katrine water, prepared by Professor E. J. Mills, D.Sc., F.R.S., Anderson's College, has been issued. The results are in parts per 10,000: total solid impurity 3.10; organic carbon, 0.152; organic nitrogen, 0.008; total combined nitrogen, 0.031; hardness, 1.1; chlorine, 0.66; temperature, 7.0° Centigrade.

The water was sampled on 15th November. It was light brown in colour, and contained a considerable amount of suspended matter. (Compare 19th September 1845.)

---

23 November 1784

Balloonery 1.

A big crowd gathered in St Andrew's Square to watch the daredevil aeronaut Lunardi make his balloon ascent. While the subtile bladder was being inflated, a band played; when it took off, all the chimes of Glasgow mingled with the cheers of the spectators, the huzzas of the dignitaries, the catcalls of the cats, the vilependencies of the pious, the awestriking of the idly curious, the leaps, waves, stampings and gesticulations of the demonstrative, the frenzied caressings of wood of the superstitious and the loosening of the restrictive parts of the garments of fainted ladies.

Two and a half hours later, Lunardi landed near Hawick in Selkirkshire, to the astonishment of the natives — a close encounter of the third kind. A month later he was back in Glasgow, to repeat his triumph (see 5th December) and make a tidy sum by advertising "aerial excursions" for the public.

From today's *Glasgow Herald:*

24 November 1858

"GLASGOW Martinmas Wednesday Fair, This great feeing market was held on a Wednesday in the Bights, at Graeme Square. The market was rather dull, and a great number of servants left without being engaged: in general, servants submitted to a reduction of wages. First class ploughmen, formerly at £14, accepted of £12 for the half year. As usual, the streets were thronged with Jockies and Jennies, who uncouth behaviour excited no small amusement among the town's onlookers."

A picturesque sight, evidently, the market in human flesh.

Thomas Chalmers (1780-1847) was on this date appointed minister of Glasgow's Tron Church, a position he held until 1820, when he moved to St John's. He was reckoned one of the greatest evangelical orators of his age. He was a pioneer of the movement towards the disruption of the established Church and the formation, in 1843, of the Free Church. He also believed in bringing the Kirk up to date in matters of science and economics, and in tightening its control of education and poor relief. Poverty, he believed, could be relieved through the taking of collections, and piety by home missions. And during all these good works, he wrote theological, philosophical, expository and devotional treatises. His astronomical discourses held in the Tron on Thursdays were very well attended, and when published rivalled the latest production of Sir Walter Scott as a bestseller.

25 November 1814

Civic dignity can be a frosty thing, and it is good to see it thaw now and again. Today the magistrates of Glasgow, who had recently refused permission for the city's coat of arms to be used on a backcloth for a pantomime, relented and gave their lordly consent. They should, of course, have done so in the first place. Quite apart from Glasgow's distinguished association with the art form, we have

26 November 1958

long felt that the legends of St Mungo's doings, as illustrated in said coat of arms, would make an excellent Christmas panto. With ingredients such as adultery, angling, spontaneous combustion and kindness to animals, it would have something for everyone. (See 13th January for St Mungo's adventures.)

27 November 1916

Andrew Bonar-Law, one of the two Prime Ministers furnished by Glasgow, failed to impress quite a number of people, including Asquith. On this date Asquith is reported as delivering (to Lloyd George) this crushing appraisal:
"He has the brains of a Glasgow baillie."

28 November 1638

The first book to be printed in Glasgow was a controversial blockbuster snappily entitled *The Protestation of the General Assemblie of the Church of Scotland, and of the Noblemen, Barons, Gentlemen, Burrowes, Ministers and Commons, Subscribers of the Covenant, lately renewed, made in the High Kirk, and at the Mercate Crosse of Glasgow, the 28 and 29 November 1638.* The printer was George Anderson. (For more about the said Assembly, see 21st November.)

29 November 1837

On the occasion of this month's election of the Provost, 15 councillors voted for each of the two candidates, Dunlop and Fleming. Both were leading merchants in the city, Fleming being the popular one and Dunlop having the support of the Tories. The retiring Provost, William Mills, insisted he had the right to give the casting vote, which he did in favour of his friend Fleming. But Bailie Henry Paul argued that Mills had by this stage demitted office, and was therefore not competent to vote. As senior acting chief magistrate, the casting vote should be *his*, and he decided for *his* friend, Henry Dunlop.

Both candidates tried to take office. Both

squeezed into the Provost's chair. The proceedings were in grave danger of developing into a farce, so it was decided to refer the problem to the Courts. In the meantime, Glasgow was to have two provosts! Both men took the oath of office, and agreed to act jointly in the signing of documents and the chairing of meetings. This absurd state of affairs continued until the Court of Session gave a "lengthy decision" in favour of Dunlop.

---

30 November 1923

Today John MacLean died at the age of 44. The immediate cause of death was bronchial pneumonia, but it was a combination of overwork and the deprivation and maltreatment he had suffered in the prisons of Calton, Duke Street, Peterhead and Barlinnie that destroyed the health of the greatest spokesman of the Scottish workers. The news was greeted with shock and dismay. 10,000 followed his coffin to Eastwood Cemetery, where he was buried on 3rd December.

MacLean was born in Pollockshaws, Glasgow, in 1879. His family were exiles from Mull, victims of the Clearances. His father died when he was eight years old, leaving his mother to bring up the children as best she could. It was not an easy life. MacLean learned something of poverty at first hand. While attending Pollock Academy and Queen's Park School, he learned something about inequality, too. In 1896 he began his career in teaching, as a pupil teacher in Polmadie School. MacLean had a religious upbringing. He was also a voracious reader. Soon his Christianity was replaced by a firm belief in the materialist doctrines of Marxist history and economics — around 1900 he read *Capital*. Not content with theoretical study, he threw himself into its application to the situation he found about him. He joined the Social Democratic Federation, a revolutionary Marxist group, in 1903, helped organise meetings, demonstrations and, most importantly, educational courses in economics and Marxist theory.

It was the coming of the First World War that

brought about MacLean's first serious confrontations with the government of the day. The war issue had split the socialist movement, some being as jingoistic about it as any Tory. MacLean was utterly opposed to it from the start. He recognised it as a war by and for the bosses, at best an irrelevance to working people and their aspirations, at worst a murderous exploitation of their lives and labour. He went out and said so.

The first arrest was in September 1915, for "using language likely to lead to a breach of the peace". He was fined £5, but refused to pay and was jailed for five days.

It was the first of a string of prison sentences MacLean was to collect. Arrests followed on such charges as obstruction, making statements likely to prejudice recruiting, encouraging mutiny, encouraging disaffection, sedition, impeding the production and transport of war material, and so on. His battle with the authorities had its ludicrous aspects: the plain clothes police at his rallies, taking down wildly inaccurate reports and trying to look inconspicuous, the claim that he had told workers to sell their German alarm clocks so they would sleep in in the morning and miss work, the charge that he had advised workers to use "their guns". Of course, the main charges were substantially true. MacLean *was* opposed to the war effort and anything to do with it. When he came to speak for himself in the High Court, rather than defend himself, he went straight into the attack.

Needless to say, he kept being found guilty and given heavy sentences: three years penal servitude, five years, three months, 12 months. Though sustained pressure from his supporters forced the government to grant his early release, the experiences of imprisonment (including hunger strikes, force-feeding, inadequate or drugged food) took a severe toll.

MacLean's work and sacrifices had come to the notice of Lenin, who described him as one of the "isolated heroes" who were the precursors of revolution: "Liebnecht in Germany, Adler in

Austria, MacLean in England (*sic*)". In 1918 he was appointed first Soviet Consul for Scotland. The British Government flatly refused to recognise or deal with him. It should be made clear that, honoured though he no doubt was by the appointment, he was quite explicit that the role he envisaged for Scotland in the socialist community was one of independence from the Soviet monolith. Scotland was not to be "dictated to by Moscow".

By 1920, MacLean had grown convinced of the need for an independent Scottish socialism, a concept rejected by the Communist Party and by most of the Left. His experiences travelling and campaigning in England had demonstrated the wide gulf between the state of political awareness of the Scottish workers and that of their southern counterparts. The revolution could not wait for them to catch up. Perhaps too he was influenced by the example of Irish Republicanism. In August 1920 he published the proclamation *All Hail the Scottish Workers' Republic*. The foundation in February of 1923 of the Scottish Workers' Republican Party marked his final break with "British" socialism.

It was while campaigning as the SWRP candidate in Gorbals for the General Election later that year that John MacLean died.

The foregoing is a bald and very sketchy outline of MacLean's life and work. To assess the man is a more difficult task.

MacLean was not a politician. One cannot imagine him making the pragmatic compromises the practice of politics demands. He was not even a great popular leader, lacking the demagogue's egoism and talent for seizing on and exploiting events to his advantage. He had no personal interest in power. He was neither a great writer nor a great speaker — as an orator he lacked "charisma", and both his speeches and prose writings tended to lurch from clumsy rhetoric to rather uninspiring factuality. He was not a great original thinker. He did not develop Marxist theory significantly, though he was the first — perhaps the only one — to apply it to the notion of an independent Scottish republic. He was not a figurehead, or a "star", or a symbol. He was not, or was only incidentally, a martyr. What, then, was he?

A teacher, certainly, and something of a preacher. He never lost sight of the absolute primacy of education, of having a working class made up of informed and critical individuals. After all, teaching was his trade and his vocation. Leaders are seldom over-enthusiastic about educating those they lead, but MacLean was only a leader by direction and example. Behind his instruction there was something of the West Highland preacher's fiery austerity. MacLean was a moralist, not in the usual sense of the word nowadays, though he was by personal inclination rather a puritan. It was the sin of greed he attacked, and cruelty, and injustice — these he saw above all as inalienable attributes of a particular economic system: capitalism. He had an extraordinary capacity for seeing through events to their causes, of grasping simple truths however obscured by lies and hypocrisy. It was this very directness that caused his enemy to reveal its true nature in those savage courtrooms.

In himself, he was inclined to pacifism and was by all accounts the most kindly of men. He had no great facility for wit, but possessed an enduring sense of fun. He was well liked.

John MacLean was a *good* man, by which we mean to infer a quality essential to him, like the colour of his eyes. It is simply not possible to imagine him behaving in certain ways, such as altering his course from what he believed in. He could never, as the others arrested along with him did, have changed his plea to "guilty", said "sorry" and thrown himself "on the mercy of the court". This was not bloody-mindedness: he just knew, in all humility, that he was right. There is usually something repellent in such certainty, but we do not feel that in MacLean's case.

He has left no political heirs. His vision of a Scottish Workers' Republic has few adherents today and seems as remote of achievement as ever. Several political parties pay selective homage to him; none has the right to do so. The Labour Party, which he would heartily despise could he see it, mutters the odd shamefaced platitude when it has to, the SNP, still largely bourgeois-reformist in outlook, tries to extract from him the honey of nationalism while avoiding the sting of Bolshevism. The Communist Party, who with chilling cynicism attributed his espousal of Scottish autonomy to mental derangement brought on by his sufferings in prison (the internment of dissidents in mental hospitals is a logical development of this way of thinking), patronise him as a kind of high-minded but errant primitive. There are one or two left-wing republican groups, but these exist in political limbo, that is to say, without a power base.

Soviet Consul or not, if he had lived longer MacLean would surely have rejected the later perversions of Communism in the USSR and the appalling tyranny it became. Otherwise, he would most likely have found himself in the wilderness. Seeing old photographs of John MacLean, whether in full flight of oratory, buoyant above a sea of flat hats, or with his family, or alone and looking out at us with an air of self-containment and startling candour, we have an illusion of a time when issues were simpler, heroic even. Yet, amid all our cynical complexities, the steady gaze of the dominie still confronts us from the bitter sepia, hardens into a question.

1 December 1931

Percy Joseph Sillitoe was appointed Chief Constable of Glasgow. While it is certain that he should have the credit for introducing the police-box or "Tardis" system, it is probably only a myth that he was responsible for breaking up the Glasgow gangs. As the song puts it:

There came up once to Glesca Sir Percy Sillitoe,
To rascals he's an enemy, to criminals a foe.
They say he broke the gangs, but it really isnae true,
For they didnae stop the fechtin till they a' signed aff
*   the broo.*

Nevertheless, his name is to this day revered by the blue-rinse brigade at Scottish Tory Party conferences.

---

2 December 1685

Sir John Maxwell was fined the sum of £8,000 sterling for sheltering Presbyterians in Haggs Castle. On refusing to pay, he was imprisoned for 16 months. He died shortly after being released.

---

3 December

Today is our day for a story. It is by a man called Mr Tom Leonard and it is called:

MR CHESTY BURNS THE FRIED BREAD

It was a lovely sunny morning in Glasgow, and Mr Chesty was hanging face down over the side of his bed.

That nasty old night phlegm was draining to the top of his lungs.

Poor Mr Chesty!

Cough, cough, cough! At last "The First of the Day" arrived, and Mr chesty wrapped it in a nice fresh Kleenex.

Mr Chesty peeped.

It was a Mr Happy. "Glasgow's miles better!" chirped the little fellow.

Mr Chesty found he could cough up Mr Happys whenever he wanted. And every time Mr Chesty coughed up a Mr Happy, he wrapped it in a nice fresh Kleenex, and put it in the floral bin beside the gas fire.

Soon the floral bin beside the gas fire was full of Mr Happys. "Glasgow's miles better! Glasgow's miles better!" sang the floral bin.

Mr Chesty sat listening to the floral bin. It was just like the Glasgow Orpheus Choir.

"Can you sing 'The Garden where the Praties Grow'?" asked Mr Chesty. But the floral bin did not know the words.

So Mr Chesty went to make his breakfast.

Mr Chesty put his morning slice of bread in the frying pan, with his morning slice of Lorne. Then he spotted something outside in the garden.

It was a giant inhaler! Mr Chesty went outside to investigate.

The inhaler was almost as big as Mr Chesty himself! Mr Chesty read the label:

CHESTY'S MAGIC INHALER
EXPIR MAR 1995
TWO PUFFS ANYWHERE IN GLASGOW
BEFORE OR AFTER MEALS
STATE DESTINATION CLEARLY

Mr Chesty sat down on the magic inhaler. He pressed the top of the canister twice, and held on tight. "The Burrell Collection!" stated Mr Chesty, clearly.

Puff! Puff! went the magic inhaler — and rose into the air!!

It was the happiest day of Mr Chesty's life. He saw all the Glasgow museums. He saw all the galleries. He saw all the parks. He saw the Cathedral. He saw Provand's Lordship.

He had lunch with the Lord Provost at the City Chambers. He heard a symphony concert by the Scottish National Orchestra. He joined in all the coughing between the movements!

But of all the wonderful places Mr Chesty visited that day, his favourite was the Burrell Collection in Pollok Park.

Do you know who Sir William Burrell was? Can you guess why Mr Chesty felt so proud?

Sir William Burrell was one of Glasgow's most generous and patriotic sons, who had helped his country by selling it ships during the First World War.

Then he had encouraged local business, by spending all the money in Big Peter's cash-and-carry in Maryhill.

One of your no-nonsense Glasgow men, Sir William had liked nothing fancier on his floors than a half-inch of reasonably dry sawdust. So he hung all Big Peter's carpets and rugs on his walls.

"Sir William was one of us," mused Mr Chesty, proudly.

That day was the most marvellous day that the whole city of Glasgow ever saw or heard. For as Mr Chesty flew back and forth over the city on his magic inhaler, the most marvellous thing began to happen.

In all the Mr Happy clinics, people gathered at the windows, waving an tapping on the windows with their little inhalers. "Rat-a-tat-tat! Rat-a-tat-tat!" The sound gathered in unison over all the city. "Rat-a-tat-tat! Rat-a-tat-tat!"

It was Morse Code. "Glasgow's miles better! Glasgow's miles better!" tapped the happy inhalers.

At last Mr Chesty felt it was time to go home. "Home!" he stated clearly to the magic inhaler, pressing the top of the canister twice. But nothing happened. "Home, magic inhaler!" said Mr Chesty a little louder.

But all the metered doses had been used up, and the magic inhaler wasn't magic any more. So Mr Chesty would have to walk.

As Mr Chesty walked home, it was late, it was dark, and it began to rain. It rained so hard, it was like walking through a sea of boiling gob-stoppers.

"I'd forgotten tomorrow was Fair Friday!" sighed Mr Chesty.

But that wasn't all that Mr Chesty had forgotten. For when he arrived home, he found that his slice of fried bread had been burnt to a frazzle. And the slice of Lorne was a wee black postage stamp!

"I'll try to scrape that in the morning," yawned Mr Chesty, and went to his bed.

As Mr Chesty climbed into his bed, he coughed up "The Last of the Day". Mr Chesty wrapped it in a nice fresh Kleenex, and slipped it under the pillow.

It was Mr Pneumonia. "Is it fuck!" said Mr Pneumonia. "Is it fuck!" But Mr Chesty didn't hear Mr Pneumonia's nasty bad language. For Mr Chesty was fast asleep.

It was Mr Chesty's lucky night. Already he was dreaming his favourite dream.

In Mr Chesty's favourite dream, he won a magnificent sports trophy. Can you guess what it was called?

THE CAPSTAN FULL-STRENGTH BLOW FOOTBALL
SILVER QUAICH

Happy Mr Chesty! Glasgow's miles better!

---

4 December 1677

One hundred and thirty-six houses and shops were destroyed by fire, and 600 families made homeless. The heat at Glasgow Cross was so intense that the clock of the Tolbooth caught fire — the prisoners held within, mostly Covenanters, were saved from certain death only by the crowd's action in releasing them.

After attributing the disaster to God's justice, due punishment for the awful carrying-on of the citizens, the Town Council went on to limit the amount of timber that could be used in buildings. This must have been the first serious attempt to tame the Tinderbox of Europe.

"Lothian Tam", a Dissenting preacher, was involuntarily elevated when his leg became entangled in the rope of Lunardi's balloon. This was on the occasion of Lunardi's second ascent from Glasgow. It may have crossed Tam's mind as he swung from the rope that Lunardi's previous effort had taken him 70 miles away. However, at a height of about 15 to 20 feet, Tam was successfully brought to earth by a jerk or "yerk" on the rope. He was uninjured, and Lunardi only got as far as the Campsies. (See also 23rd November.)

5 December 1785

Balloonery 2.

Date of the account in a Glasgow newspaper of a great destructive fire at a warehouse at 74 Buchanan Street, on the corner of Exchange Square. The premises belonged to several silk, muslin and yarn traders. Damage was estimated at £100,000 in this, the worst fire in the city for many years.

6 December 1856

The text below is of an inscription in Hamilton Parish Churchyard to the memory of certain Covenanters, citizens of Hamilton, who were unfortunate enough to fall into Royalist hands after Bothwell Bridge:

> "At Hamilton lie the heads of John Park, Gavin Hamilton, James Hamilton and Christopher Strang, who suffered at Edinburgh December 7th, 1666.

> "Stay passenger, take notice what thou reads;
> At Edinburgh lie our bodies, here our heads,
> Our right hands stood at Lanark, those we want
> Because with them we sware the Covenant."

That is, their right hands were cut off and placed on the public ports of Lanark, that being the place where they took the oath of the Covenant.

7 December 1666

The great English essayist and opium eater, Thomas De Quincey, who died on this date, was about Glasgow a good deal in the years between March 1841 and June 1843. A major reason was his

8 December 1859

interest in astronomy and his friendship with Professor Nichol, the holder of the chair in that subject at Glasgow. De Quincey lodged with Nichol, before taking rooms in the High Street, opposite the College. Strangely, he simultaneously rented rooms in Renfield Street, purely to accommodate his vast and hopelessly disordered library.

From 1846 to '47 he lodged at No. 112 Rottenrow, with a Mrs Tosh as his landlady. A long-suffering one no doubt, for De Quincey was somewhat eccentric in his habits. Carlyle describes him as "one of the smallest man-figures I ever saw; shaped like a pair of tongs, and hardly above five feet in all". He had "a beautiful child's face". Scrupulously negligent where his appearance was concerned, he wore whatever shabby, ink-stained and threadbare clothes were to hand. But he was fussy about his food. "Madam," he said once to Prof. Nichol's cook, "owing to dyspepsia affecting my system, the possibility is that additional derangement of the stomach might take place, and consequences incalculable distressing arise — so much so, indeed, as to increase nervous irritations and prevent me from attending to matters of overwhelming importance — if you do not remember to cut the mutton in a diagonal rather than a longitudinal form."

While in Rottenrow, De Quincey wrote for *Tait's Magazine*, but owing to his habit of carelessly jotting down his writings on any old scraps of paper, much of his Glasgow output must have been lost or destroyed, perhaps swept up by an exasperated Mrs Tosh.

We cannot leave De Quincey without mentioning his notorious opium habit. Towards the end of his life, he was taking 8,000 drops of laudanum — tincture of opium — every day, enough to fill seven wine glasses. There are reports of similar quantities being imbibed by Glaswegian addicts around the same time. Of course, this was long before the famous Strathclyde Police Drugs Squad did so much in Glasgow to control the traffic in dangerous drugs.

The superstitions regarding witchcraft and allied arts which flourished during the reign of that expert, Jamie the Saxt, did not leave Glasgow untouched. The case of Kate Hopkin was today referred to Glasgow Presbytery: she was accused of taking part in a ritual known as "turning the riddle" in order to discover the guilty part to a theft. This folk alternative to the detective and judicial processes was a simple affair, and if adopted today could go a long way towards easing the pressure on the CID, not to mention all the delay and congestion at Glasgow Sheriff Court. All one has to do is balance a sieve or riddle on a pair of tongs, which must be held by two fingers only. The name of the suspect is then uttered. If the sieve trembles, he or she is undeniably guilty.

9 December 1601

The wanderer who strays over the Bridge of Sighs and up and through Glasgow Necropolis cannot fail to be struck by the varied and exotic examples of memorial architecture that accost him. It seems that, in the booming of last century, a lifetime spent accruing wealth and importance could have reached no more enviable conclusion than a fancy big tomb looking down on Glasgow. There are Catacombs, "Egyptian" vaults, a "Moorish Kiosk", a classical Mausoleum . . . the following example appeared in the *Glasgow Herald* of 10th December 1858:

10 December 1858

> "THE NECROPOLIS. A monument has just been erected in this beautiful cemetery to the memory of the late Robert Baird Esq. of Auchmedden. It is in the form of Scipio's tomb in Rome . . . another (of the) many elaborate *in memoriam* monuments which stud our city of the dead."

No doubt if Publius Cornelius Scipio had died 2,000 years later he would have wished his tomb to be in the form of that of Robert Baird Esq. of Auchmedden in Glasgow. (See also 12th March.)

11 December 1787

When their employers attempted to cut wages by 25 per cent, the weavers of the Calton took direct action. They wrecked looms, broke into warehouses and burned employers' stock, and stoned officers and police who tried to prevent them. The military was called in, the Riot Act was read in Duke Street. Then the soldiers fired, killing three and wounding several others.

The handloom weavers of Calton and other suburban weaving villages had developed what was originally just another cottage activity into a full-time home industry, using yarn from the factories rather than the limited supply previously spun by their women. By the latter 18th century, they had formed substantial and prosperous communities, with an extraordinarily rich and diversified culture. Widely read in all manner of subjects from Shakespeare to Tom Paine, the weavers were often keen amateurs in such varied fields as ornithology, botany, engraving, acting and poetry, and were intensely involved in religion, philosophy and, above all, radical politics, giving major support to movements such as the Friends of the People and the United Scotsmen.

It was an impressive society, and too good to last. Earnings failed to keep pace with rising inflation during the Napoleonic Wars. The trade was increasingly swamped by outsiders prepared to accept lower wages (with the exception of the fine quality work, virtually anyone could master the craft in a few months). And the weavers effectively failed to have a minimum wage rate fixed, an agreed scale of prices for their work and protection from unskilled entry to the trade. While the Court of Session ruled in favour of some of their demands, the manufacturers were left free to ignore them. This, of course, they did, and in 1812 the weavers were driven to take strike action.

The great strike of 1812 affected the entire country, and lasted for nine weeks. The strike was well organised, well disciplined and non-violent. Yet the authorities broke it, by the dubiously legal arrest of the strike leaders, who were tried and imprisoned for the "crime" of taking part in a combination to raise wages. Apparently the English Combination Acts were to be applied in Scotland as well.

From then onwards the industry went into a slow but painful decline, partly due to the competition of the factories now producing cloth on power looms, partly to the vast numbers continuing to enter the trade, swollen by veterans of the wars. Wages fell drastically, from around 30s. to 40s. a week in 1800 to around 7s. 6d. (or even 4s. 6d. for lower grade work) in 1830. In fact, it was only in the making of the poorest grades of cloth, which could be produced cheaper by seated labour than by machine, or in the very highly skilled and specialised weaving of Paisley shawls and suchlike, that the handloom could hold its own. It was not enough. By the end of the 19th century, the age of the handloom weavers was over.

William Stirling, testatory benefactor of Glasgow's first public library, is born. Passing over any important or significant aspects of his life, let us follow him in later age to the home of James Wardrop, merchant of Glasgow. "Jemmy" Wardrop has been rated a bit of a wag, in pursuance of which reputation he has hit on the idea of inviting all the hunchbacks of Glasgow to dinner. Quite a number turn up, though we know the names of only three of them, including William Stirling. One glance at the assembled company is enough to convince W.S. that he is getting the mick took. He is not amused. He gives Wardrop a piece of his mind, then leaves in dignified dudgeon. Jemmy realises he has gone over the score and tries, with some success, to mollify the remaining guests with lavish hospitality. But public opinion, taking Stirling's side, withholds its chuckles. He gets religion, and begins preaching, but no one can make head or tail of his sermons. He dies in relative obscurity. The moral of all this is, don't get a hunchback humphy.

12 December 1723

13 December 1814

Mr Hunter has lost a bottle of rum to Mr Monteith about a substance found in the toasted cheese.

(Minutes of the Board of Green Cloth)

---

14 December 1905

Hugh Watt, Liberal MP for Glasgow Camlachie, appeared at the Old Bailey charged with attempting to persuade three men to murder his wife, Julia.

Watt, elected MP in 1885, was a wealthy, flamboyant playboy who wanted to be in high society. He lived in the West End of Glasgow with his wife, daughter of a rich Glasgow merchant. After being elected, Watt gradually sold off the import/export business he had inherited for close on £1 million. Then he and his wife moved to London, to a luxurious house in Knightsbridge. Watt rarely visited his constituency after that.

The Glasgow couple gave many parties attended by high society freeloaders. At one of the parties Watt met Lady Violet Beauchamp, wife of Sir Reginald Beauchamp, soldier/explorer and landowner.

Lady Violet quickly became infatuated with Watt, waylaying him frequently in the street. Watt was flattered and soon infatuated with the little green-eyed brunette.

Julia Watt did her best to stop the affair, forbidding Lady Violet the house. One afternoon Julia found Lady Violet in her bedroom in her husband's passionate embrace. Mrs Watt complained to Sir Reginald and eventually the cuckolded parties sued for divorce.

Mrs Watt was granted a *decree nisi* which meant that her husband couldn't marry Lady Violet, nor could he set aside a property agreement he'd made with his wife.

Frustrated to the point of madness, Watt contacted three petty crooks and offered them large sums of money to go to the house in Knightsbridge and murder Mrs Watt. The crooks took the money, laughed behind the "Scotch toff's" back and did nothing.

Watt then offered a private investigator £1,000 to

murder Julia. The man refused and reported the matter to Scotland Yard. Watt was then arrested on a conspiracy to murder charge.

The trial lasted eight days. Watt was found guilty and sentenced to five years penal servitude.

From discharged prisoners came stories of a gentleman who was living in luxury in Parkhurst Prison. The gossip in society circles was that Lady Violet, one of King Edward VII's favourites, had persuaded the monarch to ensure that Watt would be made comfortable in jail.

The public were amazed when Watt was released after serving less than a year of his sentence. Lady Violet met him at the prison gate and took him off for a champagne breakfast. Then the couple retired into comfortable obscurity.

Julia Watt, a shrewd Glaswegienne, never had her *decree nisi* made absolute, never set aside the property agreement. Not only did she get a large share of Watt's fortune, but she sued Lady Violet for libel and received £2,000 in damages.

EYEWITNESS ACCOUNT
by JOSEPH BROWN, SUBWAY MINER

15 December 1894

"How far underground were you?"

"When the fire broke out? Three hundred yards forward of the shaft in St Enoch's Square. Right up at the face, on the far side of the airlock and inside the tunnelling shield, under the river. About eight o'clock on Friday night, Will Cameron the lockman stumbled forward half-blinded, crying 'Fire! Get above ground! The timbers at the lock entrance are on fire!' Then we saw smoke — down at the lock still, but thickening all the time. We knew it was bad straight away. It's what all miners dread, a fire underground, and you're caught the wrong side of the lock. Every time you go down you dread it. Someone had to get the news to those above ground or we were done for. We could see Will was too done in to go back again. So John McCluskey said he'd go. We soaked his shirt and breeks. But we weren't to know if he got through—"

"The fire was in the airlock?"

"No. Outside. On the far side. But a fire in pitch and timber makes a great smoke and this was seeping in through the lock hatches and the chinks in the tunnel lining. We could watch it crawling towards us like a black beast—"

"How many were you?"

"Thirteen, with Will Cameron, who could have saved himself as easily as come forward to warn us. When we saw we couldn't get back through the lock we lay down to die. Some cursed Will for making thirteen. Some cried aloud, what would become of wives and bairns if they died there, in the gloom, under the Clyde. Then Will cries, 'Whist! Hold your greet'n.' And sure enough — air! Hissing from the pipe we use for caulking the lining plates after we've bolted them in. It meant McCluskey had got through. And the engineman had kept his head, remembered the airline. It's no more than an inch across but it did us. We kept the air playing in our midst, passing it from man to man. Some put the nozzle to their faces and sniffed up the fresh air. I tell you — I never smelt air sweeter. If that pipe had failed in the fire we'd have been done in a few minutes. As it is we managed a full twelve hours till they broke through from the other tunnel — that's six feet of digging and two lots of lining to batter through. We got out at eight on Saturday morning. Three years I've been mining this subway — through running sand and roof falls and flooding — but that's a shift I don't want to work again. That McCluskey! See him! Some hero, but!"

---

16 December 1610

Following a plague of leprosy in the mid-14th century, the pious Lady Marjory of Lochow had founded a leper hospital on St Ninian's Croft, in Hutchesontown. This area, of wide green fields, remained otherwise uninhabited until 1794.

Yesterday, the Town Council of Glasgow laid

down the conditions of behaviour for lepers entering the city. They were to:

> "gang onlie upon the calsie (street) syde, near the gutter, and sal haif clapperis and ane claith upon their mouth and face, and sal stand affar of quhill they resaif almous (receive alms), or answer under the payne of banisching from the toun and Hospitall."

We wonder whether they also had to call out "Unclean! Unclean!" or, being Glasgow lepers, "Clarty! Clarty!".

Nowadays you can walk from one end of Hutchesontown to the other and not see a single leper. There are about as many of them in the area as there are damp-free and inhabitable houses.

This year Mr Wylie and Mr Lochhead joined forces as operative upholsterers in Glasgow. Two years later they added funeral undertaking to their concern. Hitherto this had not been a distinct business in Scotland, and a funeral was a complicated, not to say pricey, affair. The coffin had to be ordered from the joiner, hearse and mortcloth from somewhere else, refreshments from the baker and wine and spirit merchants, and so on. And even after the corpse was interred, there might be the necessity of guarding it from "resurrectionists" until it was nicely decomposed. Wylie and Lochhead offered an all-in package deal, even down to burial space. Aside from the convenience, this could save the bereaved customer as much as 50 per cent. Their timing was immaculate. 1832 was the year of the most appalling cholera epidemic in Glasgow. Whylie and Lochhead made a killing, as they say.

Later, they were to move to Buchanan Street, to an impressive warehouse of their own design with all mod. cons., including a novel "hoisting machine".

"This apparatus," writes Mr Dawson Burns (see 24th April), "affords no small treat to many who visit the establishment (and they are not few) who

17 December 1729

can be elevated in the world with a pleasing ascending motion. . . ."

Wylie and Lochhead diversified: they introduced an omnibus service for Glasgow and district, and moved into the house furnishing for which they are perhaps best known. Though it might be unfair to claim they owed it all to the little cholera virus, it is nevertheless substantially true.

---

18 December 1810

A charming (and startling) pastoral picture is presented by this advertisement from today's *Glasgow Herald:*

> "To let; the thatched cottage and garden of Sauchiehall. The Tenant will have an abundant supply of milk from the Dairy (which will enable him to furnish curds and cream on the easiest terms), as also fruits in season from the extensive gardens of Willow Bank."

"Willow Bank" is, in fact, a fairly direct English translation of the "Sauchiehall" (orig. *Sauchie Haugh*) that gives southern visitors such problems. Needless to say, no splinter of a sauch survives near that street.

---

19 December 1777

A letter from King George to Lord MacLeod orders the raising of a Highland regiment of foot. This is to become the Highland Light Infantry, the regiment that Glasgow remembers as its own. To read through its battle honours is sufficient to show the scope of its involvement in most of the fighting that went on: Hindoostan, Roleia, Seringapatam, Corunna, Fuentes D'onor, Budajoz, Pyrenees, Salamanca, Toulouse, Nive, Waterloo, Sebastopol, Egypt, Carnatic, South Africa, Modder River, Mysore, Sholingus, Central India, Orthez, Vittoria, Almaraz, Bilsaco, Cape of Good Hope, Assaye, Vimiera, Cruidad Rodrigo, Nivelle, Peninsula, Tel el Kebir, Mons, Loos, Ypres, Somme, Arras, Palestine, Hindenburg Line, Archangel, Gallipoli, Mesopotamia. A glittering list, yet one name is omitted: Glasgow University. But a skirmish did take place there in 1810 which should be

remembered if only as a foot note to swell that catalogue of glory.

One November morning, several students lounging around the West part of the College grounds noticed a substantial number of squaddies of the 71st (HLI) trespassing within the "sacred enclosure". Horrified at this insult to the *alma mater*, they resolved to eject the intruders forthwith. A large force of red gowns mustered under the command of one William Couper (later President of the Faculty of Physicians and Surgeons of Glasgow and Professor of Natural History) and, rushing uphill, pressed home their attack. Although taken by surprise, the Highlanders were soon reinforced from the nearby barracks. They drove the students back towards the Hunterian Museum, where a fierce stone battle ensued. Several of the museum's window's were broken. In the meantime, the College professors had contacted the regiment's officers, who arrived at the scene and called off their men.

Much later, one of the students involved recalled the engagement in much the same terms he used when describing the battles of the Peninsular War, in which he had served as a chaplain. One of its heroes later became a Professor of Mineralogy, not, we are told, as a result of any aptitude for the science, but rather for the accuracy of the volleys of *minerals* he directed against the 71st and as a reward for "his extraordinary valour in defending the Museum from the violence of the redcoats".

Who would not sleep with the brave?

A Glasgow man of Burmese origin, Mr Muang Mya, of 23 Blackburn Street, was giving evidence today in an undefended divorce action at the Court of Session. As a Buddhist, the form of oath he opted to take was rather different from "I swear by Almighty God . . . ." etc. It went:

20 December 1958

> ". . . that I am unprejudiced, and if what I shall speak shall prove false, or if, by colouring truth others shall be led astray, then may the three Holy Entities, Buddha,

Dharma and Pro Sangha, in whose sight I now stand, together with the devotees of the twenty-two firmaments, punish me and also my migrating soul."

We like it. It makes a nice change. And what it promises is more precise, more plausible and infinitely more practical than "the truth, the whole truth and nothing but the truth".

---

21 December 1908

On the evening of this day the body of Miss Marion Gilchrist was found by her maid Helen Lambie. She was lying in a pool of blood in the dining room of her house at 15 Queen's Terrace, West Princes Street, Glasgow. Subsequently, Oscar Slater was wrongly arrested for her murder and served 19 years in prison before being pardoned. (See 8th June 1928 and 14th September 1914.) A diamond crescent brooch was stolen from the house and this item played an important part in the miscarriage of justice.

---

22 December 1817

St Andrew's R.C. Cathedral, completed at what was for the time the enormous cost of £16,000, was opened on Clyde Street. Doak and McLaren Young call it the first serious attempt at Gothic revival in Glasgow. Prior to its building, Glasgow's Catholics had to put up with some pretty makeshift accommodation for their worship: in 1792, a temporary chapel was used in a tennis court in Mitchell Street, giving a new dimension to the word "service".

---

23 December

Last-minute shoppers trundle their bunions from store to store, as above them Glasgow's famous Christmas decorations sparkle festively in the frosty air. A merry scene, yet it is with gloom and unease that we take up the pen, a sense of deep foreboding that the season's gaiety fails to dispel. If we were required to summarise the problem in not more than two words, those of "Mister" and "Happy" would inevitably be deployed.

Perhaps it all began towards Christmas '83 when, among the usual fairy lights, a huge figure of Santa Claus appeared in George Square. Rearing up in black jackboots, it faced the City Chambers with right arm raised stiffly, more, it seemed, in salute than in benediction. Then the municipal buildings themselves came out in yellow blotches. On closer inspection these were revealed to be the city's new coat of arms. This has proved much simpler to draw than the old one, being just a yellow amoeba with a rictus, which is like a smile but more desperate. At the time, though, it was rather like seeing stickers on the lapels of a respectable businessman's pinstripes.

It was the first intimation the citizens of Glasgow had of the bloodless coup that swept the "Mister Men" to power in the city. Mister Bendy, Mister Greedy, Mister Silly and Mister Kelly, along with Little Miss Givings and Little Miss Takes, began at once to put into operation their programme of recovery through infantile regression. Almost overnight, Glasgow was inundated with images of a jaundiced thalidomide endomorph, inchoately human, the entropic blob of the future.

This is the image that haunts us now, which we fear will have a horrible manifestation this Christmas. The omens and the signs have been unmistakeable; the second coming is at hand. Are we prepared? How will we react when the great addled yolk, bestriding George Square like a Colossus, booms from its megaphone throat, *"Ho! Ho! Ho! Glasgow's Miles Better! Ho! Ho! Ho! Glasgow's Miles Better!"*, fixing on the city and the world a gaze as blank and pitiless as the sun?

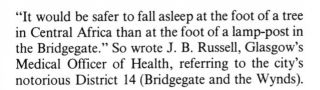

"It would be safer to fall asleep at the foot of a tree in Central Africa than at the foot of a lamp-post in the Bridgegate." So wrote J. B. Russell, Glasgow's Medical Officer of Health, referring to the city's notorious District 14 (Bridgegate and the Wynds).

24 December 1888

Most of the homes in this area consisted of one room. Infant mortality was 1:5 during the first year of life. One-third of these children never saw a doctor. By his exposure of these and similar facts, Russell probably did more than anyone else of his day to stimulate concern about slum housing, and what he called "the inhabitants of the uninhabitable".

25 December 1915

Christmas morning, and the Minister of Munitions, Lloyd George, at last fulfils his promise to visit Glasgow. Not with seasonal greetings and a sackful of goodies, but to explain to recalcitrant strikers in the munitions industry why they should go back to work and help win the war. Earlier that year, over 10,000 engineers from 26 factories had gone on strike for an extra 2d. an hour. The Clyde Workers' Committee had emerged from this, originally as an informal monitor of events on Clydeside, then as the main voice of opposition to Government policies in the industry, particularly the dilution of labour.

Around 3,000 turned up, mostly CWC workers. Lloyd George badly miscalculated the mood of the meeting, launching into a tirade of jingoistic rhetoric. He was shouted down, and the meeting ended in turmoil.

The Government, convinced now more than ever of the threat of the CWC, reacted with a heavy hand to the public humiliation of one of its Ministers. The socialist newspaper *Forward*, which carried the only truthful account of the meeting, was suppressed by troops, and unsold copies impounded. The leaders of the CWC were arrested and deported from Clydeside. Resistance disintegrated as the Dilutions Commissioners split the workforce by negotiating plant by plant. Conscription was introduced in January 1916.

The strike had failed, but a precedent of militancy and repression had been set.

When the new carillon of 16 bells was erected in Glasgow Tolbooth on this date, the following tunes were played, viz: *The Queen's Anthem, Mariners, Innocent, Caller Herrin' Scots Wha Haw, Christmas Chimes, Christmas Hymn, Hark the Herald Angels Sing, Chime Again, Beautiful Bells, Duncan Gray, Rule Britannia, British Grenadiers, Marsellaise, A Highland Lad, March of the Cameron Men, God Save the Queen.* The bells replaced musical bells which were completed in 1736 at a cost of £316. 1s. 9d. They played the following tunes, viz: Sunday, *Easter Hymn;* Monday, *Gilderoy;* Tuesday, *Nancy's Tae the Green Wood Gane;* Wednesday, *Tweedside;* Thursday, *The Lass o' Patie's Mill;* Friday, *The Last Time I Came o'er the Muir;* Saturday, *Roslin Castle.*

26 December 1881

Yesterday, five persons who appeared before the Kirk Session were ordered to make public repentance for "keeping Yule", as Christmas was still known. At the same session, the baxters (bakers) of Glasgow were required to make known the names of those to whom they had supplied "Yule bread".

For the reformed kirk, then, Christmas was a piece of Papish and/or pagan nonsense. It was not easily suppressed — they were still passing laws against it at the end of the century — but they succeeded in subordinating it to the serious business of Hogmanay and Ne'er Day, at least until the Victorians revived the fashion and the 20th-century Triumph of Mammon. In deference to indigestion and overdraft, we have allowed God's birthday to pass by without comment.

27 December 1538

The funeral took place in Westminster Abbey of William Thomson, Lord Kelvin, the greatest physicist and applied scientist of the Victorian age. He was Professor of Natural Philosophy for 50 years at Glasgow University, which he had entered at 11 years of age.

He was very much the Victorian scientist-as-

28 December 1907

inventor, extending his theoretical grasp of physics into material inventions, in particular those connected with ships and nautical apparatus. He designed a new compass, and sounding equipment. His work on submarine telegraphy led to the laying of the first telegraph cable under the Atlantic. He also studied radioactivity and encouraged the research of the Curies. As an associate of James White in the firm of Kelvin and White, he involved himself in the manufacture, as well as the invention, of scientific instruments. Apparently, he was a rotten lecturer as well. He never used notes when lecturing and, in order to keep himself up to scratch, offered his students a prize for the best set of notes they could come up with.

He is remembered by a public toilet for birds in the form of a bronze statue seated near the putting green in Kelvingrove. By its feet babbles that tributary of the Clyde after which he was lorded. The Kelvin is a perjink river, and takes care in its wayward progress to avoid the more unsalubrious parts of the city. In the name "Kelvinside" it has the distinction of defining a peculiarly grotesque form of middle-class accent for which it is virtually impossible to devise an orthography.

The name "Kelvin" itself is from the Gaelic sources "coille" and "abhainn", and means "wooded river". To be sure, it cuts a bosky vale. As the poet sang:

> *O sylvan Kelvin! Where thy streams*
> *Mellifluously meaunder,*
> *Athwart the streetlamp's sunny beams*
> *It was my wont to wander.*
> *There, at some witching hour of day,*
> *I used to go a lot,*
> *Along the path that winds its way*
> *Up to the Pewter Pot.*

Now, the Pewter Pot . . . but we could carry digression too far.

The results of a series of surveys conducted by the Education Department of Jordanhill College revealed the heroes of the average Scottish 14-year-old to be, in order of merit, Winston Churchill, "mother", Elvis Presley and the Pope.

The survey also showed that the commonest spare-time activity of this hypothetical bairn was reading. This, the department suspected, meant comics. But why should they jump to such a conclusion? It might have been French novels, or existentialist philosophy (see 17th August).

By an Act of the Scots Parliament this year, students at the Universities of Glasgow, St Andrews and Aberdeen were granted the dispensation of begging. This was a valuable privilege, at a time when unlicenced begging was punishable by mutilation, banishment and death, and it is to be hoped that they showed more gratitude than their present-day counterparts who seem to think the world owes them a living. Stop all their grants, say I, give them each a gaberlunzie and send them out on the streets!

(Disgusted, Hyndland.)

The old year dances on tottery legs towards a midnight burial, as the new year kicks restlessly in the womb of the future. It's Hogmanay, of course, a strange and terrible time, a time of horrible pleasure, of deadly serious levity, of drinking-yourself-sober. A time when words of ritual significance are on everyone's lips: "Thank God it's only once a year."

There's no need to go into what happens. We all do it. Evelyn Waugh gave the concisest definition of Hogmanay: "People being sick on pavements in Glasgow". But while we're still capable of taking it in, let us have an etymological digression ("Ah'll jist hae anither hauf . . ." "Sit doun, faither, the boay's goat the mike . . .").

Hrrrmph! Even the Scottish National Dictionary admits confusion regarding the origins of this strange word, so richly connotive of hoggish houghmagandie, hangover and Huguenot hegemony. It seems it first makes its appearance in early 17th-century Scotland as "hagmonay". This comes (possibly) from the North French dialect word "hoginane", itself (perhaps) derived from the 16th-century French "aguillaneuf", meaning (maybe) a gift given at the new year (l'an neuf). Over the centuries it has undergone a dizzy number of permutations, suggesting Scots have been as incapable of spelling during it as of anything else. These are the forms given by the SND: hogmanae, hogminay, hogminae, hogmaenay, hogmenai, hogmaynae, hoguemennay, hogmonay, hogmoney, hagmenay, hagmane, hug-me-nay (a Gallovidian perversion), huigmanay, hoghmanay, hagmonick, hangmanay, hanginay, hogernoany and huggeranohni (Shetland). It sounds as if they have the best time in Shetland.

Regarding the moral and medical dimensions of the ritual, we regret . . . but soft, the Bells!

DONG! . . . take in graphic
DONG! . . . "Dear auld Glasgow toun,"
DONG! . . . take in graphics
DONG! . . . "For it's goin' roun' an' roun'!"
DONG! . . . "SUM HOMO LABORANS VULGARIS"
DONG! . . . "As anyone here can see,"
DONG! . . . "Bot quhan twa drinkis I on Sabbath-een taik"
DONG! . . . "Is leamsa a'Ghlaschu!"
DONG! . . . "Eh?" . . .
DONG! . . . "Glasgow belongs to me!"
DONG! . . . "A Happy New Year to all wur readers!"
DONG! . . . and this is where we came in. . . .